文学翻译中的连贯模式研究

以《红楼梦》及其英译本为例

李晰 ◎ 著

上海交通大学出版社
SHANGHAI JIAO TONG UNIVERSITY PRESS

内容提要

本书以系统功能语言学为框架,以《红楼梦》及其英译文为语料,阐述了文学翻译中的语篇连贯模式。连贯是一个多维度的概念,其构成是概念功能和语篇功能共同作用的结果。本书深入探索了连贯在词汇语法层的实现,并讨论了不同翻译中的连贯模式,揭示了语言类型学差异、译者风格、翻译目的等对翻译中连贯实现的影响。

本书针对的读者群体为语言学和翻译专业的研究生、教师及学者。

图书在版编目（CIP）数据

文学翻译中的连贯模式研究:以《红楼梦》及其英译本为例 / 李晰著. 一上海:上海交通大学出版社,2023.11

ISBN 978-7-313-28199-9

I.①文… II.①李… III.①《红楼梦》—英语—文学翻译—研究 IV.①H315.9②I207.411

中国国家版本馆CIP数据核字(2023)第143997号

文学翻译中的连贯模式研究
——以《红楼梦》及其英译本为例
WENXUE FANYI ZHONGDE LIANGUAN MOSHI YANJIU
—— YI《HONGLOUMENG》JIQI YINGYIBEN WEILI

著　　者:	李　晰		
出版发行:	上海交通大学出版社	地　　址:	上海市番禺路951号
邮政编码:	200030	电　　话:	021-64071208
印　　制:	上海万卷印刷股份有限公司	经　　销:	全国新华书店
开　　本:	710 mm×1000 mm　1/16	印　　张:	15.5
字　　数:	256千字		
版　　次:	2023年11月第1版	印　　次:	2023年11月第1次印刷
书　　号:	ISBN 978-7-313-28199-9		
定　　价:	99.00元		

前　言

　　连贯是一个重要的语篇特征,然而,学界对于连贯的定义并没有形成共识。目前对于连贯的研究角度有认知语言学、心理语言学、语用学、语篇语言学等。文学翻译涉及不同的源语和目的语读者与文化,在翻译中如何实现语篇连贯也是文体学及翻译学应该关注的话题之一。本书以系统功能语言学为框架,将连贯视为一个多维度的概念。连贯是概念功能和语篇功能共同作用的结果,其在词汇语法层的实现体现了语篇连贯的模式。因此,本书通过深入阐释源语及目的语语篇的连贯模式,将连贯的概念具体化,并探索了翻译中连贯的实现。

　　本书的第1章是引言,介绍了本书的研究背景、研究理据、研究视角、研究语料、研究目的、研究问题等。

　　第2章是文献综述,主要从连贯的定义、连贯研究的角度、连贯研究的理论框架、连贯与翻译的关系、《红楼梦》中的衔接及连贯研究等角度梳理了国内外的研究成果。

　　第3章是连贯研究的理论框架介绍。从系统功能语言学的角度出发,介绍了层级、元功能、语境等重要概念,并且探讨了衔接与连贯的关系,提出了一个描述语篇连贯模式的框架,具体描述了这一框架在系统功能语言学层级—功能中的定位,将连贯模式视为经验功能、逻辑功能以及语篇功能在语法词汇层面的实现。

　　第4章是具体的研究方法,包括语料库构成、语料库工具、分析步骤等。

　　第5章从逻辑功能的角度出发,探讨了其在连贯构成中的作用。由于逻辑功能决定小句之间的逻辑关系及连接方式,语篇语义发展也是逻辑关系发展的过程,因此逻辑功能体现了语篇连贯的一个方面。本章对比了源语及目的语两个语篇在词汇语法层对逻辑功能的实现,具体描述了英汉语言之间的差异以及译者差异。

第6章从语篇功能的角度出发,分析了源语及目的语两个语篇各自的衔接链构成,发现在翻译过程中衔接链显化,具体对比了同一链和相似链,探讨了英汉语篇差异的原因。

第7章综合分析了经验功能、逻辑功能和语篇功能在语篇连贯方面的具体实现。以衔接链为基础,分析了构成衔接链的衔接词所处的小句的逻辑环境以及经验环境,解释了连贯作为一个多维度的概念在具体语篇中的构成以及在翻译中的实现。

第8章系统回顾了研究结果,分析了研究不足,并对未来的研究提出了建议。

总之,本书通过理论框架构建,借助语料库工具的定量分析、文本分析以及实证举例,深入阐述了语篇的连贯模式,解释了翻译中连贯模式的具体实现,并探讨了译者风格及翻译策略。本书对于语言学研究、文体学研究以及翻译学研究均具有参考意义。

本书是根据笔者的博士论文修改而成的,因此借此书付梓之际,笔者要感谢在笔者的读博生涯中给过笔者指导、鼓励和支持的所有人。首先感谢澳大利亚麦考瑞大学的两位导师——吴灿中博士和 Annabelle Lukin 副教授。他们在笔者研究生涯的开端教会笔者什么是语言学研究以及如何做语言学研究,他们严谨的治学态度和高效且充满鼓励的指导让笔者备受鼓舞。当笔者遇到困难时,灿中和他的夫人富有同理心的勉励和宽慰让笔者走出困境,笔者至今仍旧十分怀念他们举办的家庭聚会。Annabelle 总能在笔者的研究遇到瓶颈时指出问题所在,当笔者因为觉得自己的理论基础差而信心受挫的时候,她总能坚定地鼓励笔者且为笔者指明可行的研究角度,还能在百忙之中不厌其烦地修改笔者的文稿。作为成功的事业女性,她是笔者职业生涯的楷模。希望此后笔者能一直谨遵两位导师的教诲,严谨治学、为人师表。

在笔者的博士论文写作过程中,悉尼的学术环境为笔者的快速进步提供了良好的土壤。笔者非常有幸能够在麦考瑞大学获得和韩礼德、韩茹凯夫妇交流的机会,并得到他们的鼓励。麦考瑞大学的David Butt副教授和Annabelle Lukin副教授开办的每周研讨会对于笔者加深对系统功能语言学的理解提供了非常大的帮助。悉尼大学James Martin教授每周五举办的系统功能语言学研讨会也使笔者获益匪浅,在那里能够接触到不同学校的知名研究人员,聆听他们最新的研究成果,还能在会后与研究前辈和同行们一起讨论、进步。

笔者还要感谢读博期间的同学和朋友们:李龙、于海玲、陈祎、严琨、陈思佳、郇昌鹏、韩潮、Noon Owatnutpat、Neda Karimi、Qandeel Hussain、Nicole Guo等。他们都给过笔者鼓励和支持,他们的友谊使笔者四年的读博生涯充满了精彩瞬间。

本书得以出版离不开笔者的工作单位中国科学院大学的支持。笔者有幸获得中国科学院大学2020年度青年教师科研能力提升项目的支持,使得本书的出版成为现实,也为笔者获得2022年教育部人文社科基金青年项目立项打下了良好的基础。同时也感谢中国科学院大学外语系的领导和同事,他们共同创造的宽松又温暖的工作环境使笔者始终对工作充满激情。

时光匆匆,从笔者读博踏入学术领域以来已近十载。笔者已从当初迷茫不知所措的博士生成长为能够独当一面且教学与科研兼顾的青年教师,很感激自己遇到了如此多的良师益友。回首这些年的学术道路,虽磕磕绊绊且有遗憾,但笔者获益良多。学术写作使笔者的思维更加深刻,也更能够体会工作与生活平衡带来的精神上的丰盈。希望以后笔者能保持乐观积极的人生态度,从容面对困难,成为一个为社会创造价值的人。

Contents

Chapter 1

Introduction

This research explores coherence as a means of gaining insights into the translation of a Chinese literary text and its English translations. A systemic functional linguistic framework proves well suited to tracing the multifaceted nature of coherence and the inevitable nuances that arise in its transference through translation. Analyzing the lexical and grammatical patterns of coherence in the source and target texts can provide insight into how they convey meaning, as well as differences between the Chinese and English versions that point to the translators' approaches. The linguistic study of the literary text and its translations extends beyond traditional concerns over equivalence to consider stylistic shifts. Patterns of transference and difference across the source and target texts serve as a window into contrasting assumptions and priorities in the source and target linguistic and cultural contexts. This study illuminates the complex interplay between text and context that both enable and challenge the preservation of coherence in translation. The findings contribute to an understanding of linguistic and translation theory enriched by consideration of the relationship between language and cultural context.

1.1 Background

This research is a comparative study of the patterns of coherence of a Chinese novel, *Hong Lou Meng (HLM)*, and its two English translations, focusing on the transference of coherence from Chinese to English in translation. In translation studies, the application of linguistics has made significant contribution to both the practice and study of translation, which accordingly broadens the field of linguistic studies (Baker, 1997; Catford, 1965; Munday, 2009; Nida, 1969). Systemic Functional Linguistics (SFL) takes an important part in the study of translation. Much research has been carried out in translation using SFL theories and methods (Baker, 1997; Bell, 1991; Hatim and Mason, 1990; House, 1997; Huang, 2002; Kim, 2007b; Matthiessen, 2001; Pagano, 1994). Their research has made great progress in the translation studies from linguistic approach. Various aspects of using SFL in translation have been studied, but limited work has examined coherence from the SFL perspective.

Since Halliday and Hasan conducted research on the mechanism of cohesion in English, the study of coherence has become a big concern in Halliday and Hasan's approach to text linguistics, and it has been studied by other scholars at different times (Campbell, 1995; Harabagiu, 1999; Reinhart, 1980; Seidlhofer and Widdowson, 1999; van Dijk, 1977; Wolf and Gibson, 2006). Though much research has been done on coherence, no consensus on the definition of coherence is reached so far. The concept of coherence varies according to different scholars: it has been defined from a cognitive perspective (Hobbs, 1979; Kintsch and van Dijk, 1978), in relation to theme progression (Danes, 1974), and also from different strata of systemic functional perspective [Eggins, 1994; Halliday and Hasan, 1985 (1989); Hasan, 1984; Hu, 1994; Sanders and Noordman, 2000; Seidlhofer and Widdowson, 1999; Tanskanen, 2006]. This research adopts the systemic functional linguistic approach in the description of coherence, and makes a comparison of the source text (ST) and the target texts (TTs) of a literary text.

The importance of linguistic study of a literary text lies in the fact that the interpretation of the linguistic patterns can be related to the understanding of the text and the context. Widdowson [1983 (2014): 46] argues that what distinguishes our understanding of literary text is identifying patterns of linguistic organization and inferring the particular meanings that linguistic elements take on within those constructed patterns. Through the lexicogrammatical patterns of coherence recognised in the Chinese and English texts, the transference of them in translation indicates the ways of realising coherence in different languages and by different translators. The stylistic study of literary text translation is beyond the traditional issues of equivalence and faithfulness (Pagano, 1994: 213). Hence, the comparative study of Chinese and English coherence from the perspective of SFL can give better insight of the study of both linguistics and translation.

1.2   Rationale for the research

The present research undertakes to determine the different patterns of realising coherence in both Chinese and English texts. It chooses the perspective of coherence from a systemic functional linguistic view as the entry point to compare a Chinese source text and its two English translations, so as to illuminate how coherence is kept and achieved in translation.

Coherence has been the focus of text linguistics for a few decades; however, there has been little research on coherence in Chinese-English translation from functional and textual linguistic approaches. In addition, Chinese and English are quite different typologically, both having their own ways of realising coherence. Coherence is taken as the essential condition to distinguish text from non-text (Zhang, 2012: 272), therefore, being coherent is the basic characteristic of a source text to be understood and translated into another language. In this research, it is assumed that all source and target texts are coherent. The object of study is therefore not whether they are coherent or not, or to what extent they are coherent, but how they differ in realising coherence.

It is necessary to examine the feasibility of SFL applied in analysing the differences of coherence in both Chinese and English. One benefit of SFL is that it can provide an overall view of different languages, and can describe both Chinese and English texts from a multi-dimensional view. The description can therefore set the two language texts in the same framework, which provides a basis for a comparative study. To compare the ways that the source and target texts realise coherence, the study will elaborate how the two English target texts handle the transference of coherence and how they are different from the Chinese source text and from each other based on the different properties of SFL.

1.2.1　Systemic functional linguistics: some basic concepts

Systemic functional approach is comprehensive and multidimensional. From the SFL perspective, Webster (2009: 5) defines language as "a particular kind of semiotic system which is based on grammar, characterised by both a stratal organisation and functional diversity". Stratification and metafunction are two key concepts of SFL.

Stratification is the layering of meaning in a language, which enables us to draw a systemic description of language from context, semantics, lexicogrammar and phonology or graphology (Halliday, 1994). The significance of stratification can be seen by comparing the protolanguage of a young child with the language of an adult. In an infant's language, meaning is expressed only by sound, so his/her language only has two strata: content and expression (Halliday, 1975). With the evolution of the protolanguage to language, a purely abstract network of interrelations appears, in which meanings can be organised in their own terms. The "content" expands into lexicogrammar and semantics (Halliday, 1984). The organisation of lexicogrammar mediates content and expression. Lexicogrammar is the core of the stratification plane, because it is the intermediate level which is purely internal to language, neither related to the experiential world nor to the articulation of human sounds: it is the source for the creation of meanings. This research focuses on the lexicogrammatical level and also the semantic level that is realised by lexicogrammar to explore the semantic and lexicogrammatical patterns used to build coherence in Chinese and English texts.

Metafunction is also an essential concept in SFL. Language has three basic functions: ideational, interpersonal and textual. The ideational function construes human experience and is divided into two components: the experiential and the logical. The logical function "sets up logical-semantic relationships between one clausal unit and another" (Halliday, 2003: 17). The interpersonal function is about the personal and social relations of the speaker and the addressee, in this case, the writer/translators and the readers. There is a third function that creates a coherent text. This is the textual metafunction of language. It has an enabling or facilitating function to the other two since "both the others — construing experience and enacting interpersonal relations — depend on being able to build up sequences of discourse, organising the discursive flow and creating cohesion and continuity as it moves along" (Halliday and Matthiessen, 2004: 29–30). The metafunctional principle has shaped the organisation of meaning in language (Halliday, 2003: 18).

The analysis in two different languages can be made equivalent in terms of stratification and metafunction, thus setting a basis for a comparative and translation study of Chinese and English.

1.2.2　Cohesion: foundation of coherence

According to Halliday and Hasan [1985 (1989): 94], "cohesion is the foundation on which the edifice of coherence is built", and "the basis for textual coherence lies in cohesion" (Hasan, 1984: 210). Cohesion is "the set of linguistic resources that every language has (as part of the textual metafunction) for linking one part of a text to another" (Halliday, 1985: 48). Despite an essential property of texts, cohesion itself does not make a text coherent, instead, the way that the cohesive devices are deployed distinguishes text and non-text, and one text and another [Halliday and Hasan, 1985 (1989): 54]. In this research, cohesion is treated as a key factor in building up coherence of the text. In order to establish how cohesion contributes to the creation of coherence, the focus of the research is on the ways how cohesive devices are configured in the texts.

The classification of cohesion proposed in Halliday and Hasan [1976; 1985 (1989)] not only applies in English, but also in Chinese. Both languages have grammatical (reference, substitution, ellipsis) and lexical (repetition, synonymy, antonymy, meronymy) cohesive devices. Hasan (1984) divides cohesion into non-structural and structural cohesion. In this research, "cohesion" refers to the non-structural cohesive relations, because they are considered as "crucial to the creation of coherence" (Hasan, 1984: 183). The coherence of a text is mainly based on the non-structural cohesive devices. In Chapter 3, the grammatical cohesive devices (i.e. reference, substitution, ellipsis) of the two languages will be listed as fundamental elements for further analysis of the patterns of coherence.

1.2.3 Summary

In this research, the focus is on the two metafunctions, ideational and textual, of both the Chinese source text and the English target texts from the strata of semantics and lexicogrammar. The shaded parts in Table 1-1 show the location of the current research in the stratification-metafunction matrix. It does not mean that coherence is defined as the combination of ideational and textual functions at lexicogrammatical level, but that the joint effect of realisation of the ideational and textual meanings at lexicogrammatical level: transitivity, clause complexes and the cohesive chains configure the patterns of coherence of the text. This study attempts to explain how coherence is realised with these aspects, and how the lexicogrammatical patterns of that realisation give parameters for comparing the coherence patterns of different language texts in translation.

Table 1-1 The location of current study in the stratification-metafunction matrix

	Ideational		Interpersonal	Textual
	Experiential	Logical		
Context				
Semantics				
Lexicogrammar	Transitivity	Clause Complexes		Cohesive Chains

1.3 Translation: A functional approach

This research explores and interprets translation problems from the functional approach.

1.3.1 Previous research

Translation studies are closely related to modern language, comparative literature and linguistics (Munday, 2009: 4-5). It provides a research method based on the research results and theories of some other disciplines (such as linguistics, anthropology, and cultural studies). Translation scholars adopt new ideas from other fields, such as information science, cognitive science, and psychology (Neubert and Shreve, 1992: vii). At the same time, the innovation and development of translation studies stimulate the development of other disciplines.

Since the 1990s, text linguistics has been introduced into translation by many scholars and begun to play a significant role in translation study. Neubert and Shreve (1992) view translation as a textual process and state that translation study should be concerned primarily with the text as a unit of analysis. Hence, a general and comprehensive analysis of the source and target texts rather than only the syntactic or lexical comparison in translation becomes the focus of consideration, because meaning is not sentence-bound in the text-linguistic model (Neubert and Shreve, 1992: 23).

Translation is defined by Catford (1965: 20) as the replacement of textual material in the source language (SL) by equivalent textual material in the target language (TL). The key issue of translation studies is to seek equivalence between source text and target text. From the systemic functional point of view, the equivalence of source and target texts can be assessed from different strata, metafunctions and ranks, and the study of translation equivalence is not limited to language itself, but can expand to the context and culture.

Since the introduction of text linguistics into translation studies, the research on translation has come to a new stage. Great progress has been made in translation study under the guidance of text linguistics. Many translation researchers have taken functional linguistics as their framework of analysis and research, for it has the same focus as the purpose of translation, both focusing on the text and the relationship between the text and the context. Research has shown that SFL can make a good model for translation from various perspectives (Baker, 1997; Hansen-Schirra, Neumann, and Steiner, 2007; Hatim and Mason, 1990; Kim, 2007a; Munday, 2009; Steiner and Yallop, 2001).

At the end of the last century, a new paradigm was introduced into translation studies: the corpus. Baker (1993) was one of the first scholars to tie corpus linguistics and translation studies together, and in the following 20 years, corpus-based translation studies have developed considerably with the joint effort of

Munday (1997), Stewart (2000), Zanettin (2002), Olohan (2004), etc. Laviosa (2004) comprehensively reviews the development of corpus-based translation studies from 1993 to 2004. The establishment of parallel corpora in translation studies provides us with an extensive view to evaluate and improve translation quality and to better understand source and target languages. This research adopts a corpus-based approach in the analysis of source text (ST) and its equivalent target texts (TTs) in order to be able to describe and compare the characteristics of the ST and the TTs and also to make the methodology replicable in other translation studies.

1.3.2　Translation model in the present research

The comparative study of coherence patterns in the present research is based on the model of both Halliday (2001) and Matthiessen (2001) towards translation studies.

1.3.2.1　Halliday's view of a good translation

Halliday depicts a model of translation and translation evaluation in *Towards a Theory of Good Translation* (2001). He states that "a text has meaning at all linguistic strata" (Halliday, 2001: 14). In his evaluation of good translation, he also follows Catford's (1965) definition of translation and equivalence. The equivalence of the source text and target text is actually the comparison of the systems of the two languages that lie behind the texts. When observing the translation, the translator and linguist take different stances. The linguist assumes that "you can theorise the relationship of translation only by referring to language as a system" (Halliday, 2001: 14). The translator's perspective tends to be instantial, as it requires engaging with language at the textual level when thinking about how to create an effective translation (Halliday, 2001: 14). The divergence of the two different stances can be solved when seeking "equivalence" in translation under a systemic functional framework.

The three parameters in SFL — stratification, metafunction and rank — can provide a comprehensive model for translation from order, content and strata. Halliday proposes the notion of "equivalence value" attached to ranks, strata and metafunctions in translation (Halliday, 2001). Generally speaking, the higher the equivalence value is, the higher the rank and stratum are. In metafunction, the ideational equivalence is taken for granted, and the higher value of equivalence is achieved by the interpersonal and textual meanings. "A 'good' translation is a text which is a translation (i.e. is equivalent) in respect of those linguistic features which are most valued in the given translation context" (Halliday, 2001: 17).

1.3.2.2   Matthiessen's translation environments

In *The Environments of Translation*, Matthiessen (2001) contextualises translation from the most global to the most local environments of language within the dimensions of systemic functional theory (i.e. stratification, rank, metafunction) as a descriptive model. Translation is modelled as a mapping of meanings, and we can map not only between two lexicogrammatical systems but also between two semantic systems (Matthiessen, 2001: 66).

He contextualises translation in the lexicogrammar of English, and identifies the environment relevant to the location of translation from the most global environments of language to the most local ones. The widest environment is context. Table 1–2 shows the location of translation in the stratification-instantiation matrix. Translation is from one text to another. It is in the instance pole of the cline of instantiation, and it can happen at any stratum in the stratification. The comparison between SL and TL texts are to be taken at lexicogrammatical and semantic levels. The lexicogrammatical manifestations of coherence patterns in the ST and the TTs are compared in this research to see how translation equivalence or shifts take place. The equivalence and shift are evaluated thus: "The wider the environment of translation, the higher the degree of translation equivalence; and the narrower the environment, the higher the degree of translation shift" (Matthiessen, 2001: 78). Catford (1965: 49) defines translation equivalence in this way:

> The SL and TL items rarely have "the same meaning" in the linguistic sense; but they can function in the same situation. In total translation, SL and TL texts or items are translation equivalents when they are interchangeable in a given situation. This is why translation equivalence can nearly always be established at sentence-rank — the sentence is the grammatical unit most directly related to speech-function within a situation.

Table 1-2　The translation location in the stratification-instantiation matrix
(Matthiessen, 2001: 98)

Stratification	Instantiation	
	potential	instance
context		
semantics	semantic system: networks of ideational, interpersonal and textual meanings; their construction as texts, sequences, etc.	text: semantic selection expressions, and their representation as meanings
lexicogrammar	lexicogrammatical system: networks of ideational, interpersonal and textual meanings; their construction as clause complexes, clauses, groups, etc.	lexicogrammatical selection expressions, and their manifestation as wordings

1.3.2.3　Summary

The systemic functional translation model has a direct guiding effect on translation, which makes the model highly operational and practical.

In the present research, the equivalence of a literary text in translation is investigated. The translation aims to rebuild the context of situation of the ST in the target language culture. As the highest value of equivalence can be achieved in context, which is realised by semantics and lexicogrammar at the content plane of a language, the analysis of the linguistic features of the ST and the TTs is also taken at the highest rank — the clause — to reach as high as possible translation equivalence.

1.4　A brief introduction to *HLM*

The data used in this research come from a Chinese classic novel *HLM* and its two most famous complete English translated versions, *The Dream of the Red Mansions* (translated by Yang Xianyi and Gladys Yang) and *A Story of the Stone* (translated by David Hawkes and John Minford). The corpus in the current research consists of 3 chapters of the Chinese source text and its two accordant English target texts. To supplement the present research, another corpus consisting of 30 pieces of dialogue between the two main characters,

Baoyu and Daiyu, throughout the first 80 chapters of the novel and its two English translations is also applied.

HLM is one of the four great classics of Chinese literature. It was written mainly by Cao Xueqin in the middle of the 18th century during the Qing Dynasty, and is widely considered a masterpiece of Chinese literature and a pinnacle of Chinese fiction. HLM is a typical type of traditional Chinese novel, with captions for each chapter. It has been verified that the first 80 chapters of the novel were written by Cao Xueqin, while the later 40 chapters were finished or compiled by Gao E and Cheng Weiyuan.

Taken as a semi-autobiography of the author Cao Xueqin, born in an extremely notable aristocratic family, which, however, declined before he was a teenager, *HLM* tells a story of the decay and destruction of beauty. Based on the main plot of the tragic love story between the hero Jia Baoyu and heroines Lin Daiyu and Xue Baochai, the novel describes the life of an aristocratic family (the Jia) and the process of how it, and the lives of three other notable families, the Shi, Wang and Xue, go from great prosperity to decline. In the frame of the love story, a stone was abandoned by the Goddess Nv Wa when she was melting rocks to repair the sky. Then, the stone visited the human world through being born into a baby boy's mouth, and experienced the worldly things with the boy for his whole life. The baby boy was Jia Baoyu, the incarnation of the formal attendant Shenying in the Palace. He once watered a Crimson Pearl Plant when he was still in heaven. After his incarnation, the Crimson Pearl also went down to the world and took the form of a girl, Lin Daiyu. She only took the girl's form to repay him the water he shed on her with her tears. Since the stone had experienced all the things which happen in the human world with his master Baoyu, and all his experience was engraved on itself, the novel has the title "*Shi Tou Ji*" (which means *A Story of the Stone*).

The novel has aroused great interest among readers and scholars over hundreds of years. The field study devoted to this novel is called "redology", which has become an academic subject in China, in East Asia and elsewhere in the world. Though a novel, *HLM* is more like an encyclopaedia of Chinese society in the 18th century, for it contains almost every aspect of the different social classes, from aristocratic to common life, and it also reflects the customs, activities, medicine, architecture, cuisine, opera, music, mythology, and religions in that time. Therefore, the novel represents the Chinese culture in almost every aspect of that time.

The author Cao Xueqin was a master in the use of language, whether in traditional Chinese poetry, classical Chinese, or written dialogues. The novel was written in the vernacular rather than classical Chinese, and it used the Beijing dialect, which is the basis of the modern Standard Chinese. In *Modern Chinese Grammar* (1959), Wang Li, an authority in Chinese linguistics and also Halliday's Chinese teacher, took the language used in *HLM* together with another novel *Legend of Heroes and Heroines* as the foundation of modern Chinese grammar. In the preface of that grammar book, Zhu Ziqing said that even though it has been more than 200 years since the publication of *HLM*, the grammar is the same with modern Chinese; there are only a few changes in the lexis. Most of the examples in the book are from *HLM*, because the language used in *HLM* is formal Chinese [Wang, 1959 (1985)]. The novel can still be a good resource of linguistic study of modern Chinese language (Feng, 2008; Hou, 2012; Liu, 2010; Zhao, 2011).

The translation of the novel into other languages is a difficult task, because the various aspects of language and culture that *HLM* reflects make the novel a rich resource for cultural, aesthetic, historic and linguistic study. The richness of the novel also imposes difficulty for the study of the translation of the novel.

The study of *HLM* is a subject known as redology, which involves many aspects of research and divides into different branches. However, the redological study is more like historical research, and among all the redological studies, the translation and linguistic studies of *HLM* constitute only a small part.

1.4.1 *HLM* in translation studies

Li (1993) proposes that the study of translation of *HLM* specifically be termed "*HLM* translatology", which would include the translation of *HLM*, the history of *HLM*, and *HLM* translation theory and methodology (Li, 1995). Since the first English translation of *HLM* in 1830, the novel has been translated into 23 languages and there are now more than 60 translated versions in all different languages (Li, 1995). The versions were completed at different times and by translators of different backgrounds, which provides a large body of resources for studying the translation methods that were used.

The overview of the English translation studies of *HLM* in China from 1980 to 2003 was done by Yan (2005). She categorises the research into 13 groups based on research topics, and analyses each of them in terms of research methodology. The translation study of *HLM* is combined with many other subjects like linguistics, aesthetics, and art and so on. Many translation theories are adopted such as Nida's function equivalence (Nida, 1969; 1993) and Newmark's semantic translation (Newmark, 1977). However, the translation study on *HLM* is far from enough compared with *HLM* redologic studies. Therefore, it calls for further and more research on this aspect, especially on research methodology.

Wen and Ren (2012) have found that the studies on English translation of *HLM* in China grew steadily from 1979 to 2010, especially after 2000. Since 2000, more than 10 papers have appeared each year. Wen and Ren (2012) divide the studies into two groups: general studies, which include the translation study of culture, different versions of the novel and the history of its English translation; and specific studies, which include the study of different features within the novel such as poems, dialogues, names, chapter titles, idioms, figures, etc. Their research shows that there are far fewer general studies of *HLM* than specific ones.

The study perspectives on *HLM* vary, but the descriptive and qualitative research efforts are far more than the quantitative ones. In addition, there is still a long way to go in expanding the methodology and the theoretical framework, so as to do more translation process research and to build up *HLM* translation as a subject. This current research can make some contribution to these efforts.

1.4.2　Linguistic studies of *HLM*

In recent years, the study of *HLM* has not been limited to literary criticism, and the translation study of *HLM* has also not been restricted to translation criticism, but both have expanded to other fields like linguistic perspectives, such as corpus-based studies and functional linguistics.

The construction and applied studies of a Chinese-English parallel corpus of *HLM* were funded by the Chinese National social and scientific program. The corpus is "the first annotated parallel corpus with one source text and three target texts" (Hou, 2012: 28), and was built up by Professor Liu Zequan at Yanshan University in China in 2005. This program has made a foundation for corpus-based study of English translations of *HLM* and also provides a perspective to the translation of other classical works. Liu (2010) has reviewed the results from his corpus programme and conducted applied research on lexical and textual translation with a combination of qualitative and quantitative methods. He has also explored the different styles of four translators of *HLM*, quantitatively comparing the characteristics of each translation with respect to lexicon and sentences on the basis of this corpus (Liu, Liu, and Zhu, 2011). Another translation corpus on *HLM* was constructed at Shanghai Jiao Tong University in 2008.

Feng (2008) has compared Yang's and Hawkes' versions in terms of the translation of rhetoric, cultural terms, idioms and lexical frequency to explore how the source and target language cultures influence the translators and their translations. This research is very useful in using a corpus in translation studies and statistical evaluation to show the differences between the works of different translators. Feng highly evaluates Hawkes' version as it shows rigor in the domestication of terms, lexis and collocations, and colloquial and written style of language used in translation. Feng's research reveals the influence that the different cultural backgrounds of the translators have on the translation styles.

Li, Zhang, and Liu (2011) also adopt a corpus-assisted analysis of *HLM* to investigate translators' styles. They build a parallel corpus consisting of the first 15 chapters of the source Chinese novel and its two English translations, the versions by Yang and Hawkes. Using corpus tools in the research makes the study of translators' styles systematic and reliable. Their research focuses on the type-token ratio (TTR) and average sentence length of the two translations. The statistical results show that Yang's version uses a wider range of vocabulary. The differences of the two translations are mainly caused by the different ideological and cultural backgrounds and translation philosophies of the translators. First, the two groups of translators have different translation purposes. Yang's purpose is promoting China to the outside world, while Hawkes and Minford aim to introduce a Chinese classic to the English world. Secondly, English and Chinese show their own features in connecting clauses into a sentence. The different mother tongues of the translators therefore lead to longer sentences in Hawkes' version than Yang's. Their research provides a perspective on investigating the translators' styles through their linguistic habits and stylistic patterns.

HLM and its English versions are also studied from functional linguistic perspectives. For example, the cohesion in the novel is studied to evaluate how the different English versions are well cohesively organised or whether they are in accordance with the Chinese source text (Zhang, 2010; Zhu, 1998). Hou (2011) investigates the nominalisation, a nominalised transform of finite clause, in the translation of literary prose in HLM based on three different English translations. The nominalisation in Hou's research is investigated from its semantic role in the clause, and the results indicate that nominalisation in translation is the joint effort of grammar, lexicalisation, co-text, and context of a language. These different perspectives together contribute to different translator styles.

In summary, the linguistic research on *HLM* is still in the initial stages compared with studies of other aspects of the novel. Firstly, most of the research on the translation of *HLM* is about the translation evaluation of a specific subject, such as poems, cultural items, and names. Secondly, the research method used is mainly qualitative and descriptive rather than quantitative. Thirdly, the study of cohesion in *HLM* and its translations is so far insufficient, for most studies just compare different ways of realising the cohesive devices with a few examples.

The research done for this book connects the linguistic research of literary text with translation from the starting point of coherence. As a specific genre, literary text has its own contextual features. The systemic functional linguistic investigation of the features will provide a perspective on analysing literary text in a quantitative and descriptive way. Furthermore, coherence is closely related to the interpretation of literary text in both the original and target language cultures. The coherence patterns in the source and target texts are indicative of the translators' choices and styles in translation.

1.5   Aims and research questions

The purpose of this study is to examine how coherence is realized differently in the source text and the target texts of *HLM* from a functional linguistic perspective, using corpus tools. This approach aims to offer a new framing for evaluating the translation of this novel as well as other literary works.

1.5.1 Aims of the research

This study aims to discuss the different patterns of realising coherence in the source and target texts of *HLM* from the functional linguistic point of view with the aid of corpus tools, so as to provide a new perspective on assessing the translation of this novel and also on other literary works. By evaluating the Chinese text and its two English translated versions, the study will consider how the similar and different ways of realising coherence are dealt within different languages and by different translators. Since coherence has been studied for longer time in relation to English, there is abundant research on the coherence of English text, while the number of research efforts on Chinese coherence is relatively few (Zhu, Zheng, and Miao, 2001). Therefore, through the comparative study of both Chinese and English, this research also tries to enhance the research of the characteristics of coherence patterns in these two languages and to provide a methodology for the study of the patterns of coherence and its translation.

In addition, through a systemic functional linguistic analysis of literary texts, this study intends to view translation from a linguistic perspective. Linguistics can give us a point of view to look at a text and will help us develop a consistent analysis of the text, and the linguistic analysis of literature is also one of the most active and creative areas of literary studies. (Prince, Traugott, and Pratt, 1981: 39–40). What this research does is to give a specific systemic functional linguistic description of a literary text, and to compare texts in two languages in order to develop a framework for the translation of the patterns of coherence.

1.5.2 Research questions

A highly operational and plausible model for analysing the realisation of coherence needs to be set up to make the results practical, comprehensive and reliable. The model should be able to present characteristics of coherence both in Chinese and English.

Firstly, the comparison of Chinese and English texts mainly focuses on the ideational meaning of the texts, because "the most fundamental difference between the two languages seems to be in the division of labour between the two ideational modes of construal — the logical and the experiential" (Matthiessen, 2001: 67). The clause complex contributes to the logical development of the text, and the transitivity construes the experiential meaning. Secondly, cohesion sets the basis for textual coherence studies. The combination of the ideational and textual meanings together construes the patterns of coherence. After identifying the ways of realising coherence in Chinese and English, the translation of coherence can be processed to supplement translation studies and therefore to make some contributions to the development of the two disciplines: text linguistics and translation studies.

Based on the above discussion, the following research questions are raised:

(1) How are the patterns of coherence realised in the text by the mutual effect of the ideational and textual metafunctions?

(2) What are the similarities and differences in the realisation of coherence in the Chinese source text and the English target texts?

(3) How are the patterns of coherence kept and transferred in translation from Chinese into English?

(4) How do the patterns of coherence in the two TTs indicate the translators' styles?

(5) What does the variation in coherence patterns between the two translations suggest?

1.6   Structure of the research

This research comprises eight chapters. Chapter 1 introduces the background of this research, states the rationale and research problems, and outlines the aims and research questions of the research. This part also introduces *HLM*, the data of this research, and briefly reviews the linguistic studies of the English translation of this novel. The significance of the linguistic research on this novel has also been addressed in this part. Chapter 2 reviews the relevant studies on coherence and the translation of it. The different opinions on the relationship between cohesion and coherence are reviewed and discussed and then the view that cohesion is the foundation of coherence is adopted. The domain of the current research is derived from the review of the previous literature. Chapter 3 sets the research in a systemic functional linguistic framework, and describes the key notions related to the analysis of data in this study. Through the systemic functional linguistic description and the comparison of cohesion in English and Chinese, this chapter makes the comparative study of the two languages within the same framework. Chapter 4 presents the methodology and the corpus tool used in this research. Chapter 5 tries to explain the effects that the logical metafunction has on the construction of logically related sequences of meaning. It shows the results of the clause complex analysis of both the Chinese source text and the English target texts, and explores how the patterns of clause combination are transferred in translation. Chapter 6 relates the realisation of textual coherence with the textual metafunction via cohesive chains. It presents the cohesive chains and the difference in the ways of realising them in the three texts. Chapter 7 discusses how the ideational and textual meanings together construct the patterns of coherence in Chinese and English translated texts. By comparing the ways of realising coherence in the Chinese text and the two English texts, this chapter evaluates how the patterns of coherence are displayed in different language texts and by different translators. Chapter 8 is the conclusion. This part summaries the results in the previous chapters, discusses the implications for the research in the field of coherence and translation, proposes suggestions for future research, and also points out the limitations of this research.

Chapter 2

Literature Review

The present research is a comparative study of coherence between a classical Chinese novel and its English translations. It focuses on the coherence patterns of the text, and how the coherence of the Chinese source text is handled when translated into English target texts. Coherence in this study is closely related to translation, and in order to compare the two languages and translations, what "coherence" is needs to be clarified. In this section, the study of coherence and its development will be reviewed to provide a theoretical basis for the present study.

2.1   Coherence

In text linguistics, coherence has long been considered as an important issue in defining the characteristics and properties of a text. It has been discussed from different perspectives, such as SFL (Beaugrande, 1980; Campbell, 1995; Fries, 2004; Hu, 1994), cognitive linguistics (Givón, 1995; Kintsch and Van Dijk, 1978; Wei, 2004), and computational linguistics (Fais, 2004; Harabagiu, 1999; Sinclair, 1991). Coherence, within the systemic functional linguistic perspective, begins with the study of cohesion, which reveals the formation and characteristics of English texts. The concept of cohesion and the relationship between cohesion and coherence are vital in the understanding of coherence.

2.1.1   Cohesion

Cohesion contributes to coherence by "linking one part of a text to another"

(Halliday and Hasan, 1989: 48). By making a sequence of sentences hang together as a coherent text, it is considered as the aspect of texture that upholds textuality (Hatim and Mason, 1990: 210). Evidence in Harabagiu (1999: 2) shows that "the coherence structure of a text builds up from its cohesion structure".

Halliday and Hasan (1976) make the most comprehensive explanation and analysis of cohesion in English. "Cohesion is defined as the set of possibilities that exist in the language for making text hang together" (Halliday and Hasan, 1976: 18). Cohesion is not only something within the text, but is also related to its context of situation, which the hearer or reader constructs in the process of understanding the text. When readers can understand the relations of a clause with others in a text, cohesive relations are established. Cohesion occurs "where the interpretation of some elements in the text is dependent on that of another" (Halliday and Hasan, 1976: 4).

Halliday and Hasan (1976) identify several forms of cohesion within the text, and present a clear framework for cohesion analysis. They propose three cohesive devices, or connectors: grammatical connectors, lexical connectors, and logical connectors. The term grammatical connectors refer to reference, substitution and ellipsis. Lexical connectors refer to lexical collocation. They also classify lexical cohesive relation into two types: reiteration and collocation. Logical connectors are used to connect two ideas that have a particular relationship, and they are also called conjunction. Logical connectors can be further classified into four types: additive, adversative, causal, and temporal. Since the influential publication by Halliday and Hasan (1976), research on cohesion has remained popular. Halliday and Hasan observe that the purpose of cohesion study is to discover the characteristics of a text as distinct from a collection of sentences, because "cohesion concerns how the text is constructed as a semantic edifice" (Halliday and Hasan, 1976: 26), and "it is the underlying semantic relation of sucession ... that actually has the cohesive power" (Halliday and Hasan, 1976: 229).

While Halliday and Hasan's (1976) view has been very influential in the study of cohesion, there are also other scholars who hold various views on the function of cohesion.

On the basis of Halliday and Hasan's definition of cohesion, Tanskanen (2006: 7) specifies cohesion to the connection of the grammatical and lexical elements of a text.

De Beaugrand and Dressler (1981: 3) think that cohesion concerns ways in which the components of the surface text are mutually connected within a sequence. Widdowson (1978: 26) states that cohesion refers to the combination of sentences and parts of sentences to ensure propositional development. In this sense, cohesion is not restricted to grammatical and lexical devices.

Apart from the above illustrated explanation of cohesion, Hasan's work on cohesion has been extended and developed further by several scholars. Many scholars, for example, have extended and applied Halliday and Hasan's (1976) explanation of non-structural cohesion, both in English (Taboada, 2000; Tanskanen, 2006; Thompson, 1994) and Chinese (Hu, 1994; Zhang, 2004). Being comprehensive and explanatory, Halliday and Hasan's categorisation of cohesive devices is used for this research.

2.1.2   Cohesion and coherence

The concept of cohesion is defined as a semantic one. Cohesion refers to relations of meaning that exist within the text (Halliday and Hasan, 1976: 4), while coherence refers to the property of "unity" and of "hanging together" (Hasan, 1984: 181).

Since the publication of *Cohesion in English* (1976), "cohesion" has been a widely accepted concept; but "coherence" is still regarded as a "rather mystical notion" (Sinclair, 1991: 102). Cohesion and coherence are discussed at the same time by many scholars (Parsons, 1991; Sunday, 1983; Tierney and Mosenthal, 1983). The most controversial issue concerning the relationship between cohesion and coherence is whether cohesion is the basis of textual coherence (Fulcher, 1989).

2.1.2.1   Cohesion as the prerequisite for coherence

To study coherence, an understanding of cohesion is necessary. "Cohesion is a necessary though not a sufficient condition for the creation of a text" (Halliday and Hasan, 1976: 298–299). Hasan (1984) divides cohesion into two types: non-structural cohesion and structural cohesion. She states that non-structural relations are crucial to the creation of coherence. Here, non-structural relations refer to the cohesive devices mentioned in *Cohesion in English* (1976).

On the basis of Halliday and Hasan's view, Zhang (2012) takes cohesion as a semantic bond, which forms cohesive ties and network; and coherence a textual unity of these ties, cohesive network, and the context of situation. The coherence of the text is built upon the semantic bonds of the text.

Baker (1997) views coherence as a network of relations contributing to the organisation of the creation of a text. Cohesion is the surface expression in a text, while coherence lies below the surface expression in a text. Huang (1988: 11) holds a similar view to that of Baker, observing that coherence is the deep connection on contents of a discourse, while cohesion is the superficial connection of forms of a discourse. He concludes that the study of coherence often contains the study of cohesion. Even though the two scholars' view is different from Halliday and Hasan's, they treat cohesion as necessary in the study of coherence.

However, whether cohesion is in fact necessary for coherence is a controversial issue. Unlike Halliday and Hasan [1985 (1989): 9], who define cohesion as the foundation on which the edifice of coherence is built, Eggins (1994) views cohesion and coherence as two aspects of a text; and does not consider cohesion as the only standard for deciding whether a text is coherent or not. When we find the text not "hanging together", there are two dimensions to look at: "its contextual properties: what we call its coherence; and its internal properties: what we call its cohesion" (Eggins, 1994: 87). Coherence is referred to as the way clauses or sentences relate to the context. Thus, cohesion and coherence are two properties of a text: they together construct a text; and whether a text is cohesive or coherent depends on the perspectives from which the readers look at the text, either internal or external of the text. Enkvist (1978: 110) finds that "the formal cohesive links on the textual surface fail to reflect an underlying semantic coherence", but a well-formed text must have not only semantic coherence, but also sufficient surface cohesion to make sure that readers are able to chapture the coherence (Enkvist, 1978: 120).

Halliday and Hasan [1985 (1989): 48] argue that cohesion plays an important but not exclusive role in creating coherence, in that it "embodies the internal semantic relationships" of a text:

> An important contribution to coherence comes from cohesion: the set of linguistic resources that every language has (as part of the textual metafunction) for linking one part of a text to another. [Halliday and Hasan, 1985 (1989): 48]

Against Hasan's (1984) claims about the relations between the quantity of cohesive devices and perceptions of coherence, Parsons (1991) reports that a higher number of cohesive devices does not result in a higher quality of coherence, i.e. readers do not find the amount of cohesion in a text significant for its perceived coherence. He examines 16 students' essays in chain interaction analysis, and lists the relevant tokens, peripheral tokens, central tokens and non-central tokens and also the ratios of relevant to peripheral, central to non-central, central to peripheral and central to total tokens of each text. Then, the essays are graded for coherence by eight informants and are evaluated into five categories: poor, below average, average, above average and good. The results of the evaluation show the lack of correlation between ratios relevant to peripheral and coherence, but underline the crucial role that the percentage of central tokens in coherent texts. The importance of the ratio of central to total tokens is emphasised by Parsons, and is also considered as related to the coherence of a text. Therefore, he further develops Hasan's cohesive harmony, pointing out that it would seem that those texts which have central tokens organised into long chains are being perceived to be more coherent (Parsons, 1991: 425).

Zhang (2004) divides the procedures of encoding textual coherence into four steps: ① analyse all the cohesive devices in the text; ② explain all the cohesion; ③ build up the context on the basis of the explanation of cohesion; ④ tie cohesion and context together and construe the unity of textual coherence. He presents the view that cohesion corresponds to coherence, and specifies the role that cohesion plays in textual coherence. Zhang's approach contributes to the analysis of textual coherence with reference of cohesion.

2.1.2.2　Cohesion and coherence as two different properties

There is another perspective on the relationship between cohesion and coherence, which does not deny the relation between them but the cause and effect relation between them: some authors believe that some texts can be coherent without cohesive devices; while some also believe that cohesive devices do not lead to coherence in the text.

This perspective of the relationship between cohesion and coherence is thus to see them as two properties which do not determine each other. For Thompson (1994: 147), cohesion is a textual phenomenon, while coherence is a mental phenomenon, and it is in the mind of the writer and reader and cannot be identified or quantified in the same way as cohesion. Tanskanen has a similar view. She claims that cohesion is a textual property, while coherence depends upon the communicators' evaluation of the text (Tanskanen, 2006: 21).

Widdowson (1978) believes that cohesive sentences are not definitely coherent, and that sentences without cohesive devices may be coherent. He states that cohesion can be described in terms of the formal (syntactic and semantic) links between sentences and their parts. But discourse is not dependent on overt cohesion of this kind. Regarding overtness, Blum-Kulka (2000: 299) defines cohesion as an overt relationship between parts of the text, signalled by language specific markers. He gives an example to show that a coherent text isn't necessarily cohesive, within this definition:

> A: That's the telephone.
> B: I'm in the bath.
> A: OK. (Widdowson, 1978: 29)

Blum-Kulka's idea is supported and developed by Brown and Yule (1983), who are critical of Halliday and Hasan (1976) for appearing to postulate that it is necessary for a text to explicitly display some of the features of cohesion in order to be identified as a text. Brown and Yule give examples of texts that display few if any markers of cohesion, and consider that the reader or listener will assume that the sequence of sentences constitutes a text (1983: 195). The cohesion in the text is not necessary in the interpretation of the coherence of the text; rather, the readers' shared knowledge is more important. Similar views are expressed as "coherence also works without cohesion but not the other way around" by Koch (2007: 2); and as "coherence of the text is not guaranteed by the presence of cohesive ties" by Coulthard (1994: 174).

Widdowson (2007: 46) further expresses his view on the relationship between cohesion and coherence thus: cohesive devices are only effective to the understanding of a text when they enable readers to construct meaning that makes contextual sense and to derive a coherent discourse. This point of view doesn't treat cohesion as the basis of coherence, only as the explicit expression of coherence.

Hasan has taken into consideration the above points of view, and argues in response:

> Whenever scholars have attempted to prove that it is possible to have texts without cohesion, in order to demonstrate their point they have normally created what I would describe as "minimal texts" consisting of either a single message by one participant, or one message per participant. [...] However, in describing the attributes of a class of phenomena we need to start with typical members; and it cannot be denied that discourse whether spoken or written is typically productive of much larger — non-minimal — texts, which display the full range of possibilities open to texts in general. [...] So in order to support our statements about text in general, we must take non-minimal texts into account, since this will permit generalisations about minimal texts as well, while the reverse is not true. [Halliday and Hasan, 1985 (1989): 78]

Even though some minimal texts can be coherent without cohesive devices, most texts have cohesive devices; and the relationship between the cohesive devices and coherence is also investigated.

Cohesive devices are used as "an index of textual coherence", in Tierney and Mosenthal's (1983) study of *Cohesion and Textual Coherence*, to explore to what extent they contribute to textual coherence. A quantitative method is adopted in measuring the ranking of coherence in students' essays; the percentage of each cohesive category and subcategory is made; and the rating by three raters is used to determine the relationship between cohesive patterns and coherence. The result is not positive about the causal relation of cohesion to textual coherence. They make the conclusion that "a cohesion index is causally unrelated to a text's coherence" (Tierney and Mosenthal, 1983: 228).

For Van Dijk (1985), cohesion is neither a sufficient nor necessary condition for discourse coherence. It is not the individual word meanings or referents that determine discourse coherence, but the whole propositions as they relate to facts. The facts actually refer to the real world, or knowledge of the world and situations, which can be interpreted as the context.

Giora (1985: 699) claims that "cohesion as a linear relation that obtained between pairs of sentences is neither a necessary nor a sufficient condition for text coherence". She views cohesion as a by-product of coherence, not an independent requirement of textual coherence, and it cannot account for coherence. The function of cohesion is only to help mark or identify the discourse topic, and the coherence of a text is perceived by readers through the linked topics that are controlled by the cohesive devices: it is more intuitive than textual.

The issue that whether cohesion is necessary for coherence is debated from different perspectives. Even though some scholars think that cohesion is not the prerequisite of coherence study, they cannot deny that cohesion and coherence are closely related and that the study of coherence is often related to cohesion. In the present research, as Halliday and Hasan's view elaborates, cohesion is taken as necessary in the study of coherence.

2.2　The definition of coherence

The above section has shown different views on the relationship between cohesion and coherence. As to what coherence is, different scholars have their own views, and each of them makes sense within the terms of their own approach. Table 2-1 is a brief summary of the research on the definition and scope of coherence from different perspectives throughout the past few decades.

Table 2-1   Summary of the literature on the concept of coherence

Author	Date	Perspective on Research of Coherence	Genre
Van Dijk	1977	Cognitive linguistics	Book
Widdowson	1978	Pragmatics (illocutionary acts)	Book
Kintsch and van Dijk	1978	Psychological referential coherence	Article
Reinhart	1980	Pragmatics	Article
Sanford and Garrod	1981	Psychological linguistics	Book
Brown and Yule	1983	Cognitive and psychological linguistics	Book
Hasan	1984	Cohesive harmony	Chapter
Giora	1985	Discourse topic	Article
Crystal	1985	General linguistics	Book
Cook	1989	Encyclopaedia of language	Book
Petofi	1990	Encyclopaedia of language	Book
Nunan	1993	Language education	Chapter
Campbell	1995	Cognitive linguistics	Book
Rickheit and Habel	1995	Discourse processing/Cognitive linguistics	Edited book volume
Hu, Zhu and Zhang	1996	Systemic functional linguistics	Book
Zhang	1999	Text linguistics	Article
Taboada	2004	Text linguistics	Book

From the above table, we can tell that the notion of coherence has been taken as a significant component in text-linguistics, cognitive linguistics, psychological linguistics and computational linguistics.

Traditionally, the classification of the study of coherence is from two dimensions: one is from the text producer's point of view [Halliday and Hasan, 1985 (1989); Hasan, 1984]; the other is from the reader's point of view (Van

Dijk and Kintsch, 1983). The first point of view is from linguistic analysis; while the latter is from the psychological or cognitive linguistics, because it views the processing of a text as an interaction between the text and the prior knowledge or memory schemata of the listener or reader (Carrell, 1982: 482).

2.2.1 The linguistic view of coherence

Within a systemic functional perspective, a text "hangs together", which is a characteristic of coherence (Halliday and Hasan, 1985: 48). This indicates that any point in a text establishes content connection backward and forward. In semantics, coherence is expressed as "connectivity" and "consistency or unity" (Zhang, 1999). Coherence is a semantic concept: it is determined by the context of situation, and is realised through lexicogrammar and phonology. Neubert and Shreve (1992: 94) view a coherent text as having "an underlying logical structure that acts to guide the reader through the text". Their definition, however, needs to be further explained in terms of a logical structure.

Huang (1988) combines different views, and suggests that a coherent text should have certain cohesive devices, and follow semantic and cognitive principles. Clauses must be connected in meaning, and must be logical in sequence.

Realising the concept and mechanism of coherence, many scholars have conducted research on the coherence of texts. In her study, Tanskanen (2006) focuses on the role of lexical cohesion in collaboration and communication in the co-creation of texts. She distinguishes between the channel and communicators of texts; and adopts two analyses to understand the role of cohesion in discourse organisation, cohesive chains and texts. A main purpose of her research is to discover how cohesion contributes to coherence; or rather, whether cohesion has some effect on the reflections of collocation and communicative conditions in cohesive strategies. This research uses a different method from Hasan's concept of cohesive chain to study the collaboration contributing towards coherence in text. Calculating the cohesive pairs in text is the main part of the study. Even though the results show some differences in the cohesive pairs and portions of collocation among different types of text, they do not make clear the problem of coherence.

Reinhart (1980) does not rely only on SFL, but also adopts certain concepts from pragmatics to make an explanation of coherence. She distinguishes between explicit and implicit coherence, and defines the conditions for well-formedness: connectedness (cohesion), consistency and relevance; which can be seen as elements relating to text coherence. Her contribution is significant to the present research in terms of proposing cohesion, especially repetition, as contributing to textual coherence.

Giora (1985) adopts the idea of coherence by Reinhart (1980), and proposes her own conditions for text well-formedness: ① its discourse topic is the proposed one; or ② it is treated as a digression; or ③ it is a piece of background information. Her definition of text coherence is slightly different from well-formedness: it emphasises hyper theme or discourse topic of the text, which means that it defines coherence in terms of "aboutness".

Fries (2004) views coherence as a multidimensional concept. Four factors together contribute to the perception of coherence: social interaction; textual; overall generic structure; and an understandable and relatively self-consistent world conveyed by the words. Each factor is a continuum. A text can be coherent in one aspect, but not coherent in another. Coherence is thus "a multidimensional continuum which is always contextually bound" (Fries, 2004: 44).

The linguistic perspective of defining coherence sets text as the entry point of coherence study, which is also the focus of the present research.

2.2.2   The schematic view of coherence

For other schema theoreticians, coherence of a text rises from the individual's background knowledge, which enables comprehension of the text as a coherent whole on the basis of psychological constructs. According to Koch (2001: 2), "cohesion is described as a textual phenomenon whereas coherence is a mental one and also works without cohesion but not the other way around". Coherence is maintained by interaction of textual knowledge with readers' prior knowledge of the world (De Beaugrande, 1980: 19)

Cohesion relates only to the ways in which the actual words in a text are mutually connected by the grammatical forms within a sequence. Coherence concerns how the concepts and relations of the textual world are mutually accessible and relevant (De Beaugrande and Dressler, 1981: 3–4).

Brown and Yule (1983) also consider that the discussion of coherence should be beyond semantics. They have identified three aspects of the speaker's or writer's interpretation of coherence in discourse: "① computing the communicative function (how to take the message); ② using general socio-cultural knowledge (facts about the world); and ③ determining the inferences to be made" (Brown and Yule, 1983: 225). Their perspective of coherence does not target the language itself, but around it. They ascribe the coherence of a text to the speaker's or writer's intention. When people are interpreting linguistic messages, they make an assumption of coherence. However, they do not give a clear view of what coherence is; and their theory focuses on analysing the coherence in discourse beyond the text rather than within the text.

Van Dijk (1977: 93) takes coherence as a semantic property of discourses, but the interpretation of coherence relies on readers' knowledge, which is about the context of the discourses.

Derived from Van Dijk's (1973) coherence constraint, Werth (1984) views coherence as a superordinate term of cohesion, collocation and connectors; and it covers all forms of discourse connectivity, formal, lexical, logical and semantic. He considers that all the forms of connectivity result in semantics. In this sense, "coherence includes both formal and semantic connectedness" (Werth, 1984: 73). His definitions of cohesion, collocation and connectors are slightly different from the Firthian view, in that he thinks that they are semantic-pragmatic in nature. Werth then infers that, in literary studies, the coherence is usually called "theme", and is also studied by Van Dijk (1972; 1980) by the notion of "macro-structure". They set two conditions for a coherent discourse: "if its respective sentences and propositions are connected, and if these propositions are organised globally at the macrostructure level" (Kintsch and Van Dijk, 1978: 365).

Campbell (1995: 5) defines coherence as unity; and it is the relation between text and context of situation. For Widdowson (2007: 51), cohesion does not account for the coherence of a text, but the extent to which the text relates externally to the contexts, to the schemata that readers are familiar with in the particular social-cultural context.

Based on these definitions of coherence from the cognitive perspective, which examine how people interpret the meanings of the text or discourse rather than examining the linguistic signals themselves, several works have been conducted to clarify the cognitive perspective.

Sanders and Noordman (2000) have studied the cognitive status of coherence relations, which are referred to as cognitive entities that affect the processing of text. They also study linguistic markers that signal relations, by implementing an experiment to verify the role of linguistic markers and coherence relations. The results show that the linguistic markers facilitate the encoding of coherence relations.

Fries (2004) views coherence not as a single aspect of a textual feature, but as a multidimensional concept. Fries lists four factors that contribute to the perception of coherence: ① Can what is said be referred to as some understandable social interaction (2004: 12)? ② Does the language that is produced exhibit a normal texture (2004: 21)? ③ Does the language that is produced have an expected overall generic structure (2004: 33)? ④ Does the language that is produced construe an understandable and relatively self-consistent world and a set of values toward what is said about that world (2004: 36)? These factors interact with each other, and each one is gradient; but they work together at different strata to form the coherence of a text. He emphasises the interpretation of these factors from the interpreter's point of view.

Coherence is also studied from the comparative linguistic point of view. Taboada (2000) presents a view of how to measure cohesive relations in a comparative way. The data in her research are of a specific genre, namely task-oriented conversation, which is conversation completed under a certain topic given by the researcher; and the results therefore may not be applicable to other genres of conversation. Taboada (2004) also makes an overview of cohesion and coherence in dialogues on the basis of Halliday and Hasan's (1976) work. Her work contributes considerably to an understanding of the ways of realising cohesion and coherence in both English and Spanish through the application of Cohesive Harmony, Thematic Progression and Rhetorical Structure Theory (RST). The method is of relevance to the comparative study between other languages. It provides a practical way of analysing the construction of coherent texts or discourses in a bilingual corpus and also a method for generic study.

Wei (2004) conducts a significant research on the difference between the methods for realising coherence in these two languages from the cognitive perspective. He also distinguishes two types of mechanism of discourse coherence, inner and outer, and makes a valuable comparison of Chinese and English.

It can be concluded from the above review that no single theory can form a complete framework for explaining coherence nor comprehensively clarify textual coherence. Nevertheless, the research efforts on coherence complement each other and provide a view of it at different levels, such as context, semantics and lexicogrammar. To make further studies on coherence, what constitutes coherence, and how coherence works in the systemic functional linguistic framework, both need to be clarified.

2.2.3 Definitions of coherence in the frame of the function-rank matrix

Despite the various definitions on coherence, each one has its own perspective. Different views on coherence from the functional linguistic approach are presented and framed in Table 2-2 in the function-rank matrix, to present, categorise and relate the previous research views on coherence.

Table 2-2　Previous definitions and studies of coherence
framed in the function-rank matrix

		Ideational		Textual
		experiential	logical	
Context	Widdowson (1978); Hasan (1978) Generic Structure Potential; Beaugrande and Dresser (1981); Giora (1985) hyper theme; Campbell (1995); Eggins (1994); Seidlhofer and Widdowson (1999); Toboada (2004)		van Dijk and Kintsch (1978; 1983); Garrod and Doherty (1995)	Reinhart (1980) connectedness (cohesion); consistency and relevance

(continued)

| | | Ideational | | Textual |
		experiential	logical	
Semantics	van Dijk (1977); van Dijk (1985)	Zhang (1999)	Mann, Matthiessen and Thompson (1987; 1989) RST; Huang (1987); Knott(1994); Computational Linguistics; Harabagiu (1999); Sanders and Noordman (2000); Wolf and Gibson (2006)	Danes (1974) Thematic Progression; Halliday and Hasan (1976) cohesion; Hasan (1984) Cohesive Harmony; Tierney and Mosenthal (1983); Werth (1984); Lorentz (1999); Tanskanen (2006)
Lexicogrammar			Neubert and Shreve (1992)	

It can be inferred from Table 2-2 that the definition and study of coherence mostly full within the ideational metafunction, especially the logical component, and the textual metafunction, at contextual and semantic levels in a language. The previous research benefits the present research in terms of defining coherence, and also has provided a framework for the later research of coherence within the function-rank matrix.

2.3   The studies of coherence derived from systemic functional linguistics

Since coherence is such an important concept, it is necessary to review different theories that have been influential in its study. Apart from each defining coherence in a specific frame, these theories have framed the study of coherence in a practical model, and inspired many research efforts in the application of their models to the study of coherence for various types of texts and fields.

2.3.1   Thematic progression

Theme is the departing point of the message, and it locates and orients the clause within its context (Halliday and Matthiessen, 2004: 64). Theme is at the clause level of a text; and the thematic development works at the text level to organise the text as a cohesive whole. Danes (1974) distinguishes three types of thematic progression, and takes them as the representations of the connexity which shows the type of coherence in a text. Fries (1981) has utilised the choice of theme and thematic progression in his framework to investigate the overall organisation of a text.

Thematic types and progression are taken as a means of text coherence. There have been studies focusing on the application of thematic progression in translation, for example, Kim (2007a; 2007b) investigates how theme works in Korean with a small scale of corpus, finding that elliptical subjects play a vital role in contributing to thematic progression and in creating a cohesive text. The textual effect that thematic progression plays in creating meaning in the target text has also been studied by other scholars (Kim and Huang, 2012; Mundays, 1998; Ventola, 1995). Their works relate translation studies to the systemic functional framework, especially focusing on the textual metafunction in the meaning creation process.

2.3.2 Rhetorical Structure Theory

Rhetorical Structure Theory (RST) is a descriptive theory of a major aspect of the organisation of a natural text. It was developed in the 1980s as a result of exhaustive analyses of texts, as described in Mann and Thompson (1987).

Matthiessen (1995) sees a text as a univariate organisation with nesting rather than ranked units. It is characterised as the connecion of relations, which realises text coherence. RST shows how text units are structured and combined by adding a rhetorical relation between segments (Mann and Matthiessen, 1990: 3), and describes the relations in fuctional terms (Mann and Thompson, 1987: 2).

Acording to Mann and Thompson (1987), RST provides a general way to describe the relations between clauses in a text, whether or not they are grammatically or lexically signalled. It is a useful framework for relating the meanings of conjunctions, the grammar of clause combining and non-signalled parataxis. It has been used as an analytical tool for a wide range of text types. It is also useful in analysing narrative discourse. It provides a framework for

investigating Relational Propositions.

Since the coherence of a text depends in part on these Relational Propositions, RST has been useful in the study of text coherence (Mann and Thompson, 1987: 3). RST provides a system of text structure, which can be seen as a pattern of textual coherence.

Although RST was initially devised to guide computational text generation, it has since become popular in analysing text organisation and textual coherence. The application of RST has also expanded to other fields, such as pedagogical application, writing in second language acquisition, and translation.

2.3.2.1　Previous studies on RST

The relations that connect the parts of a text have been investigated for a long time, and have been given different terms: rhetorical predicates (Grimes, 1975), coherence relations (Hobbs, 1979; Kehler and Kehler, 2002; Sanders, Spooren, and Noordman, 1992), clause relations (Hoey, 1983), and rhetorical relations (Mann, Matthiessen, and Thompson, 1989; Mann and Thompson, 1987). Since RST was originally used for text generation in computational linguistics, the study of rhetorical relations and coherence has also flourished in this field.

Hovy (1988) adopts RST to describe a method of planning paragraphs to be coherent. Then, in *Approaches to the Planning of Coherent Text*, Hovy (1990) uses relations from RST, operationalised as plans, to construct coherent paragraphs. He proves that RST relations support both the creation of paragraphs at macro-level and the composition of parts of sentences at micro-level.

Knott and Dale (1994) discuss the relationship between implicit and explicit relations and cue phrases from the perspective of computational linguistics and natural language generation. Using a substitutability test, they have built up taxonomy of relational phrases and observe which relations they signal in linguistic phenomena. Later, Knott and Sanders (1998) model coherence relations in the construction of text from the reader's and writer's views. They propose two methods for investigating relations; and examine the methods that lead to the classification of relations and cue phrases, both psychologically and linguistically. The results show that the two methods are compatible with and complement each other. Therefore, their research provides a cross-linguistic methodology to explore the coherence relations in explaining cognitive and also linguistic views of language.

Taboada and Mann (2006) review the application of RST, and investigate whether the relations in the text can be signalled or not, and whether cohesion and coherence are independent from or interrelated with each other. They do not make a comprehensive review of RST, but focus on the fields in which RST is used in analysing textual coherence.

Taboada (2006) makes a detailed elaboration of the discourse markers in terms of relevance to the relations they mark, and describes how and when the rhetorical relations are marked. Although this research addresses the relationship between the rhetorical relations and discourse markers, it cannot clearly show how they contribute to the coherence of texts. Later, from a different perspective from the previous research, Taboada (2009) discusses the signalling of relations, which she recognises as the explicit marking of the presence of relations.

Renkema (2009) divides coherence relations into additive and causal relations. Some relations that have conjunctions are called explicit relations. His research provides useful suggestions and information for further research on RST and coherence, especially on how to find the discourse markers and how they work in discourse.

RST has also been used in cross-linguistic studies, as it provides a basis for contrastive rhetoric study. Cui (1986) makes a contrastive analysis between English and Chinese rhetorical structures. The results of Cui's research shed light on the comparison and contrast between the two languages, the combination of RST with other textual measurements such as cohesion, and also on translation.

There are also scholars who have applied RST in the Chinese context.

In *On Rhetorical Structure Theory*, Wang (1994) makes a brief review of RST, and focuses on the application of the theory to text analysis. He claims that implicit relations are as important as explicit relations, and that they contribute significantly to the coherence of texts. He points out that the rhetorical relations are recursive, and provides a theoretical basis for the implicit relations. In this sense, RST is crucial in revealing the coherence and interpersonal function of texts. However, how to grammaticalise and realise rhetorical relations needs to be further investigated.

Jiang (2006) points out seven problems in the coherence of students' essay writing. This study applies and explains RST and how it contributes to the coherence of texts, and thus it is a useful study for further research. It also shows that RST has a pedagogical function in essay writing.

Most of the research efforts reviewed above have tried to elaborate the relationship between RST and textual coherence, and have made contributions to the application of this theory across various fields. Still, more research needs to be done if we are to clarify the mechanism of coherence within the RST framework.

2.3.2.2   Relations between SFL and RST

Rhetorical relations are defined from four parts, which can be simplified into two: constraints and effect. The constraints on the spans generally refer to the status which they might have on the readers. The effect states a condition which (plausibly, in the analyst's view) the writer wants to achieve by employing the spans and the relation (Mann and Matthiessen, 1990). The effect is particularly helpful in explaining coherence of texts (Mann and Thompson, 2000).

According to Mann and Thompson (1987), the function of rhetorical relations is expressed through the locus of effect. To be specific, the rhetorical relations can be classified on the basis of the locus of effect, whether on nucleus only or on nucleus plus satellite.

There is a correlation between rhetorical effect and metafunctions.

> Each relation functions according to just one metafunction.
> All relations whose locus of effect is nucleus plus satellite function according to the ideational metafunction.
> All relations whose locus of effect is nucleus alone function according to the interpersonal metafunction.
> There are no relations whose function corresponds to the textual metafunction. However, the order of spans of a relation functions textually. (Mann and Matthiessen, 1990: 14–15)

Matthiessen and Thompson (1988) suggest that a text can be seen as being organised in dependency terms by a set of relations that depict the relationship between one part of a text and another, primarily in an asymmetrical relationship based on a notion of nuclearity.

On the other hand, SFL provides a theoretical basis for text planning and generation (Bateman, 1990: 2). RST is located within the SFL framework in the description of a text and also in exploring the unity of a text, to be specific, the coherence of a text. The connection between RST and SFL has also been explored by other scholars.

Matin (1992) uses RST to analyse conjunctive models; but he puts these relations in reticulum presentation. RST is considered "a preference for 'hypotactic' dependency which leads to multilayered rhetorical structures of considerable 'depth'" (Martin, 1992: 260).

Stede (1999) discusses the differences between rhetorical structure and thematic structure in text generation. The ordering of the text units is very different for these two methods, as RST focuses on nucleus-satellite relations, whereas themes are the results of choice. However, he does not make clear how to relate building a discourse marker lexicon to theoretical structure and thematic structure. Taboada and Lavid (2003) tie rhetorical analysis and thematic analysis together to characterise conversations in generic terms. Their research opens up a window for further research into any of these rhetorical, thematic and generic structure studies.

Stuart-Smith (2007) explores the relations not only at a functional level but also at a clausal level. Her research emphasises the hierarchical organisation of a text, and is suggestive in combining RST with Generic Structure Potential in terms of the study of coherence.

2.3.2.3　Criticism of RST

While popular, RST has also received criticism.

Moore and Pollack (1992) claim that RST analyses are inherently ambiguous. Mann and Thompson argue that one analysis will be preferred, depending on the intent that the analyst ascribes to the speaker (1987: 30). However, Moore and Pollack are not convinced by this statement. They give examples to show that the relation between two clauses is not settled: it can be informational, but can also be intentional. They believe that RST's major failure is that it does not adequately support multiple levels of analysis.

Knott and Dale (1994) think that it is inevitable for RST to have some defaults, and they point out the problems with the proliferation of relations. The hypothesis of RST is not completely reasonable, in that not all texts can be analysed by rhetorical relations, while even incoherent texts can be analysed with rhetorical relations between text spans.

Another criticism of RST is that it relates segments at a semantic level. Andriessen, De Smedt, and Zock (1996: 261) view the relation between two segments as multivalent. Moore and Pollack (1992) distinguish two co-existing levels of discourse relations, intentional level and informational level, which is contradictory to the RST assumption of one single preferred rhetorical relation between two segments.

However, despite certain deficiencies in RST, it remains an important tool in the analysis of textual coherence, and its combination with other frameworks is plausible.

2.3.3 Cohesive harmony

Cohesive harmony was first proposed by Hasan (1984) to identify the coherence of a text. Coherence is explored in terms of cohesive harmony in her influential article "Coherence and Cohesive Harmony". She lays the foundation of coherence on cohesion: cohesive devices do not make coherence, but the way of calibration of cohesive relations contributes to coherence. According to Hasan, the study of cohesion in a text is actually the study of its cohesive ties. "Two-ness" is the central idea of cohesion: the semantic bond between any element of the cohesive device and some other element in the textual environment creates cohesion. The two elements thus form a cohesive tie. The density of occurrence of cohesive ties is closely related to the degree of coherence (Hasan, 1984: 185–188).

Halliday and Hasan [1985 (1989)] then propose three semantic relations: co-referentiality, co-classification, and co-extension. These three relations tie two members of a tie; and the existence of such a tie is essential to texture. Co-referentiality ties two or more items that have the same referent into a cohesive chain. Co-classification ties items from the same class. Co-extension ties items referring to something within the same general field of meaning. By the three relations, a set of items, each of which is related to the others, can form a cohesive chain. Cohesive chains can be divided into two types: identity chain (members of the chain are in a co-reference relation), and similarity chain (members of the chain are in a relation of co-classification or co-extension).

Armstrong (1991) points out that cohesive chains cannot guarantee the coherence of a text, and that relations between the chains need to be analysed, through what is called chain interaction analysis. Thompson (1994) argues that chain interaction is just a contributing factor in the creation of a cohesive monologue. The systematic relationship between clause relations, lexicogrammatical cohesion in a monologue is explored by Thompson, and chain interaction is used as a main factor in measuring the coherence of a monologue. More research needs to be conducted on discourse types other than monologues.

Taboada (2000) adopts a comparative method to measure cohesive relations in both English and Spanish, but finds that the interaction of cohesive chains is low, which may indicate that other genres of data need different measures of cohesive harmony.

Despite the fact that cohesive harmony is more plausible in small texts than big texts, it is playing a significant role in identifying the mechanism of coherence in a text. The key concepts within cohesive harmony are also adopted in the present research in determining the patterns of coherence in the text.

2.3.4　Summary

The above-mentioned methodologies are all applied to different text types in explaining the coherence of a text, and each is explanatory to some degree. In the present research, these different aspects of coherence studies will be taken into consideration, and a method for the analysis of coherence patterns in systemic functional linguistic framework will be proposed in Chapter 3 and Chapter 4.

2.4　Coherence in relation to translation

New ideas from other disciplines have invigorated translation studies

(Neubert and Shreve, 1992: vii). And meanwhile, the innovation and development of translation studies stimulate the development of other disciplines. "Any theory of translation must draw upon a theory of language — a general linguistic theory" (Catford, 1965: 1). One of the goals of the present research is to discover how coherence is transferred and expressed in translation from a linguistic perspective.

2.4.1　Coherence in translation

Since the introduction of text linguistics into translation study, the research on translation has arrived at a new stage. Many scholars have adopted SFL as their analysis and research framework, and have made tremendous progress in translation study.

2.4.1.1　House's application

House (1977) provided a text translation model, which, however, has received considerable criticism. House improved her model in *Translation Quality Assessment: A Model Revisited* (1997) by introducing Halliday's register analysis into her early model. This new model compares the characteristics of the source language text and the target language text, and evaluates translation from the perspectives of language, register and genre. It realises register analysis through the comparison of lexicon, syntax and text. She distinguishes three main textual aspects: ① theme-dynamics (various patterns of semantic relationships by which "themes" recur in texts); ② clausal linkage (a system of basically logical relations between clauses and sentences in a text); ③ iconic linkage (two or more sentences cohere because they are isomorphic) (House, 1997: 45). House's text translation model supplements Halliday's by describing the text from the three contextual variables, Field, Tenor and Mode, from the perspective of her own approach. She suggests two basic types of translation: overt and covert; which are differentiated by whether the source text is culture specific or not. The model provides a very practical functional linguistic approach to translation studies, and sheds light on achieving the equivalence of the source language culture and target language culture in translation. However, as the author acknowledges, an overt translation can never reach "functional equivalence" (House, 1997: 112).

2.4.1.2 Baker's application

In *In Other Words: A Coursebook of Translation*, Baker (1997) divides textual equivalence into five levels: equivalence at word level; equivalence above word level; grammatical equivalence; textual equivalence; and pragmatic equivalence. She examines literary equivalency from three perspectives: thematic and information structure; cohesion; and coherence. And in dealing with cohesion analysis in translation, she adopts Halliday and Hasan's (1976) approach. According to Halliday and Hasan (1976), cohesion is realised in English using reference, substitution, ellipsis, conjunction and lexical cohesion. In the traditional way, reference means the relationship between a word and what it points to in the real world in semantics; but in the textual sense, "reference occurs when the reader has to retrieve the identity of what is being talked about by referring to another expression in the immediate context" (Baker, 1997: 181). The continuity of reference results in cohesion. Substitution and ellipsis are both grammatical relations. The former refers to the replacement of one item (or items), while the latter means the omission of an item. Conjunction involves the use of formal markers, such as additive, adversative, causal, temporal, continuative and so on, to relate sentences, clauses and paragraphs to each other (Baker, 1997: 190–191). Lexical cohesion refers to certain words in organising relations within a text (Baker, 1997: 202). Different languages prefer to use different cohesive devices; and the general level of cohesion differs across languages and even within the same language. The density of cohesive devices also varies in different texts. Therefore, the translator should take into account the above differences between languages so as to produce good translations.

In terms of the translation of coherence, Baker defines it as equivalence at pragmatic level, which refers to how utterances are used and interpreted in context (Baker, 1997: 217). Whether a text is coherent or not depends on its readers and the situations the readers are in. Therefore, a translator has to consider the target readers' knowledge range and expectations they have about such things as the organisation of the world, the organisation of language in general, the organisation, and conventions of particular text types (Baker, 1997: 222). Baker sets up her own model in analysing cohesion and coherence in translation studies.

Despite that her model adopts Halliday and Hasan's cohesion analysis in seeking textual equivalence in translation, she does not consider that cohesion could result in coherence. She treats coherence as one property of the text which needs to be understood by the target readers with shared knowledge. For the purposes of the present research, cohesion in both the source text and the target text helps to build up the coherence of the texts, for the cohesive devices contribute to relating the texts with the context. Therefore, Baker's view of the equivalence of coherence in translation is not adopted in this book.

2.4.1.3 Hatim and Mason's application

In *Discourse and the Translator*, Hatim and Mason (1990) view translation as a communicative event happening under a certain social context. Through reviewing a range of translation studies, they explore the relationship between translation and linguistics, the influence of linguistics on translators, and the guiding effects of linguistics on translation studies.

Hatim and Mason emphasise the role that context plays in translation. Malinowski (1935) points out that both verbal and non-verbal texts should be related to their environment, to make them situationalised. This is referred to as the context of situation, which includes participants in speech events. For Hatim and Mason, the key point of translation is to see the meaning of texts as something negotiated between the producer and the receiver. Apart from knowing the intentions of any source language text, the translator can also make judgments about the effects that the translated text has on target language readers (Hatim and Mason, 1990: 65). Translating can be viewed as the process of transforming one semiotic entity into another, under some conditions of equivalence related to semiotic codes, pragmatic actions and general communicative requirements (Hatim and Mason, 1990: 105).

Texture is also important in translation, and it is explored from three perspectives: coherence, cohesion, and thematisation. Hatim and Mason define coherence as the continuity of sense in the text, and cohesion as the surface reflection of coherence in the text (Hatim and Mason, 1990). They claim that the translator needs to reflect the coherence from the source text to the target text. "Coherence, once it has been retrieved from the ST, can easily be re-established in the TT (by using recurrence or co-reference), but not the same pronominal means" (Hatim and Mason, 1990: 197). They think that the analysis of cohesive devices and cohesive ties are important in translation; otherwise, the motivation in the ST of such ties would be weakened (Hatim and Mason, 1990: 201).

Hatim and Mason's model sets a practical and comprehensive framework for the translation of coherence. However, it only describes the components of the textual coherence; as to how to determine textual coherence, it does not provide detailed exemplification. Therefore, to supplement and further develop the previous study, in this book, a framework for the analysis of the coherence patterns of the text will be presented.

2.4.1.4 Summary

All the above-mentioned literature has been influential in relating translation with linguistic theories, especially with text linguistics. There are also other scholars who have approached translation studies from a systemic functional linguistic perspective (e.g. Bell, 1991; Hansen-Schirra, Neumann, and Steiner, 2007; Kim, 2007a, 2009; Kim and Huang, 2012; Munday, 2009; Steiner, 2001; Trosborg, 2000). They have contributed to expanding the scope of text linguistics and have also enriched translation studies.

Further research needs to be conducted on analysing the patterns of coherence both in Chinese and English, and how they are dealt with in translation.

2.4.2 The study of coherence in translation

Apart from the above-mentioned research on the model of coherence translation, there are scholars who have worked on the translation of coherence from other perspectives. Their works approach the study of coherence not only in a general framework, but also from some specific entry points; and have broadened the study of coherence in wider frameworks.

Wang (1998) divides coherence into three levels: the morphological level, the lexical level, and the clausal level, and also distinguishes unmarked and marked coherence. Being cohesive and coherent at the semantic level is taken as unmarked coherence; being grammatically incoherent at the semantic level, and being generally coherent but partly incoherent at the semantic level, are taken as marked coherence. Coherence at the clausal level not only involves cohesion but also thematic progression. The translator has to consider the three levels of coherence, to be specific, morphological, lexical and clausal levels, to achieve high quality coherence in translated texts. Wang highly values the importance of coherence in translation, since he assumes that the source text is coherent. Then, the target text readers' misunderstanding and confusion can be blamed on the inappropriate transference of the coherence of the source text. Hence, the study of coherence is vital to effective translation.

Krein-Kühle (2002) studies the use of the demonstrative "this" in translation. She claims that cohesion and coherence are interrelated, and that one of the ways of keeping coherence in translation is to adopt cohesive devices. She examined the use of "this" as a demonstrative determiner and a demonstrative pronoun in English and its German potential equivalents, and discovered that: ① the interplay between the cohesive devices helps to establish not only the cohesion but also the coherence or the continuity of sense in the target text; and ② cohesion in the target text contributes to preserving the sense and inference so as to establish the coherence at the text-in-context level. Krein-Kühle's study proves that coherence in German target texts is maintained and upheld by cohesive means. Her study, however, only focuses on the use of "this", and there are more cohesive devices to be considered in text-in-context based research. We can have more insights into how cohesion and coherence are produced in source texts and their translations across text genres and types (Krein-Kühle, 2002: 51).

Zhao (2002) views cohesion and coherence as two essential qualities of translation. He claims that the transference of the source text to the target text must maximise the mapping of both cohesion and coherence, which serves as an important parameter for the translation quality assessment. He attributes the transference of cohesion to the shift of two grammars from the source text to the target text, and also of coherence to the relevance with the theme. According to Zhao, when translating poems, it is considered better to keep the equivalence of both form and function between the source and target texts in terms of cohesion and coherence.

Wang (2005) identifies coherence as a multi-dimensional concept reflected in grammar, semantics, pragmatics, and stylistics. He believes that cohesion is an important condition for coherence, but not a necessary one. He clarifies the mechanism of semantic coherence, and explains how to identify and reconstruct semantic coherence via cohesion in the translation of a novel. In the specific genre of a novel, semantic relations in the specific context can show different poetic values. As a result, the translator should keep the semantic relation of the source text to maintain semantic coherence in translation. He points out certain translation problems regarding lexical cohesion in the transference from the source text to the target text, and emphasises the importance of collocation in establishing context so as to maintain textual coherence. His study reveals the importance of cohesion in the study of coherence within the context of literary translation.

In later work, Wang (2006) classifies coherence as unmarked and marked. Usually in translation, translators would assume the source text is coherent, but sometimes the source text lacks cohesion, so they have to decide whether to add some cohesive ties in the target text. Wang (2006) believes that the translator should keep the coherent model of the source text in the reconstruction of coherence in the target text. He establishes his own way of analysing coherence in the source text, and also proposes some strategies for dealing with coherence in the translation of fiction. These two articles of Wang have been an inspiration for the present research in the reconstruction of coherence in translation, especially in literary texts.

Zheng (2009), adopting De Beaugrande and Dressler's (1981) perspective on coherence, defines a coherent text as a sense of continuity as the result of merging concepts and relations into a network of knowledge space centered around main topics. This continuity of senses is viewed as the basis of coherence. In order to maintain coherence from the source text to the target text during translation, the author proposes four solutions: ① retention of the continuity of senses of a text in translation; ② reconstruction of the target text for the purpose of continuity; ③ coherence complementary in translation; and ④ the extracting and foregrounding of topic sentences in translation. These four approaches can serve as the means of keeping textual coherence in translation.

Another approach to applying cohesion and coherence in translation is from the corpus linguistic view. Since Baker (1993) published "Corpus linguistics and translation studies: implications and applications", the corpus-based approach of translation studies has gained increasing attention. Translation scholars will be able to discover the nature of translated text as a mediated communicative experience thanks to the availability of vast corpora of both original and translated texts, as well as the development of a corpus-driven methodology (Baker, 1993: 243).

Of the later development and application of corpora in translation studies, some studies are related to the transference of cohesion and coherence. For example, Hansen-Schirra, Neumann and Steiner (2007) conduct a quantitative analysis of cohesive devices in English and German parallel corpora, which shows the differences in their cohesive patterns, thus revealing the explicitness and explicitation in translation. Their research benefits the methodology of the study of coherence in translation in the way that the cohesive devices are dealt with.

A corpus-based approach is adopted in cohesion studies in translation by Bystrova-McIntyre (2012) between English and Russian. She compares the means of every cohesive device, and the global textual features in three kinds of texts: non-translated texts, human-translated texts, and machine-translated texts. She assumes that the way a text is produced would be reflected in the use of cohesive devices and other global textual features, and examines the means of text production in three different genres of text: literary texts, newspaper texts, and scientific texts, using a corpus linguistic approach. The results of this research show significant differences in the use of cohesive devices and other global textual features in the three genres of texts. The corpus-based methodology in this study is intriguing in the combined approach of comparative studies, translation studies and translation pedagogy. Her study shows the value of an approach to translation study based on corpus linguistics, and gives some brief cohesive patterns in different genres of texts.

2.5　Cohesion and coherence in *HLM* studies

The study of cohesion and coherence can also be traced in the linguistic and translation studies of *HLM*, although such study in this area is relatively rare. There are only a few articles on the cohesion of *HLM* and its translation. Most of them involve the application of Halliday and Hasan's cohesion theory to the comparison of the source text and different versions of target texts of *HLM* (Pan, 2008; Zhang, 2010; Zhu, 1998); but they haven't given detailed explanations of how the cohesion mechanism works in the source and target texts.

Zhao (2011) has studied the explicification of cohesion in translation by comparing the conjunctions, adverbs, and conjunctive phrases in the source text and in two English translated versions (Yang and Hawkes) of *HLM*. It appears that, in translation, both translators adopted the explicification strategy and supplemented the cohesive devices of the target texts. The results show some personal differences in using these devices in the translated versions, thus indicating the features of each translator.

The research on the cohesion of *HLM* and its translation is, however, insufficient. The problem of all the above research efforts on the transference of cohesion and coherence in *HLM* translation is that they haven't made clear the relationship between cohesion and coherence. None of these researchers provide their own analytical model for coherence translation studies, but only apply cohesion theory in the translation of *HLM*. To the knowledge of the present author, to date little work has been done on the coherence of *HLM* and its translation.

Therefore, this calls for further study on the framework of utilising cohesion as one of the factors in building up the coherence of the text, and also of the translation of coherence.

2.6   The location of coherence analysis in the present study

The present research develops a model for coherence analysis capable of generating a framework for describing coherence in Chinese and English texts and also in translation.

As a multi-dimensional concept, coherence is the collective effect of the different metafunctions. It can also be probed from different ranks in the systemic functional framework. Since lexicogrammar is the core of the language, the patterns of coherence can be realised in lexicogrammar through different systems in different metafunctions. Table 2–3 shows the aspects of the description of coherence within the function-rank matrix.

Table 2–3　The location of coherence in the function-rank matrix

Stratification	Metafunction	
	Logical	Textual
Semantics	RST	
Lexicogrammar	Clause complex	Cohesion; Cohesive chains

Based on the above summary of the factors that contribute to coherence, we can state that the coherence in a text can be analysed in the framework of SFL in terms of the collective effects of the ideational and textual metafunctions at the lexicogrammatical level, and it is realised by transitivity, clause complex and cohesive chains in combination with each other.

2.7　Summary

The research on coherence of a text has been carried out from different perspectives; and coherence has always been an important issue in the study of text linguistics and translation. Different definitions of and research on coherence have widened the scope and methodologies of the study of coherence from different perspectives.

Cohesion is taken as a main factor contributing to textual coherence in the present research. Despite the research taking cohesion and coherence as two separate properties, in the analysis of coherence, cohesion remains an important component.

Halliday and Hasan (1985) outline the scope of coherence, and Hasan (1984) analyses the extent of coherence in a text. In some of their expressions, we can observe that texture can be seen as coherence in a vague sense; for example, "the parts of a sentence or a clause obviously 'cohere' with each other, by virtue of the structure. Hence, they also display texture" (Halliday and Hasan, 1976: 6); and "cohesive ties between sentences stand out more clearly because they are the ONLY source of texture [emphasis in original]" (Halliday and Hasan, 1976: 9). Halliday and Hasan have been criticised for arguing that cohesion is the basis of coherence in a text, and for taking texture to mean coherence (Carrell, 1982: 481). Eggins agrees that a text has texture; but she views it as the result of contextual coherence and cohesion (1994: 94–95), created through the patterns of cohesion (1994: 112). In the present study, the difference between texture and coherence is not distinguished; but the lack of distinction between texture and coherence is only to make clear that the study of coherence cannot be done without the study of cohesion.

Taking consideration of the different definitions and scope of coherence, it is preferable to choose the view that cohesion forms the basis of coherence study. The coherence of a text is displayed in the way that the cohesive devices connect with each other in the structure of the text, and "variation in coherence is the function of variation in the cohesive harmony of a text" [Halliday and Hasan, 1985 (1989): 94]. In addition, the configuration of coherence patterns in the systemic functional linguistic framework can not only provide a methodology for the analysis of coherence in different genres of texts, but also contribute to the comparative and translation study of texts in different languages.

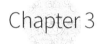

Chapter 3

A Systemic Functional Framework for the Study of Coherence

From the systemic functional linguistic view, the present study attempts to investigate the patterns of coherence in terms of the integration of the different metafunctions: the experiential, logical and textual, and lay out a methodology for analysing coherence patterns in Chinese and English.

This chapter consists of four sections. Section 3.1 depicts an overall map of SFL. Section 3.2 is concerned with the cohesive devices in the formation of cohesive chains. Section 3.3 combines the elements mentioned in the previous two sections and locates them in the SFL map, for the analysis of coherence in the present study. Section 3.4 describes the Chinese grammar from the systemic functional perspective, "to map between two lexicogrammatical systems as well as between two semantic systems" (Matthiessen, 2001: 66) in English and Chinese. This mapping is crucial in translation studies by allowing for alignment between the two languages and comparisons to be made within the same unit.

3.1 Systemic functional linguistic theory

SFL "provides the linguistic community with the first comprehensive systemic description of the clause and group/phrase grammar of language", and is the foundation model of language description not only of English but also of other languages (Hasan, Matthiessen, and Webster, 2005: 793). Systemic functional grammar is a choice system: instead of viewing language as the expressed, it views language as a meaning potential, and focuses on the grammar of language. Some key notions of systemic functional grammar will be clarified: metafunctions (ideational, experiential, logical, interpersonal, and textual), systems, stratification (semantics, lexicogrammar, and phonology), rank, context and instantiation (instance, potential, and register probability) (Halliday and Matthiessen, 2004; 2013).

3.1.1 Stratification

Language is seen as a complex semiotic system with various levels, or strata. The content plane of a language includes two levels, semantics and lexicogrammar; and the expression plane includes phonology. The linguistic system all together comprises three strata: semantics, lexicogrammar, and phonology. These strata are related by realisation: semantics is realised by lexicogrammar, which is realised by phonology. In other words, each lower level realises the higher level.

"The heart of language is the abstract level of coding that is the lexicogrammar" (Halliday, 1985: 8). As the intermediate level, the lexicogrammatical level is purely internal to language. In contrast, the semantic level relates upwards to the context of the language and the phonological level relates downwards to the soundings. According to Halliday (1992), language is a meaning potential and that grammar is the powerhouse of language. Lexicogrammar shows how language construes meanings and how the meaning is to be potentially expressed with patterns. The focus on language meanings or wordings should be on lexicogrammar rather than on semantics, even though both meaning and wording are important to understand "how language works" (Halliday, McIntosh, and Strevens, 1964).

As the resource for the creation of meanings, lexicogrammar is also the only level that does not relate to the experiential world nor the articulation of human sounds directly. The location of grammar in the system of language, as the inter-level between semantics and phonology, is an important aspect of the study. Beyond how lexicogrammar, semantics, and context are related to one another, we also need to consider how the lexicogrammar is organised, which depends on the system network.

There are two modes of grammatical organisation: paradigmatic and syntagmatic. The paradigmatic axis organises the grammatical resources into a set of inter-related options available for realising meanings. Paradigmatic organisation is under the principle of BEING, which shows the class-membership relation between options. The syntagmatic axis comprises structures, items or wordings that realise the options. Syntagmatic organisation is under the principle of HAVING, which shows the part-whole relation between structures. SFL treats language as the configuration of paradigmatic choices, which are presented as system networks.

Halliday (1978) first pointed out the perspective of examining any phenomenon or category, in relation to stratification, from three perspectives, "from above" "from roundabout", and "from below"; which he later defined as a trinocular perspective (Halliday and Matthiessen, 2004: 31). This trinocular vision shows the ways to understand systemic functional grammar from different stratal perspectives. The priority is given to the view "from above" (Halliday and Matthiessen, 2004: 31). Lexicogrammar is the resource for making meaning unified by mapping the structures one on to another so as to form a single integrated structure that represents all components simultaneously (Halliday, 1977: 176). Therefore, the analysis of the meaning of a text is rooted in the analysis of its lexicogrammar.

In order to determine how the different strata work in the construction of coherence, this study adopts a "from above" approach to explore coherence at the lexicogrammatical level, showing how choices make patterns of coherence.

3.1.2   Metafunction

"Metafunction" is a central notion in SFL (Halliday, 1985a; Halliday, Matthiessen, and Yang, 1999; Matthiessen, 1995). Halliday (1985b) postulates that in all languages the content systems are organised into ideational, interpersonal and textual components. Each functional component constitutes a distinct mode of meaning, which is realised by a distinct mode of expression. Since functionality is intrinsic to language, these functions are called "metafunctions" of language (Halliday and Matthiessen, 2004: 29–31). The metafunctions are used to explain the system of the language, setting up basis for the description of the functions of language. The metafunctional diversification organises both the content strata of language, which means it not only applies to the lexicogrammatical stratum but also to the semantic stratum.

The ideational metafunction concerns the interpretation and representation of the experience of the world. It is distinguished into two components: the experiential, and the logical. The experiential function is concerned with the processes of construing meanings from experiences that language has evolved; and the logical function with the very general logical relations between such experiences. Logical structures "present themselves in the semantic system as independent of any particular class or classes of phenomena", and "are not the source of rules about what goes where" (Halliday, 1979: 73–74).

While construing meanings, language is also enacting our personal and social relationships. This is the interpersonal function of language. It concerns the interaction between the speaker and the listener or the writer and the reader.

Along with these two functions, the textual function is related to the construction of a text. The textual function is the systemic resources that a language must have for creating a coherent discourse, for ensuring that each instance of text makes contact with its environment (Halliday et al., 1999: 528). It has an enabling and facilitating function for the other two functions, since the ability to construct discourse sequences, organise the discursive flow, and create coherence and continuity is necessary for construing experience and performing interpersonal relationships (Halliday and Matthiessen, 2004). It is the resource that presents the other two meanings as information organised into the text in context (Matthiessen, 1995: 18).

A text is the product of meanings of all four kinds — experiential, logical, interpersonal, as well as textual (Halliday, 1977: 181). Each metafunction is realised by its distinct set of lexicogrammatical systems: the experiential metafunction is realised by TRANSITIVITY system at the clause rank; the logical metafunction is realised by paratactic and hypotactic complexes at different ranks, with one of these, the clause rank, being the focus of this research; the interpersonal metafunction is realised by MOOD and MODALITY systems at the clause rank; and the textual metafunction is realised by the THEME system (theme-rheme structure) and INFORMATION system in the information unit at the clause rank, and by cohesion around the clause.

The logical component is distinct from the other three, in that all logical meanings, and only logical meanings, are expressed through the structure of "unit complexes": clause complex, group complex and so on (Halliday, 1977: 178). Halliday has identified the "logical component" in the linguistic system as distinct from all the others because "it is expressed through recursive structures, whereas all the other functions are expressed through non-recursive structures" (Halliday, 1978: 48). Additionally, the logical meaning "is composed of the functional and semantic relations that make up the logic of natural language" (Halliday, 1994: 216). The recursive feature of the logical meanings forms the rationale that the logical metafunction can induce logical development through the recursion of the paratactic and hypotactic relations, and "set up logical-semantic relationships between one clausal unit and another" (Halliday, 2003). Hence, the clause complex analysis in the present research is a basis for demonstrating how the connections between text segments create a logically connected whole, thus contributing to the overall coherence of the text.

3.1.2.1   Experiential Meaning

Experiential meaning is construed through the transitivity of the clause. The term "transitivity" refers to a network of systems whose origin is the "major" clause, which contains a predication (Haliday, 1967: 38). Although a full treatment of the experiential component in the syntax of the clause would take account of other features, such as the expression of time and place and other adjuncts to and conditions on the process, the discussion of transitivity has been limited to the expression of processes and the participants therein — syntactically, those functions having in general verbal and nominal realisations (Halliday, 1968: 179). Transitivity systems are thus concerned with the process types in the clause, as well as the participants in the process, and also with various circumstances of the process.

The transitive form of clause organisation is based on extension. The configuration of Actor + Process can be extended by the unfolding of the process through time, which can result in another participant, the Goal (Halliday and Matthiessen, 2004: 282). From another perspective, this configuration shows an ergative pattern within it. The process is actualised through Medium, which is not confined to a particular type of process, but is common to all types of process and clause types. The ergative perspective, in other words, represents the more general form of organisation of the clause into processes and participants (Halliday, 1968: 189):

> The basic pattern of organisation in the English clause seems thus to be more readily describable not primarily in terms of action and goal but rather in term of cause and effect ... These two patterns may be called respectively the "transitive" and the "ergative". In English, transitive and ergative coexist ... but the predominant pattern is the ergative one (Halliday, 1967: 15).

Halliday and Matthiessen (2004) believe that, probably in all languages, experiential systems are some blend of these two semantic models of process: the transitive and the ergative. The transitive pattern is linear; whereas the ergative pattern is nuclear. "The Process and the Medium together form the nucleus of an English clause; and this nucleus then determines the range of options that are available to the rest of the clause" (Halliday and Matthiessen, 2004: 289). The ergative pattern makes the Process and Medium the core of a clause; which then extends to other Participants, such as Agent, Beneficiary,

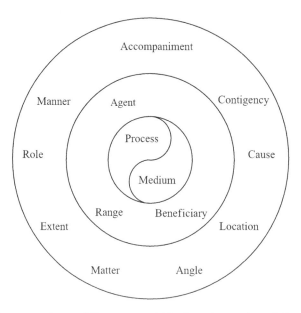

Figure 3-1 Clause nucleus of Process and Medium, inner ring of Agent, Beneficiary and Range and outer ring of Circumstances (Halliday and Matthiessen, 2004: 296)

56

Range, as well as Circumstance (see Figure 3-1). The distinction between transitivity and ergativity is important in showing how the different types of process are construed semantically in both English and Chinese, which is also instructive in the comparative study of the two languages.

Medium is associated with the process, and is the key feature in the process. Through Medium, the Process comes into existence and is obligatory in all processes, and it is the only element that is other than the process itself. The Process and Medium together form the nucleus of a clause (Halliday and Matthiessen, 2004: 288-289).

Apart from Medium, there may be also another participant functioning as the cause of the process. This participant is known as the Agent.

In English, the clause types represent the underlying grammatical selections, and restrictions on the use of specific verbs in specific clause types are rarely as rigid as they appear at first (Haliday, 1967: 52). The other elements entering into the transitive relations of the clause can be seen as "circumstantial" to the process. In addition to Medium and Agent, we can also identify Beneficiary and Range as the other ergative roles in the clause.

The Beneficiary is the one to whom or for whom the process is said to take place (Halliday and Matthiessen, 2004: 293); and it can be found as the "indirect object" in traditional grammar. The Beneficiary might then be deemed to exist outside of the transitivity system network entirely. Certain factors, however, suggest that the participant role of "beneficiary" should be taken into account, at least in part, in the context of transitivity (Haliday, 1967: 53). The Beneficiary is not limited to any class of nouns; however, the personal pronouns are more likely to be Beneficiary than any other items (Haliday, 1967: 55). It appears in "material" process, "verbal" process and sometimes "relational" process (Halliday and Matthiessen, 2004: 293). The Beneficiary specifies the Recipient, Client, or Receiver of the process.

The Range specifies the extent of the scope or domain of the process. It may occur in every type of process except the "existential" one (Halliday and Matthiessen, 2004: 293). The Range defines the scope of a process, or in certain situations, the process itself (when the verb is neutral); nevertheless, it also objects it, making it not only specific in terms of quantity or quality, but also as if it were a "participant" in the phrase, and therefore directly relevant to a beneficiary (Haliday, 1967: 61). Semantically, Agent, Beneficiary and Range share some features of participants and of circumstances: they are mixed (Halliday and Matthiessen, 2004: 295).

Apart from the nucleus and the inner ring of the clause, there is also an outer ring of elements in the clause. They are represented as Circumstances, which are adverbial groups or prepositional phrases.

Based on causation, the ergative form concerns whether the cause is external to the action or not (Halliday, 1968: 185). In determining the coherence patterns from the experiential meaning, the analysis of the ergative roles of the elements in the clause can indicate the causation relation of the cohesive devices, which can thus be taken as contributing to the coherence pattern of the text.

Although there is research on the metafunctional profile of English text (Lukin, 2002; Matthiessen, 2001), and also on the metafunctional profile of the grammar of Chinese (Halliday and McDonald, 2004), there has been few studies comparing ergativity in English and Chinese texts, even though there are ergativity studies on different languages, such as Thai (Wijeyewardene, 2012.) and Tibetan (Pin, 2012); and some typological work on the comparison between English and Chinese (Li, 2003). This research will depict a profile of the ergative patterns of the Chinese source text and the English target texts; which will not only contribute to the study of the coherence patterns of Chinese and English texts, but also to the comparison of the two languages in terms of experiential metafunction.

3.1.2.2　Logical Meaning

Matthiessen (2001) takes the translation from the "source text" to the "target text" as sequences of meaning creation. A detailed logical analysis at the lexicogrammatical level in both source and target texts will be critical in establishing the patterns of meaning creation in the two languages (Matthiessen, 2001: 115–116). The way that the logical metafunction works is to connect one unit, to be specific, the clause in the present research, with another via logico-semantic relations, to make the text a logically related whole. The connection between clauses is seen by many scholars as one critical way of construing the coherence of a text (Garrod and Doherty, 1995; Kintsch and Van Dijk, 1978; Knott and Dale, 1994; Sanders and Noordman, 2000; Wolf and Gibson, 2006). As stated before, the realisation of the logical connection between clauses is through clause complexes at the lexicogrammatical level. Therefore, the way that clauses connect with other clauses through taxis and logico-semantic relations can be taken as an important element in the interpretation of coherence.

In meaning construction, the clause is regarded grammatically as the basic unit. However, in the text, the unit construing meaning is often at the rank above the clause, which is the clause complex: "When a number of clauses are linked together grammatically, we talk of a clause complex (each single linkage within a clause complex can be referred to as one clause nexus)" (Halliday and Matthiessen, 2004: 4). A nexus is a minimal sub-complex in the unfolding complex (Matthiessen, 2002: 243). The nexus can connect with not only clauses but also nexuses, which can result in a layer and internal nesting in a clause complex. Therefore, the nature of the serial structure of clause complexes is open and dynamic (Matthiessen, 2002: 245). Clause complexes are made up of relations that link clauses depending on one another, usually one pair at a time (Halliday and Matthiessen, 2004: 367). The resources for combining clauses derive from the logical metafunction, which serves to relate clauses through interdependency relations.

The way that clauses are linked one with another is determined by two systems: ① TAXIS (degree of interdependency), via hypotaxis or parataxis; and ② LOGICO-SEMANTIC TYPE, through expansion or projection. Figure 3–2 shows how the clauses combine with the two subsystems, and also the recursion of these two subsystems. The recursion of the two subsystems demonstrates the potential of one nexus developing into a clause complex: "stop" and "go on" represent that, when a clause is related to another clause via logico-semantic relations, this process of connection can then stop or proceed iteratively. Clause complexes can get quite complex due to this possibility of looping back (Matthiessen, 1995: 140).

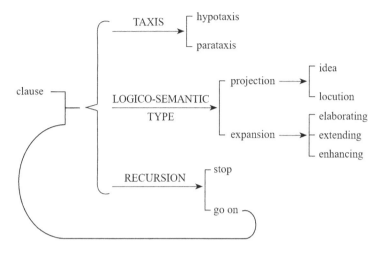

Figure 3-2　The system of clause complexing (Halliday and Matthiessen, 2004: 373)

Matthiessen (2002) has located clause complexing within the total meaning-making resource of language, stratally in the lexicogrammatical stratum, and metafunctionally within the logical function. Clause complexing is the resource for construing sequences of processes by linking clauses into complexes that are constructed out of logico-semantic relations; where the clauses are treated as equal or unequal in status (Matthiessen, 2002: 239). From above, below and around clause complexing, it "is highly indeterminate — as is every other system in language; a zone that shades into other zones. [...] It's also indeterminate in the sense that it's a constantly changing, fundamentally variable system" (Matthiessen, 2002: 310). Clause complexing can thus be related to the logical development and the cohesive sequences of the clauses, and also to the expansion of clauses.

The clauses are related to each other interdependently. The degree of interdependency of clauses is known as taxis. The structural mode of taxis is called "univariate", which is "an iteration of the same functional relationship", and "the units related in this way are interdependent" (Halliday and Matthiessen, 2004: 383-384). The two degrees of interdependency are parataxis and hypotaxis. Parataxis links units of equal status, while hypotaxis links units of unequal status. As a result, the paratactic relation is symmetrical, while the hypotactic relation is unsymmetrical. In a symmetrical relation, one clause is initiating and the others are continuing; and they are represented by numbers 1 2 3 ... In an unsymmetrical relation, one clause is dominant and the others are dependent upon it; and they are represented by Greek letters α β γ ... Any pair of clauses related by interdependency or taxis is referred to as a "clause nexus", and the clauses making up such a nexus are primary and secondary (Halliday and Matthiessen, 2004: 374–376). Table 3–1 lists the most distinctive features of the primary and secondary clauses in paratactic and hypotactic relations.

Table 3–1　Primary and secondary clauses in a clause nexus
(Halliday and Matthiessen, 2004: 376)

	primary	secondary
parataxis	1 (initiating)	2 (continuing)
hypotaxis	α (dominant)	β (dependent)

The following examples show taxis in detail:

[1] ||| The full moon smaller grows (1), || full water overflows (2). |||

[2] ||| When the tree falls (β), || the monkeys scatter (α). ||| (*A Story of the Stone*, Chapter 13)

In [1], the two clauses are in a paratactic relation; both can exist alone, and they are in an equal status with each other. In [2], the clause "When the tree falls" only sets a time condition for the clause complex, and it does not exist independently, but relies on the interpretation of the clause "the monkeys scatter"; so there is a hypotactic relationship between them.

The clause complex can work in sequence as in the above two examples; and it can also contain another clause complex, forming the nesting of clause complexes; for example:

[3] ||| Then even if the clan gets into trouble || and its possessions are confiscated, || this part of its property, as charitable estate, will escape confiscation. ||| (*A Story of the Stone*, Chapter 13)

The nesting relation of clause complexes in [3] is shown as:

β   1   Then even if the clan gets into trouble

        2   and its possessions are confiscated,

α   this part of its property, as charitable estate, will escape confiscation.

The clause complex may involve relations of both parataxis and hypotaxis, and it is often a mixture of both paratactic and hypotactic sequences, either of which may be nested inside the other (Halliday and Matthiessen, 2004: 376).

The clause nexus is not only determined by the TAXIS system but also by the system of LOGICO-SEMANTIC TYPE.

There are two fundamental logico-semantic relations between the primary and secondary clauses: expansion, and projection. Expansion means that the secondary clause expands the primary one by: elaborating it, extending it or enhancing it. Projection means that the secondary clause is projected by the primary clause as: a locution or an idea. "Expansion relates phenomena as being of the same order of experience, while projection relates phenomena to phenomena of a higher order of experience (semiotic phenomena — what people say and think)" (Halliday and Matthiessen, 2004: 377). These two fundamental logico-semantic relations, of expansion and projection, can thus be further categorised into smaller types, through the notation shown in Table 3-2.

Table 3-2　Notations of expansion and projection
(Halliday and Matthiessen, 2004: 377)

(1) Expansion		
a) elaborating	=	("equals to")
b) extending	+	("is added to")
c) enhancing	×	("is multiplied by")
(2) Projection		
a) locution	"	(double quotes)
b) idea	'	(single quotes)

Each subcategory of these two fundamental relations is elaborated as follows. (1a) Elaborating: one clause expands another by elaborating on it (or some portion of it): restating in other words, specifying in greater detail, commenting, or exemplifying. (1b) Extending: one clause expands another by extending beyond it: adding some new element, giving an exception to it, or offering an alternative. (1c) Enhancing: one clause expands another by embellishing around it-qualifying it with some circumstantial feature of time, place, cause or condition. (2a) Locution: one clause is projected through another, which presents it as a locution, a construction of wording. (2b) Idea: one clause is projected through another, which presents it as an idea, a construction of meaning.

There are three ways of expanding a clause with another one into a clause nexus: elaborating it, extending it, and enhancing it. Matthiessen (1995: 148) has taken into account the options of expansion in more delicacy. Elaborating clause complexes include expository, exemplificatory, and clarificatory options; extending clause complexes include addition (also adversative) and variation; and enhancing clause complexes include the various circumstantial relations recognised in English, e.g. spatio-temporal, causal-conditional, manner, and matter, in the context of the clause complex.

1) Elaboration

In elaboration, one clause elaborates another by restating, specifying, commenting or exemplifying the meaning of it. To be specific, the elaborating clause does not introduce any new information to the primary clause, but only further develops what is already there. Elaboration can be paratactic or hypotactic.

In paratactic elaboration, the clauses are noted as "1=2"; and it contains three types of elaboration: ① in exposition, the secondary clause restates the thesis of the primary clause in different words, to present it from another point of view, or perhaps just to reinforce the message; ② in exemplification, the secondary clause develops the thesis of the primary clause by becoming more specific about it, often citing an actual example; and ③ in clarification, the secondary clause clarifies the thesis of the primary clause, backing it up with some form of explanation or explanatory comment (Halliday and Matthiessen, 2004: 397–398). Each type is given an example in Table 3–3.

Table 3-3　Elaboration

Exposition	i.e. "in other words"	||| He spends all his time over retorts and crucibles concocting elixirs, || and refuses to be bothered with anything else. ||| (TT2)
Exemplification	i.e. "for example"	||| The sound of flutes and strings could be heard from all the houses in the neighbourhood; || everywhere was singing. ||| (TT1)
Clarification	i.e. "to be precise"	||| Haven't you ever heard the old saying, || "The beast with a hundred legs is a long time dying"? ||| (TT2)

In hypotactic elaboration, the clauses are noted as "α = β". The secondary clause functions as a descriptive gloss to the primary clause; and it can be finite or non-finite. For example:

[4] ||| You know Mr. Zhen, || [α = β] who was principal of the Jinling Provincial College? ||| (TT1)

[5] ||| For a long time Vanitas stood lost in thought, || [α = β: non-finite] pondering this speech. ||| (TT2)

2) Extension

In extension, the secondary clause extends the meaning of the primary one by adding some new information to it; and the added clause could be an addition, a replacement, or an alternative (Halliday and Matthiessen, 2004: 405).

Paratactic extension is noted as "1+2". It is known as "co-ordination" between clauses. There are three subtypes of paratactic extension. In addition, one clause is simply added to another, without any causal or temporal relationship between them. The addition can be positive ("and"), negative ("nor") or adversative ("conversely"). However, the clauses linked by the additive conjunctions, e.g. and, or, but, are not necessarily in an extending relationship. When a clause is led by, for example "and then" or "and so", the hypotactic clause is dependent, so the nexus is enhancing rather than extending. In addition, when "and this/that" refers back to the previous clause, the nexus may be elaborating. In variation, one clause is in total or partial replacement of another, and can be replacive ("instead") or subtractive ("except"). In alternation, one clause is an alternative to another.

Hypotactic extension is noted as "α+β"; and it contains the same three subcategories of extension, only with the extending clause being dependent, which can be finite or non-finite. Examples are shown below:

[6] ||| A boy like that is bound to lose the property he inherits || [1 + 2: additive] and won't benefit by the advice of teachers and friends. ||| (TT1)

[7] ||| Now, the good cosmic fluid with which the natures of the exceptionally good are compounded is a pure, quintessential humour; || [α+β: additive] whilst the evil fluid which infuses the natures of the exceptionally bad is a cruel, perverse humour. ||| (TT2)

3) Enhancement

In enhancement, the secondary clause enhances the meaning of the primary clause by qualifying it with time, place, manner, cause or condition.

Paratactic enhancement is noted as "1×2". It is also a kind of co-ordination with a circumstantial feature, which most often is time or cause. The paratactic enhancing relation can construct temporal, spatial, manner and causal-conditional sequences of clauses. For example, ||| My ma's took ill || [1×2] and I've got to go || [1×2] and fetch the doctor for her. (TT2) ||| "and I've got to go" is the result of the primary clause "My ma's took ill", and "and fetch the doctor for her" is in time sequence with "and I've got to go". Thus, the clause complex is a paratactic enhancing nexus with a nesting of a paratactic enhancing nexus.

Hypotactic enhancement is noted as "α×β". In traditional grammar, it is known as an "adverbial clause", with time, place, manner, cause and condition. It can be finite or non-finite.

[8] ||| If the old woman is deceiving us, || [condition: × β α] you naturally won't be able to find it. ||| (TT2)

[9] ||| [1 α] He had done well in the Triennial examination, || [result: × β] passing out as a Palace Graduate, || [result: ×2] and had been selected for

external service. ||| (TT2)

Expansion can be tactic relations of parataxis and hypotaxis, and also can involve embedding. Unlike taxis, embedding is not a relation between clauses, but is a clause as a constituent of another clause. Embedded expansion is not a concern for the present research, because the focus of study is the logico-semantic relations between clauses.

In addition to expansion, there is another logico-semantic relation that functions as a direct representation of a linguistic experience, which is known as "projection". In terms of the level of projection, it can be divided into "locution" and "idea"; in terms of the mode of projection, it can be "hypotactic reporting" and "paratactic quoting"; in terms of the speech function, it can be "projected proposition" and "projected proposal" (Halliday and Matthiessen, 2004: 441–442).

4) Locution

If the projected content is a "verbal" clause — what is said — then the projection is a "locution", and it is noted by the symbol. If a verbal clause is in direct speech, it is a paratactic quote. If it is in indirect speech, it is a hypotactic report. If speech function is taken into consideration, it is impossible for a minor clause to be reported directly, so this has to be a paratactic quote.

5) Idea

If the projected content is a "mental" clause — what is thought — then the projection is an "idea", and it is noted by the symbol. Just as with locution, an idea can be directly quoted or indirectly reported. Table 3-4 presents the types of projection nexus with examples of each.

Table 3-4　Types of projection nexus

		Paratactic quote		Hypotactic report
Locution "verbal	"1	"It's these two houses I'm talking about,"	α	By the way, I am sorry to say
	2	rejoined Zixing regretfully. (TT1)	"β	that last month the mother passed away. (TT2)

(continued)

		Paratactic quote		Hypotactic report
Idea 'mental	'1	"There must have been something behind all this,"	α	You don't know how
	2	thought Shi-yin to himself. (TT2)	'β	he's come into the world. (TT1)

The analyses in the present research of logico-semantic relations between clauses are all based on the above discussion.

3.1.3   Context

Following Firth (1935), who borrowed Malinowski's concepts of "context of situation" and "context of culture", Halliday views language as social semiotic, and puts language in a social-cultural context. Halliday claims that the way to understand language is in the study of texts in context, and that CONTEXT and TEXT are actually the aspects of the same process [Halliday and Hasan, 1985 (1989): 5]. "The text is an instance of the process and product of social meaning in a particular context of situation ... and the context in which the text unfolds, is encapsulated in a text" [Halliday and Hasan, 1985 (1989): 11]. No study of meaning taken apart from its complete context can be taken seriously (Firth, 1935). There are three domains of functional diversification of context: field, tenor and mode (Martin, 1992; Halliday 1978; Halliday, 1989). Field refers to what is happening and the nature of the social action that is taking place. Tenor refers to who are taking part and the nature of the participants, their statuses and roles in the text. Mode refers to the part the language is playing in the context.

Concerning the relationship between context and text, the sets of contextual systems construe the overall context in which a particular text is "embedded" (Matthiessen, 1995: 36). These contextual domains correlate with the metafunctional organisations of language (Halliday, 1978); and each of the three contextual aspects tends to be projected by one of the three metafunctions. A systematic relationship between the context of situation and the metafunctions of language has been proposed (see Figure 3–3): "the field is expressed through the experiential function in the semantics; the tenor is expressed through the interpersonal function in the semantics; the mode is expressed through the textual function in the semantics" [Halliday and Hasan, 1985 (1989): 25]. Field is realised by transitivity such as process type, active or passive voice, and actor. Tenor is realised by mood and modality such as modal verbs and adverbs. Mode is realised by theme, information structure and cohesion.

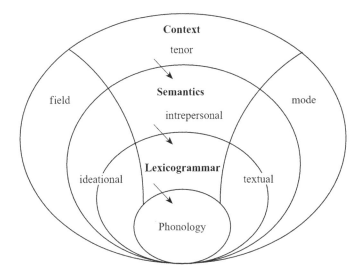

Figure 3-3   The metafunctions and contextual configuration

Context is an element that is often taken into consideration in textual coherence, as stated in the literature review in Chapter 2. The relationship between context and text explains that textual coherence is founded on the social interaction encoded in the text (Fries, 2002: 347). In the present research, consideration of the social context in which the coherent text is produced is needed to fully understand the coherence of the text. As the construction of a coherent text has been identified from the ideational and textual metafunctions, the semantic expression of the two contextual parameters, field and mode, are thus emphasised in this research.

3.1.4   Rank

Although coherence is a semantic concept, its realisation is through lexicogrammar. The first step in text analysis, in translation as elsewhere, is to identify the ranking clauses, which are the central processing unit in the lexicogrammar, because meanings are mapped into an integrated grammatical structure in the clause (Halliday and Matthiessen, 2004: 10).

The grammar of every language has a rank scale. Rank distributes the grammatical resources in terms of constituency, and it orders the units from the highest to the lowest ranking. The highest rank on the scale is clause, which is the gate way to text. The commonly recognised ranks are clause, group, and word; with a hierarchically vertical relationship between these. Each rank "consists of one or more units of the rank next below", and may "shift downgraded to function in the structure of its own rank or the rank below" (Halliday and Matthiessen, 2004: 9).

Coherence is studied at the clause rank in the present research. Clause is taken as the basic unit of analysis because, grammatically, it is the highest rank; and it can form clause complexes, which are seen orthographically as sentences. Furthermore, every language displays certain form of clause organisation (Halliday et al., 1999: 530). Clause is thus the entry point of the systemic functional grammar and is used as the fundamental unit for the experiential, logical and textual function analysis at the lexicogrammatical level.

3.1.5 Summary

SFL can set a basis for the evaluation and practice of translation. Halliday (2001) summarises translation thus:

> In any particular instance of translation, value may be attached to equivalence at different ranks, different strata, and different metafunctions. In rank, it is usually at the higher lexicogrammatical units that equivalence is most highly valued; ... in strata, equivalence is typically most valued at the highest stratum within language itself, that of semantics. Value may also attach explicitly to the level of context, especially when equivalence at lower strata is problematic. In metafunction, high value may be accorded to equivalence in the interpersonal or textual realms — but usually only when the ideational equivalence can be taken for granted (Halliday, 2001).

In this research, the equivalence of the coherence patterns in translation is studied from the highest rank, clause; from the lexicogrammatical stratum; and also from the experiential, logical and textual metafunctions.

3.2　Cohesion in the creation of coherence

As mentioned above, the textual metafunction plays a crucial role in the creation of coherence. Cohesion, as a main component of the textual metafunction, is the basis for building up coherence. However, both Halliday and Hasan [Halliday and Hasan, 1976; 1985 (1989); Hasan, 1984] have made it clear that cohesive devices alone cannot guarantee the coherence of a text. What matters more is the way that cohesive devices are linked to each other and are interpreted as a grammatically and lexically related string in a text. Fries (2004) also observes a correlation between the perception of cohesive ties and that of coherence. Markels (1981) observes that cohesion makes a random collection of sentences into a text, and imparts meaning, insight and purpose to those sentences. In the description of cohesion, the term "tie" refers to a single instance of cohesion, a term for the occurrence of a pair of cohesively connected items (Halliday, 1976: 3). The concept of a tie allows for a systematic analysis of a text's cohesive features and a systematic explanation of its textual patterns (Halliday, 1976: 4).

Hence, the analysis of cohesion should focus on how the cohesive resources, or to be specific, the cohesive devices, tie meanings together to form a text; and the analysis of the cohesive chains in the text can be seen as a crucial aspect of coherence analysis.

3.2.1　Cohesive devices

Halliday and Hasan (1976) categorise cohesion into three types: grammatical cohesion (including reference, substitution and ellipsis); lexical cohesion; and conjunction, which is on the border-line between grammatical and lexical cohesion. Hasan (1984) further sub-divides cohesion into two types: non-structural cohesion, and structural cohesion. She observes that non-structural cohesion is crucial to the creation of coherence; but that, because structure is a uniformly integrative device, it does not go far enough in the explication of coherence. Table 3–5 presents a summary of cohesive device.

Table 3–5   Summary of cohesive devices [Halliday and Hasan, 1985 (1989): 82]

Non-structural cohesion			
Componential relations			**Organic relations**
	Device	Typical tie relation	
Grammatical cohesive devices	A: Reference 　1. pronominals 　2. demonstratives 　3. definite articles 　4. comparatives	co-reference	A: Conjunctive 　e.g. causal tie 　　consession tie
	B: Substitution & Ellipsis 　1. nominal 　2. verbal 　3. clausal	co-classification	B: Adjacency pairs 　e.g. question (followed 　　by) answer; 　　offer (followed 　　by) acceptance; 　　order (followed 　　by) compliance ...
Lexical cohesive devices	A: General 　1. repetition 　2. synonymy 　3. antonymy 　4. meronymy	co-classification or co-extension	Continuatives (e.g. still, already ...)
	B: Instantial 　1. equivalence 　2. naming 　3. semblance	co-reference or co-classification	
Structural cohesion			
A: Parallelism B: Theme-rheme development C: Given-New organization			

Cohesion refers specifically to those non-structural relations that are crucial in text formation. This research investigates the resources for constructing cohesive chains, which are concerned with the grammatical and lexical devices, as explained in Chapter 2.

3.2.1.1 Grammatical cohesive devices

The grammatical cohesive devices include reference, substitution, ellipsis, and conjunction. Conjunction, making no contribution to the formation of cohesive ties and chains, is out of the scope of this research.

1) Reference

Regarding reference items, instead of being interpreted semantically in and of themselves, they make reference to something else for their interpretation. This is "the specific nature of the information that is signalled for retrieval" (Halliday and Hasan, 1976: 31). Cohesion is applied in this continuity of reference, whereby the same thing enters into the text a second time.

Traditionally, reference means the relationship between a word and what it points to in the real world in terms of semantics. In a sense of the text, reference occurs when the reader retrieves the identity of what is being discussed by referring to another expression in the immediate context (Baker, 1997: 181).

Based on whether the reference is related to the context of situation or text, reference is identified as exophoric (situational) or endophoric (textual). Exophoric reference "links the language with the context of situation; but it does not contribute to the INTEGRATION of one passage with another so that the two together form part of the SAME text [emphasis in original]" (Halliday and Hasan, 1976: 37). "Exophoric reference makes no contribution to the cohesion of a text" (Halliday and Hasan, 1976: 53), which thus is not considered in the present research. Usually, cohesion is taken as exclusively concerning endophora. Endophoric reference may be anaphoric or cataphoric, referring to the preceding text or to the following text, respectively.

Reference is divided into three types: personal, demonstrative, and comparative. "Personal reference is reference by means of function in the speech situation, through the category of PERSON [emphasis in original]"

(Halliday and Hasan, 1976: 37), and is realised via personal pronouns, possessive determiners, and possessive pronouns. Both English and Chinese have their own personal pronoun system. Table 3-6 lists the comparison of English and Chinese personal pronouns.

Table 3-6   English and Chinese personal pronouns

English				
Semantic category	Existential		Possessive	
Class	noun (pronoun)		determiner	
	Singular	Plural	Singular	Plural
First person	I me	we us	mine my	ours our
Second person	you	you	yours your	
Third person	he she it	they	his his hers her its	theirs their

(Halliday and Hasan, 1976: 38)

Chinese				
Semantic category	Existential		Possessive	
Class	noun (pronoun)		determiner	
	Singular	Plural	Singular	Plural
First person	我	我们 咱们	我的	我们的
Second person	你 您	你们	你的	你们的
Third person	他 她 它	他们 她们 它们	他的 她的 它的	他们的 她们的 它们的

There is a correspondence between English and Chinese personal pronouns, in that they can have the same function of referring backward or forward to the persons mentioned in or out of the text, while they differ morphologically. From the above table, we can tell that all Chinese possessive personal pronouns are in the form of adding a "的" after the existential pronouns.

"Demonstrative reference is reference by means of location, on a scale of PROXIMITY [emphasis in original]" (Halliday and Hasan, 1976: 37); "it is essentially a form of verbal pointing" (Halliday and Hasan, 1976: 57). The systems of demonstrative reference for English and Chinese are as follows in Figure 3-4 and Figure 3-5.

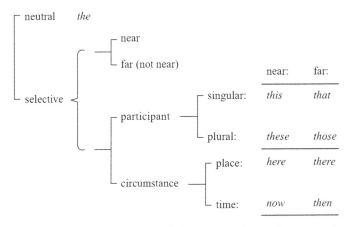

Figure 3-4   The system of demonstrative references in English (Halliday and Hasan, 1976: 57)

In demonstrative reference, the scale of proximity is interpreted according to the context of situation. To take [1] as an example, the distance "near" or "far" is based on the speaker in terms of his/her space and time:

[1]　"'All you need do, Grannie, is to make the two young people their responsibility. Let each pay for one of them.'"

"That's fair," said Grandmother Jia. "Yes, that's what I'll do."

Lai Da's old mother rose up from her stool in mock indignation.

"But this is rank mutiny! It makes me feel really angry on Their Ladyships' behalf. What, side with Her Old Ladyship against your husband's mother and your own father's sister? That's an errant breach of the laws o' consanguinity!" (*The Story of the Stone*, Chapter 43)

In [1], the first two "that" and "this" are both used as references, referring to the fact "All you need do, Grannie, is to make the two young people their responsibility. Let each pay for one of them". Grandmother Jia's and Lai Da's old mother's attitudes toward the fact is very clear in distance.

Compared with English, the use of Chinese demonstrative reference is more complicated (Zhu et al., 2001: 30), as shown in Figure 3–5

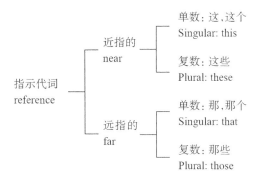

Figure 3–5   The system of Chinese demonstrative references [Wang, 1959 (1985): 213]

Although Halliday and Hasan's (1976) classification of demonstrative reference is quite similar to that of Wang's [1959 (1985)], there are some distinctive differences due to typological differences: especially the unique definite article "the", because "no other item in English behaves exactly like the" (Halliday and Hasan, 1976: 70). The distinction between the definite article "the" in English and "zero reference" in Chinese needs to be clarified. The most evident difference between English and Chinese in demonstrative reference is that English has the definite article "the", which is neither "this" nor "that" (Hu, 1994: 59). Whereas there is no such demonstrative reference in Chinese, Chinese usually adopts two ways instead to translate "the": either using "zero reference", or using "这 (this)" and "那 (that)". In Chinese, if the referent is clear in the context of situation, no definite determiner is required, and this is called "zero reference". Repetition of the referent is used in this situation (Zhu et al., 2001: 34), which will be discussed in later sections. For example:

[2] 这日天气陡寒，只见袭人早已打点出一包衣服，向宝玉道："今日天气

很冷,早晚宁使暖些。"说着,把衣服拿出来给宝玉挑了一件穿。(*Hong Lou Meng*, Chapter 89)

Today the weather had suddenly turned chilly. Xiren had already prepared a bundle of winter closthes, and said to Baoyu: "It's very cold today. You'd better keep warm in the morning and evening." Saying this, she chose a garment for him to wear. (*A Dream of Red Mansions*, Chapter 89)

In [2], the second "衣服" refers to the first "衣服", but there is no definite determiner before it: the reference is realised through the repetition of the same word "衣服", rather than using a definite determiner to refer to "衣服". This is "zero reference" in Chinese.

Comparative reference establishes indirect reference by means of IDENTITY or SIMILARITY with adjectives and adverbs (Halliday and Hasan, 1976: 37). It is further divided into general comparison and particular comparison, in terms of "likeliness or unlikeliness" and "quantity or quality", respectively. Table 3-7 shows the comparison of English and Chinese.

Table 3-7 Comparative references in English and Chinese

Comparison in English				
general (deictic)			particular (non-deictic)	
identity	similarity	difference	numerative	epithet
same equal identical identically	such similar so similarity likewise	other different else differently otherwise	more fewer less further additional so- as- equally- + quantifier, eg: so many	comparative adjectives and adverbs, eg: better so- as- more- less- equally- + comparative adjectives and adverbs, eg: equally good

(Halliday and Hasan, 1976: 76)

Comparison in Chinese			
general (deictic)			particular (non-deictic)
identity	similarity	difference	
同样的 相同的 同等的	类似的 相似的	其他/它的 不同的 别的	更 更加 再 比较 这么 比······ + adjectives or adverbs 比······ + adjectives or adverbs 了些

(Zhu, 2001: 35–36)

In terms of comparative reference, there are few differences between English and Chinese. The most distinctive difference is that English comparison can lie in the morphological change of adjectives and adverbs, while Chinese does not have morphological change in adjectives nor adverbs, but realises comparison via lexical and syntactical methods (Zhu et al., 2001: 35). For example:

[3]   I do not claim that they are better people than the ones who appear in books written before my time. (*A Story of the Stone*, Chapter 1)

[4]   想来这一段故事, 比历来风月事故更加琐碎细腻了。(*Hong Lou Meng*, Chapter 1)

I imagine this story should have more fine points than the usual run of breeze-and-moonlight tales. (*A Dream of Red Mansions*, Chapter 1)

In [3], the English comparison is realised through the morphological change of the adjective "good"; while in [4], the Chinese comparison is realised through a lexical method, adding a comparative word, "更加", before the adjective.

2) Substitution

Substitution and ellipsis are both grammatical relations. Substitution is defined as "the replacement of one item by another" (Halliday and Hasan,

1976: 88). Cohesion is created in the relationship between substituted item and the substituting one. According to grammatical function, substitution can be classified into three types: nominal, verbal, and clausal. Nominal substitution means that a noun phrase is replaced by "one" "ones" or "the same". Verbal substitution is achieved by "do" replacing a verbal phrase. In clausal substitution, "so" and "not" are used to replace an entire clause. Table 3–8 shows the forms of substitution in English and Chinese.

Table 3–8　The forms of substitution in English and Chinese

English Substitution		
Nominal	Verbal	Clausal
one ones same	do do so	so not

(Halliday and Hasan, 1976: 112)

Chinese Substitution		
Nominal	Verbal	Clausal
的 者	来 干 弄 搞	这样 这么 这样的话 不这样 既这样 不然 如果不这样 要不 是 不是

(Zhu, 2001: 45–58)

　　The nominal, verbal, and clausal substitutions in English and Chinese are equivalent to each other, semantically. The Chinese nominal, verbal, and clausal substitutions are not realised by "one" "ones" or "do" "so", but have different forms such as "的" "弄" "这样" to replace the nominal, verbal, and clausal phrases. Substitution avoids unnecessary repetition, and makes the new information in the text more distinct, both in English and Chinese. For example:

[5]   "Please send my respects to her and Lady Wang."
Promising to do so, Xifeng left. (*A Dream of Red Mansions*, Chapter 11)

[6]   探春道:"只是原系我起的意,我须得先作个东道主人,方不负我这
兴。"李纨道:"既这样说,明日你就先开一社如何?"(*Hong Lou Meng*,
Chapter 37)

"As this was my suggestion," said Tanchun, "you must let me play hostess
first. That's only fair."

"Very well then," agreed Li Wan. "You can call the first meeting
tomorrow." (*A Dream of Red Mansions*, Chpater 37)

In example [5], "do so" substitutes for the verbal clause "send my respects
to her and Lady Wang". In [6], "既这样说" refers to the entire sentence that
Tanchun said. The substituted phrases can be traced back in the previous
content, making the text cohesive through the link between the substituted and
the substituting verbs.

3) Ellipsis

Ellipsis can be seen as "substitution by zero" (Halliday and Hasan, 1976: 89).
It is "something left unsaid", but "there is some presupposition, in the structure, of
what is to be supplied" that can be understood as such (Halliday and Hasan, 1976:
142). The link between the presupposed item and the omitted item makes the text
cohesive. Ellipsis comprises three types: nominal (ellipsis within the nominal
group), verbal (ellipsis within the verbal group), and clausal (ellipsis of the entire
clause or part of the clause) (Halliday and Hasan, 1976: 147–167).

Wang [1959 (1985): 310] defines ellipsis as lacking a specific component
in form compared with a normal sentence. He also lists five different types of
ellipsis in respect of syntactic structure: subject ellipsis, object ellipsis, link verb
ellipsis, predicative ellipsis, and verb ellipsis [Wang, 1959 (1985): 312–313].
There are two conditions under which verbal ellipsis can be applied in Chinese:
one is that the verb can be substituted by modal verbs, such as "能" "敢"; the
other is in answering questions with "没有" "来", etc. [Wang, 1959 (1985): 313];
for example:

[7] "What about Bao-chai? Is she quite better?"

"Ah yes, of course!" said Aunt Xue. (*A Story of the Stone*, Chapter 8)

[8] 刘姥姥便说:"原是特来瞧瞧嫂子你,二则也请请姑太太的安。若可以领我见一见更好,若不能,便借重嫂子转致意罢了。"(*Hong Lou Meng*, Chapter 6)

"Well, of course, first and foremost we came to see you," replied Grannie Liu mendaciously, "but we were also hoping to pay our respects to Her Ladyship. If you could take us to see her, that would be very nice; but if that's not possible, perhaps we could trouble you just to give her our regards." (*A Story of the Stone,* Chapter 6)

In [7], "Ah, yes, of course!" is a positive answer to the question. It means "Ah, yes, of course! She is quite better". The entire latter clause is omitted. In [8], "领我见一见" is omitted after "若不能". "领我见一见" is the predicate in the sentence, and its ellipsis in Chinese is, as mentioned above, led by the negative form of a modal verb "能" Since the omitted items are supplied from the previous text, the texts above are cohesive, and the ellipsis doesn't confuse the readers' understanding.

3.2.1.2 Lexical cohesion

Lexical cohesion refers to word selection in organising relations within a text (Baker, 1997: 202). According to Halliday and Hasan (1976: 318), "lexical cohesion is 'phoric' cohesion that is established through the structure of the LEXIS, or vocabulary [emphasis in orignial]". They identify two aspects of lexical cohesion: reiteration, and collocation. Reiteration is defined as "the repetition of a lexical item, or the occurrence of a synonym of some kind, in the context of reference; that is where the two occurrences have the same referent". Reiteration can be the same word, a synonym or near-synonym, a superordinate, or a general word (Halliday and Hasan, 1976: 279). Collocation is "achieved through the association of lexical items that regularly co-occur" (Halliday and Hasan, 1976: 284). However, Hasan takes the notion of collocation problematic (1984, p. 195). In the present analysis, no account is taken of collocation in lexical cohesion.

Hasan (1985) outlines a more detailed componential relation of cohesive devices, including both grammatical and lexical cohesion (see Table 3–5). She divides lexical cohesion into two categories: general, and instantial. The general lexical cohesive devices, very similar to reiteration, include repetition, and other relations that can be explained by the general semantic systems such as synonymy, antonymy and meronymy. Instantial lexical cohesive devices are those dealing with relations that are not general but created by the text. They include equivalence, naming and semblance.

Cohesion via repetition is created simply because of the repeated occurrence of a lexical unit that encodes a largely similar experiential meaning [Halliday and Hasan, 1985 (1989): 81]. For example:

[9]　宝玉谈至浓快时,见她不说了,便笑道:"人谁不死,只要死得好。那些个须眉浊物,只知道文死谏,武死战,这二死是大丈夫死名死节,究竟何如不死的好! 必定有昏君他方谏,他只顾邀名,猛拼一死,将来弃君于何地? 必定有刀兵他方战,猛拼一死,他只顾图汗马之名,将来弃国于何地? 所以这皆非正死。"(*Hong Lou Meng*, Chapter 36)

Baoyu had been joining in with the greatest of pleasure, and when she stopped he responded cheerfully:

"All men must die. The thing is to die for good reasons. Those vulgar sods believe that ministers who die for remonstrating with the Emperor and generals who die in battle win immortal fame as fine, upright men — but wouldn't it be better if they didn't die? After all, there has to be a despot on the throne before ministers can remonstrate; but they court death in their eagerness to make a name, with a complete disregard for their sovereign. In the same way, there has to be a war before generals can die in battle; so they fight recklessly and try to win glory by dying, with no thought of the country's welfare. That's why I say these aren't worthy deaths." (*A Dream of Red Mansions*, Chapter 36)

In [9], "死" is repeated many times; and it is, apparently, thus the focus of the text. The repetition of "死" forms a relation in which the items are expressing a similar experiential meaning. [10] presents another example:

[10]　All men long to be immortals,

　　Yet to riches and rank each aspires.

The great ones of old, where are they now?

Their graves are a mass of briars.

All men long to be immortals,

Yet silver and gold they prize.

And grub for money all their lives,

Till death seals up their eyes.

All men long to be immortals,

Yet dote on the wives they've wed,

Who swear to love their husband evermore,

But remarry as soon as he's dead.

All men long to be immortals,

Yet with getting sons won't have done.

Although fond parents are legion,

Who ever saw a really filial son? (*A Dream of Red Mansions*, Chapter 1)

The repetition of the clause "all men long to be immortals" gives the structure of the poem a consistent pattern, so that a similar experiential meaning is kept from the beginning to the end of the poem, thus making it a coherent whole.

Synonymy refers to two items with identical experiential meaning. Antonymy is described as two items opposite in experiential meaning. Hyponymy refers to the relationship between a general class and its sub-classes. The item that refers to the general class is known as superordinate, whereas those that refer to its sub-classes are known as hyponym [Halliday and Hasan, 1985 (1989): 80].

[11] Once when Bao-chai called in to see her, the nature of her illness became the subject of their conversation.

"I suppose the doctors in attendance on this family aren't too bad as doctors go," said Bao-chai, "but the medicines they prescribe for you don't seem to make you any better. Don't you think it's time they called in someone really first-rate who could cure this sickness once and for all? Every year all through the spring and summer you have this trouble;

yet you're not an old lady, and you're not a little girl any longer. You can't go on in this way indefinitely."

"It's no good," said Dai-yu. "This illness will never go away completely. Look what I'm like ordinarily, even when I'm not ill."

Bao-chai nodded. (*A Story of the Stone*, Chapter 45)

In [11], "illness" "sickness" and "trouble" are synonyms, for they have a similar experiential meaning, all referring to an uncomfortable body condition. There are also items, such as "doctors" "medicines" "prescribe" "illness" "sickness" "trouble" and "ill", that often appear in the text together; they form a collocation relation.

Compared with grammatical ties, lexical ties are more difficult to be detected in a text. Although Halliday and Hasan (1976) do not elaborate lexical cohesion as much as grammatical cohesion, they acknowledge the importance of lexical cohesion in texture; for example in the statement that "the lexical patterns serve to transform a series of unrelated structures into a unified, coherent whole" (Halliday and Hasan, 1976: 320). Tanskanen (2006) acknowledges the importance of lexical cohesion in the interaction between cohesive elements and the knowledge of text and world held by language users. From the standpoint of the readers, Widdowson (2007: 46) confirms the positive effect that cohesion has on linking parts of a text together. Cohesive devices can connect new content to the previously established context of situation, allowing readers to comprehend it.

However sophisticated is the grammatical cohesion shown, it will not form a text unless it is matched by lexical cohesive patterning (Halliday and Hasan, 1976: 292). Grammatical cohesion and lexical cohesion work hand in hand, one supporting the other. Cohesion does not contribute to the coherence of a text directly. It is in the ways that cohesive devices are laid out or connected with each other that makes the text coherent:

> Cohesion deals with the resources in the wording for "stitching" one clause to another and another and so on. By itself, cohesion does not offer us direct information about what the "stitching" produces — the fabric

or quality of cloth; and whether it will function as a piece of clothing. In the technique of cohesive harmony, by combining choices of related lexical tokens (words, but with some specific conditions) and repetitions of grammatical roles (with some specific conditions as "repetition"), we can produce a map and a measure of semantic bonding across an extended passage of text (Butt et al., 2010: 271).

3.2.2 Cohesive chains

Texts must have cohesion, but it is how the cohesive resources are employed that distinguishes between text and non-text, as well as between one text and another (Halliday, 1985a: 54). Cohesion does not make a text coherent in and of itself, and research into the mechanics of cohesion serves as a foundation for future coherence research. The relations between the components of the clauses or groups represent the experiential meaning throughout the text, and form the horizontal threads of a text. These horizontal threads correlate with each other via the lexical tokens, which are repeated or semantically related by synonymy, antonymy and meronymy, forming the vertical dimension of a text, and thus achieving coherence. In this process, the role of cohesive ties cannot be overlooked. Cohesive ties are taken as the explicit signposts of coherence, which can help to analyse the fabrication of coherence because they signal the logical relations of segments in the text (Lorentz, 1999).

The concept of a tie allows for a systematic analysis of a text's cohesive features and a systematic explanation of its textual patterns (Halliday and Hasan, 1976: 4). To be specific, a "tie" makes the creation of cohesion evident. It is the semantic bond between two elements that creates the cohesion of a text. When examining a linguistic piece for cohesion, the focus is mostly on the ties (Hasan, 1984: 185). Hasan (1985) argues that the nature of the cohesive tie is semantic, and that the semantic relations between the two terms of any tie form the basis of cohesion. The semantic relations are: co-referentiality, co-classification, and co-extension. These three relations connect two members of a tie; and the existence of such a tie is essential to texture [Halliday and Hasan, 1985 (1989): 73-74]. Co-referentiality ties two or more items that have the same referent into a cohesive chain. Co-classification ties items from the same class. Co-extension ties items referring to "something within the same general field of meaning" [Halliday and Hasan, 1985 (1989): 74]. By these three relations, a set of items, each of which is related to the others, can form a cohesive chain.

Cohesive chains can be divided into two types: identity chain (members of the chain are in a co-reference relation), and similarity chain (members of the chain are in a relation of co-classification or co-extension) [Halliday and Hasan, 1985 (1989): 84]. The chains go a long way toward laying the framework for coherence, but they are not enough; we also need to incorporate some relations that are characteristics of those between the components of a message. This is termed as chain interaction [Halliday and Hasan, 1985 (1989): 91]. Coherence requires both the continuity derived from chain formation and the continuity of chain interaction (Lukin, 2013: 531). The minimum condition for chain interaction to occur is "when at least two members of one chain should stand in the same relation to two members of another chain" [Halliday and Hasan, 1985 (1989): 91].

Chain interaction involves relations that bring together members of two (or more) distinct chains. These relations are essentially grammatical [Halliday and Hasan, 1985 (1989): 91]. Taboada (2004) believes that cohesive chains and chain interactions are the most interesting concepts in the description of cohesion and coherence in a text. Chain interaction sets the basis for the investigation of cohesive harmony.

3.2.3   Cohesive harmony

Cohesive harmony is one of the models for the description of coherence in the SFL framework. It describes text "harmony" in terms of connecting the grammatical and lexical cohesive devices with the semantic notion of identity and similarity chains. Cohesive harmony was developed by Hasan in an attempt to measure the extent of the coherence of a text [Halliday and Hasan, 1985 (1989); Hasan, 1984]. "In any coherent discourse, threads of semantic continuity are created through the construction of cohesive chains" (Hasan, 1994: 138). Hasan's cohesive harmony is taken as the only method available to explicate the texture of a text by Lukin (2013). To elaborate the relation between cohesive chains and coherence, Halliday and Hasan [1985 (1989)] distinguish four types of tokens: relevant tokens, central tokens, non-central tokens, and peripheral tokens.

- Relevant tokens: all tokens that enter into identity or similarity chains, divided into:
  - Central tokens: relevant tokens that interact
  - Non-central tokens: relevant tokens that do not interact
- Peripheral tokens: tokens that do not enter into any kind of chain [Halliday and Hasan, 1985 (1989): 93].

The characteristics of the different kinds of tokens are important in distinguishing the tokens that take part in the creation of cohesion and coherence of a text; especially the "relevant tokens", because they are related to one another through cohesion, and they are related to the topical development of a text (Hasan, 1984: 211).

To further clarify how the tokens contribute to the coherence of a text, three hypotheses about the relation between the portions of the above mentioned tokens and the degree of coherence are proposed: ① The higher portion of relevant tokens to peripheral tokens, the more coherent the text; ② The higher portion of central tokens to non-central tokens, the more coherent the text; ③ The fewer the breaks in the interaction, the more coherent the text [Halliday and Hasan, 1985 (1989): 93–94].

These three properties of a text are called, collectively, COHESIVE HARMONY [Halliday and Hasan, 1985 (1989)]. The more cohesive harmony there is in a text, the more coherent it is (Hasan, 1984: 216).

3.3 Coherence in the SFL framework

The above description of SFL sets a framework for the study of coherence patterns. The factors that contribute to the construction of coherence in the function-rank matrix are mainly from the ideational and textual metafunctions (see Table 2–3). The patterns of coherence can be explored from the lexicogrammatical level. Thus, the mutual effect that the ideational and textual meaning have on the construction of coherence can be investigated in terms of the transitivity, clause complex and cohesion of a text. Since cohesive chains are taken as the basis of coherence, the interrelation of the experiential, logical and textual meanings is able to explain how the cohesive devices and clauses make a coherence text, and how are they representative in distinguishing the coherence patterns of a text. Therefore, the ideational and textual meanings are both incorporated in the output of coherence patterns, which might provide us an idea of how a coherent text operates with the relevant tokens, transitivity roles, and logical relations.

In the interpretation of coherence patterns, the ideational and textual metafunctions complement each other in the grammatical realisation of the patterns. In the present research, certain notions of cohesive harmony are adopted and combined with the analysis of clauses to give a view of the coherence patterns of Chinese and English texts. Furthermore, attention is paid to the relevant tokens rather than to the ratio of central tokens to the total tokens, because the relevant tokens take more responsibility for the realisation of coherence. The relevant tokens and the roles they play in clauses, and the way they are embedded in clauses, are to be investigated in this research, but chain interactions are not taken into consideration.

3.4　A systemic functional description of Chinese grammar

This research is theoretically based on SFL, and it demands uniform standards for describing both English and Chinese. Therefore, it is necessary to apply SFL in the description of Chinese grammar and to divide clauses in Chinese according to systemic functional grammar.

3.4.1　The previous studies of Chinese grammar

There was no comprehensive Chinese grammar study until the publication of *Ma's Grammar* in 1898, which is considered the first modern Chinese linguistic work. This does not mean there was no work on Chinese grammar; rather, that traditionally, although there was a long history of study on Chinese grammar, these studies were not systematic descriptions of the Chinese language, but more about the Chinese characters and words, and especially about Chinese function words.

Wang (1980: 172) categorises the study of Chinese grammar before 1949 as being in two stages: firstly, the study in the feudal age, from the end of the Han Dynasty to the end of the Qing Dynasty; and secondly, the study from the stage of Western learning being introduced into China to 1949. In the latter stage, Western linguistics is the main force in the study of Chinese linguistics. Within these two stages, the study of Chinese linguistics can be divided into four periods:

First, from the Pre-Qin Dynasty to the end of the Han Dynastry (the 21st century BC to 220 AD), primarily the Han Dynasty (202 BC to 220 AD). In this period, the study was mainly exegesis. This was only the beginning of people's awareness of grammar in ancient times. Only a few studies had been done on word classification, meaning interpretation, and word function, and they were not systematic but rather dispersed throughout different works.

Second, from the end of the Han Dynasty to the Ming Dynasty (220 AD to 1644 AD). This period witnessed the rise of phonetics in the study of Chinese grammar. There appeared works on the methods for indicating the pronunciation of Chinese characters.

Third, the Qing Dynasty (1636 AD to 1912 AD). During this period, philology, phonology and exegesis all developed on a large scale.

Forth, from the publication of *Ma's Grammar* to 1949. In this period, the influence of Western linguistic study permeated every aspect of Chinese linguistic study.

Western grammar has been brought to China since the middle of the 19th century. There appeared works on Chinese grammar, adopting the traditional descriptive method of Western grammar and western grammar research began to have a greater impact on Chinese grammar research. Two books in particular deserve to be mentioned here. One is the pioneering modern Chinese grammar, *Ma's Grammar*. It follows Greek and Latin grammars to describe the grammar of traditional Chinese. Sun (2014) believes that imitating Western grammar in *Ma's Grammar* is very important in Chinese grammar history, and that the imitations therein set a foundation for the development of modern Chinese grammar research. The main defect of this grammar book, Wang (1980: 146) considers, is that it lacks a historical view of grammar. The other key work is Li Jinxi's *A New Grammar of Mandarin*. Unlike *Ma's Grammar*, this is the first book on the systematic description of the grammar of modern colloquial Chinese. Its contribution is not only in presenting a complete grammar system for modern Chinese so as to popularise the knowledge of grammar, but also providing some valuable principles and rules for further studies on the basis of a large amount of Chinese data. *A New Grammar of Mandarin* follows the grammar of English rather than that of any other language. Compared to other Indo-European languages, English is the closest to Chinese in typology in certain respects. It is an important step to establish Chinese grammar under the framework of the English grammar (Zhang and Liao, 1985).

These two grammar books have brought the study of Chinese grammar to a new stage, studying Chinese grammar with reference to Western linguistic theories. Wang Li is one of the representatives of the era of grammar innovation (Lu, 2010: 135). He published several books on Chinese grammar, such as *Modern Chinese Grammar* (1943), *Chinese Grammar Theories* (1945), and *The Outline of Chinese Grammar* (1946), and formed his own view and system of the study of Chinese grammar. He was also one of Halliday's early teachers.

During this stage, there also appeared other linguists who did research on the comparison of English and Chinese, which further promoted linguistic research in China. In the 1930s, Zhao Yuanren published a paper on the comparison of tones in English and Chinese. Lin Yutang published a grammar book, *Kaiming English Grammar*, in 1933. Lv Shuxiang and Gao Mingkai also had their own grammar works, *An Outline of Chinese Grammar* (1942) and *On Chinese Grammar* (1948). Due to the efforts of the previous mentioned and other linguists, the study of Chinese grammar and linguistics has had a very solid foundation so as to absorb Western linguistic ideas and to create its own.

After 1949, linguistic study in China had some changes. Since 1957, when Chomsky published his *Syntactic Structures* (1957), the establishment of generative grammar meant the end of the dominating position of Bloomfield's descriptive structuralism (Shu, Liu, and Xu, 2009: 431–432). Hereafter, the study of linguistics in China has become increasingly prosperous: not only the introduction of Western linguistic theories but also the application of them into areas such as teaching, languages comparison, and testing. These theories have also promoted the study of Chinese itself.

3.4.2 The introduction and application of systemic functional grammar in Chinese studies

Of all the theories that have been introduced and applied to the study of Chinese grammar, SFL is one of the most distinguished and important. It can well explain many problems particular to Chinese, and also can be used in the comparison of English and Chinese.

In *Grammatical Categories in Modern Chinese* (Halliday, 1956), Halliday makes a relatively comprehensive description of the categories of Chinese grammar. He describes the Units, Elements and Classes of modern Chinese formal colloquial language, which sets a good basis for the later description of Chinese grammar under SFL. He identifies five units of Chinese: sentence, clause, group, word, and character. Character is typical in Chinese. Elements consists of the sentence structure, clause structure, group structure, and word structure. Classes has only three classes: clause, group, and word classes. The basic clause structures are combinations of Verbal and Noun groups, and the possible combinations are: V, N, NV, VN, NVN, NNV, VNN. These categories are very important for making a profile of Chinese grammar in later research.

From the 1960s, Halliday started to build his theory of SFL. In the 1970s, he moved to Australia and set up the Department of Linguistics in the University of Sydney, from which some very famous Chinese linguists have graduated, such as Hu Zhuanglin and Zhang Delu. They are now very active and influential in spreading SFL in China. The systemic functional grammar of English has been well elaborated by Halliday (1985b), Halliday and Matthiessen (2004), Matthiessen (1995) and other scholars (Eggins, 1994; Martin, 1992; Quirk and Crystal, 1985) over the last few decades. SFL has bloomed in many institutions in Australia, China, and all over the world.

However, the application of systemic functional grammar to Chinese is comparatively less common, because English is the home language for SFL, and it has taken time for other languages to be described. Apart from Halliday's early research on Chinese grammar, such as Halliday (1956), and Halliday and Webster (2002), more works on applying SFL to the analysis and framework of Chinese grammar have since appeared. There are scholars who have endeavoured to set up a systemic functional framework for the explanation of Chinese, such as Li and Thompson (1981), Hu (1984; 1990), Fang, McDonald, and Musheng (1995), Zhu (1996), McDonald (1998), Li (2003), and Halliday and McDonald (2004).

In this research, a comprehensive description of Chinese grammar on the basis of SFL is required.

Li and Thompson (1981) aim to provide, for the first time, a description of Chinese in functional terms. They put Chinese in a systemic functional linguistic framework, and provide terminological support for further research on Chinese and the comparison of Chinese and English using SFL.

McDonald (1998) and Li (2003) have applied SFL to Chinese grammar, and have described different processes of transitivity in Chinese. Their categorisation of the processes in Chinese grammar is adopted as the basis for the analysis in the present research.

Apart from the grammatical study of Chinese, SFL is also applied in the analysis of Chinese texts. Xu (2003) emphasises the importance of the context of situation with a comparative study of *Ru Lin Wai Shi* and its English translation. Fang (2008) probes how the expansion of system of meaning or meaning potential in Chinese is relevant to the growth of the language from a systemic functional perspective. Zhang (2008) studies the characteristics of Chinese mood system. Through search on the China National Knowledge Infrastructure (CNKI), an electronic platform of Chinese knowledge-based information resources, and also the largest one in the world, it is found that, until 2021, there are more than 10,000 papers published from the systemic functional liguistic view of Chinese, translation studies, English teaching in China, comparative studies of Chinese and English, etc.

3.4.3 The criteria for distinguishing clauses in Chinese

SFL is used to analyse Chinese in terms of clause division in this section, in accordance with the theoretical basis of English clause division. The description of Chinese in SFL has been made by different scholars from different perspectives, as elaborated in the previous section. This section focuses on the process types in Chinese, which will be the theoretical foundation for clause division in the analysis of Chinese source texts in this research.

As stated before, key concepts in SFL are, for example, stratification, metafunction, rank, and realisation. According to Halliday and McDonald (2004: 311), "metafunctions are theoretical categories, they are part of the general linguistic framework of the description; rank is descriptive terms, which may vary from one language to another". Therefore, in the matrix (see Table 3–9) below, the metafunctions in Chinese are the same as those in English, but the ranks are different. Chinese and English differ significantly in terms of rank, with the group having a lowest rank with regard to clause grammar in Chinese rather than the word does in English (Halliday and McDonald, 2004: 311).

Table 3–9 A metafunction-rank matrix for Chinese
(Halliday and McDonald, 2004: 312)

Stratification	Metafunction			
	textual	interpersonal	experiential	logical
Clause			transitivity: nuclear circumstancial aspect	logico-semantic relations and taxis
Phrase			minor transitivity	
Group: verval			aspect phase	
nominal	deixis			
adverbial	cohesion			

Halliday (1956) describes the basic structure of Chinese clauses as the combination of verbal and nominal groups. Each clause contains one verbal group, and no or one or several nominal groups.

In English, there are three main elements in a clause: process, participants and circumstances. Process defines what is going on in the state of being. Participants are the persons or objects involved in the process of what is going on. Circumstances are the features of time, place, manner, etc. (Halliday, 1994: 107–108). Although, experientially, the basic order of elements in a clause in Chinese is similar to that in English (Halliday and McDonald, 2004: 313), the process types are described in various ways by different scholars.

McDonald (1998: 72) distinguishes five different types of process as shown in Table 3–10. Unlike English, which has six process types (material, behavioural, mental, verbal, relational, existential), Chinese has five types of process. There are no behavioural process and existential process in Chinese. The ascriptive process is unique to Chinese.

Table 3–10   Process types (McDonald, 1998: 72)

material	representing the outside world, i.e., doings or happenings
ascriptive	describing the outside world, ascribing qualities or states to entities or situations
relational	identifying relationships between entities in the outside world
mental	consciously processing the outside world through the inner world of the consciousness
verbal	symbolically expressing the outside or inner world through language

In a later work, Halliday and McDonald have adjusted McDonald's previous categorisation. They categorise the ascriptive process as a relational process, so that this description is closer to that of English. Li (2003) defines four types of figure at the semantic level, and their realisation at the lexicogrammatical level. Halliday and McDonald's categorization and Li's categorisation are the same, as shown in Table 3–11.

Table 3-11   Comparison of Halliday and McDonald's categorization and
Li's categorisation of process types in Chinese

Halliday and McDonald (2004: 354)	Li (2003: 95)
Material	Mental
Mental	Verbal
Verbal	Material
Relational	Relational

In the present research, in order to avoid vagueness and ambiguity, I will adopt both Halliday and McDonald's (2004) and Li's (2003) categorisations and descriptions of process types in the analysis of Chinese clauses.

Li (2003) adopts Matthiessen's (1995) four types of figure: sensing, saying, doing, and being; and claims that figure is the fundamental unit of semantics in terms of experiential function, and that it is realised by the clause. Thus, the transitivity system represents the clause. He lists some Chinese verbs that are representative in the four process types in the transitivity system (Li, 2003: 62–72). For example, "认为" "想要" "害怕" "看见" are verbs that represent a mental process; "提到" "说" "告诉" are the verbs of saying, so they are in verbal processes. Material processes concern the material world. Relational processes in Chinese are more complicated than in English (Li, 2003: 98); but as in English are attributing and identifying the properties of one element to another.

With the criteria built up for recognising different process types in Chinese, it is plausible to divide the Chinese text into chunks as clauses under the same framework as the English text. This sets an overall framework for both Chinese and English texts in the analysis at the lexicogrammatical level and at the highest rank of clause. By doing so, the contrast and comparison between Chinese and English texts are reliable.

3.5   Summary

SFL provides a theoretical basis for the comparative study of coherence between English and Chinese. The description of Chinese and English is based on the fundamental concepts of function, rank, system, stratification and so on. This chapter emphasises the role that the experiential, logical and textual functions play in the construction of a coherent text; and highlights the clause as the highest rank in text analysis. The clause complex and logical relations between clauses connect the text as a logically related whole. Cohesion connects the clauses with cohesive devices via semantic relations. The ergative analysis of the cohesive devices in the clauses defines their causation role and the semantic variation across different languages. The lexicogrammatical realisation of the above types of analysis which are taken as the patterns of coherence can shed light on the comparative study of Chinese and English texts and translation studies.

Chapter 4

Methodology

The SFL model has a direct guiding effect on translation. It studies translation activity from the perspective of metafunctions and systems, and involves the transference and equivalence of language choices at lexical, grammatical and semantic levels. The core of translation is the transfer of meaning between two languages, which is realised by changing and replacing the source language grammar and lexis with equivalent target language grammar and lexis (Catford, 1965: 71). The text translation model serves as a practical guide to transference. The model is very influential in text analysis and translation studies, and is also studied by several scholars [e.g. Sasaki (1995), Taylor and Baldry (2001), Zhang and Huang (2002)].

Based on the description of the theoretical framework presented in Chapter 3, this chapter presents the methodology to be used to investigate the patterns of coherence in the Chinese source text and its two English target texts.

The present research is a combination of quantitative and qualitative analyses of coherence patterns in translation. Nesbitt and Plum emphasise the importance of quantitative analysis of linguistic research as follows:

> The quantitative analysis of grammar and discourse patterns has hardly begun but since language itself consists of patterns which can only be quantitatively delineated, studies of this type are central to the core questions of linguistics and important for many applications of linguistic science (1988: 6).

This chapter comprises two parts: the data used in the analysis; and the analytical tools.

4.1   Corpus

A corpus linguistic method is adopted as the tool for the analysis of texts.

The data used in this research come from one of the four Chinese classic novels, *HLM* and its two most famous English translated versions, *The Dream of the Red Mansions* and *A Story of the Stone*.

The translation of *HLM* into English started in 1830 with John Francis Davis, a British diplomat and a sinologist. Davis translated two poems from Chapter 3 under the title "On the Chinese Poetry" and published them in *Journal of the Royal Asiatic Society* (Wen and Ren, 2012). The translation of this novel into English has continued ever since. Over the 170 years since 1830, there have been 11 English translated versions of *HLM*, the most recent in 2007 (Jiang, 2007); but most of these translations are only excerpts of some poems, chapters or the major plot lines. Only David Hawkes and John Minford's and Yang Xianyi and Gladys Yang's versions are complete translations of all the 120 chapters of the original Chinese novel.

As a sinologist and professor from Oxford University, David Hawkes translated the novel in collaboration with his son-in-law, John Minford. They translated the novel as *The Story of the Stone*. Published by the Penguin Group in London, Hawkes and Minford's translation consists of five volumes, each one with a different subtitle. Hawkes translated the first three volumes, *The Golden Days* (1973), *The Crab-Flower Club* (1977) and *The Warning Voice* (1980); while Minford translated the remaining 40 chapters in two volumes, *The Debt of Tears* (1982) and *The Dreamer Wakes* (1986). This set of translations is the first complete translation of *HLM* in the English world. The data used in this research come from the first three volumes, so the translation hereafter is referred to as the Hawkes' version.

Another well known title of the novel is *A Dream of the Red Chamber*, which is also the literal meaning of *HLM*. As to the meaning of the title, there are different opinions. Zhou [1953 (2012)] claims that the "Red Chamber" originated from a Tang poem and stood for the boudoirs of the girls in the novel.

Baoyu had a dream in a girl's mansion and learned the fortune of the twelve girls in the novel, for which the title is named, "A Dream of the Red Chamber". From 1978 to 1980, a famous Chinese translator Yang Xianyi, with his British wife Gladys Yang, translated the novel into three volumes, and the title is *A Dream of Red Mansions*. Hereafter, their version is referred to as the Yang's version.

After the appearance of these two important English translations, the study of the translation of *HLM* has also grown steadily. According to CNKI, Yang's and Hawkes' versions are the most studied to date. Both versions have their own advantages. Hawkes' version is the first complete translation of the novel, and has been well received in the English world by non-academic readers and scholars. Yang's version is famous for its deep understanding of the Chinese source text. Both versions display high academic rigor.

Both Hawkes' and Yang's versions are complete translation of all 120 chapters of *HLM*; but they are slightly different in the original manuscript used as the source text. The first 80 chapters of Yang's version are based on Qi Liaosheng's manuscript, and the last 40 chapters are based on Cheng Weiyuan and Gao E's copy. Hawkes chose Cheng Weiyuan and Gao E's copy as the main source, but he also referred to the same manuscript that Yang used. In the preface to *The Story of the Stone*, Hawkes states that:

> In translating this novel I felt unable to stick faithfully to any single text. I have mainly followed Gao E's version of the first chapter as being more consistent, though less interesting than the other ones; but I have frequently followed a manuscript reading in subsequent chapters, and in a few, rare instances I have made small emendations of my own (1973: 18).

Minford also contributed to the translation of the last 40 chapters of *The Story of the Stone*. Since the last 40 chapters of the source Chinese novel *HLM* were not written by Cao Xueqin, in order to avoid ambiguity and make the overall factors under the same standard, the last 40 chapters will not be used in the present research, for either Chinese source text or English target texts. In general, in most chapters of the two translations, the differences caused by the different original copies are only a few sentences and can be neglected in the comparison of the two versions.

The two versions have received different reviews and comments domestically and internationally. Jiang (2007) claims that, even though translation studies in China tend either to prefer Yang's version or to have a similar evaluation of the two versions, Hawkes' version actually is far more influential in the English world. She selects some comments and reviews on the Amazon site of both the Hawkes' and Yang's versions, and reveals that Hawkes' version receives more stars than Yang's, and that most of the comments for Hawkes' version are positive while some are quite harsh for Yang's version. Furthermore, Yang's version is produced by a native Chinese speaker, while Hawkes' version is from a native English speaker. There might thus be some differences in translation as a result of the translators' different native languages.

For all the above reasons, *HLM* and its two English versions are chosen as the data for the present research. On one hand, this masterpiece can represent the use of Chinese written language. Although it was written over 200 years ago, the grammar is the same as standard modern Chinese. On the other hand, the similarities and differences in the two English versions must indicate differences in the author's language use and also differences in the two cultures.

The corpus in this research is parallel, consisting of the Chinese source text and its two English versions. It does not include all the 120 chapters of the novel, but only 3 chapters each. The 3 chapters come from the beginning and the middle of the novel. A chapter from the end of the novel is not chosen because, as mentioned, the last 40 chapters were not written by Cao Xueqin. Each chapter has three versions: the Chinese source text, and the two English target texts, the Yang's and Hawkes' translated versions. Therefore, there are, altogether, nine texts in this corpus, which has around 20,000 characters and 35,000 words, respectively. Biber (1993) has explained that, if well-balanced, a small-scale corpus is able to cover all the linguistic features. In the present study, three sets of data from three different chapters of the novel are used: Chapter 1, Chapter 2, and Chapter 39. To avoid confusion with the current chapters in this research, the three chapters in the novel are labelled as ch1, ch2, and ch3. Thus, for example, the Chinese source text in Chapter 1 is labelled as ST–ch1, and the English target text in Chapter 39 is labelled as TT–ch3. The ST stands for the Chinese source text, authored by Cao; and the two TTs stand for the two English target texts, indicated as Yang's (TT1) and Hawkes' (TT2) versions. In the present research, the corpus consists of only literary texts; but these texts include both monologue and dialogue, and the length of each text is enough to cover all the linguistic features we need in the analysis.

There is another corpus used as a supplement for this research. The corpus consists of 30 pieces of dialogue between the two main characters, Baoyu and Daiyu, in the novel and its two English translations. This supplementary corpus has about 40,000 words, across 80 chapters of the novel. The use of this supplementary corpus is as an application of the methodology adopted across the entire research in a larger scale. The scope of the methodology for determining the coherence patterns in the current research has been widened with the use of the supplementary corpus.

4.2　Analytical procedures

An intensive and exhaustive comparative analysis is to be conducted to interpret the coherence patterns in the original Chinese text and its two English translations. As mentioned in Chapter 3, the coherence patterns of the Chinese source text and the English target texts are measured in terms of three aspects: the lexicogrammatical realisation of meanings in the ideational metafunction; the cohesive chains in the textual metafunction; and the mutual effect that these two metafunctions have on the realisation of coherence.

Firstly, all the grammatical and lexical cohesive devices of each text will be listed. Then, from the cohesive devices, the identity chains and similarity chains can be identified. Secondly, a clause complex analysis will be conducted. All the clauses in a clause complex will be tagged with two subsystem labels, TAXIS and LOGICO-SEMANTIC TYPE. From the results, the numbers and percentages of each taxis and logico-semantic relation in each text can be compared and contrasted to see the similarities and differences in connecting clauses. Thirdly, the clauses with relevant tokens in the cohesive chains show the strings of semantic continuity in the text, thus playing an important role in construing the coherence of the text other than that of clauses. The experiential meanings that these clauses realise are crucial in connecting the text with the experiential world in a coherent way. The ergative roles of the relevant tokens are also tagged to depict a profile of the realisation of the experiential function in the ST and the TTs. Finally, analysis of the interweaving of the ideational and textual meanings in the realisation of coherence is conducted on the basis of the cohesive chains. The different patterns displayed by different texts, i.e. the ST and the TTs, can indicate the ways that coherence is realised by different languages and different translators.

4.2.1   The analytical tools used in the analysis

In the data analysis, two tools are adopted to make the analysis accessible. One is "SysFan" software for the clause complex; and the other is "SysConc" software for the frequency count of ergative patterns.

4.2.1.1   SysFan

In order to make the process of clause complex analysis easier, SysFan is used, which is a computational programme developed by Canzhong Wu in 2000. It is used to process texts through THEME, MOOD and TRANSITIVITY analyses of clauses and other systemic and functional analyses of other grammatical units. It operates at the clause rank, the highest rank in the lexicogrammatical stratum (Fang, Song, and Wu, 2008). In the present research, it also works at the clause rank to analyse the logical semantic relations between clauses. The semi-automatic setting of the software makes the clause complex analysis easy; and it can do the statistical count of the logical relations of the clauses, so as to provide a foundation for further interpretation of the data analyses.

The procedure of using SysFan in the analyses of clause complex is as follows. Firstly, all the texts are manually divided into clause complexes and clauses, and then each is given an ID. Secondly, all the texts are entered into SysFan. Thirdly, the clauses are analysed in the SysFan software. Figure 4– 1 shows a screenshot of the analyses in SysFan. It has three major parts. The upper part of the window is the control panel: it shows the location of the analysis in the systemic functional grammar system. The middle part shows the clause complex in analyses. The text ID and clause complex ID are shown in boxes as "TT1" and "TT1_1" respectively, and the clause complex is shown in the white box below. The lower part is for the process of analysing the clauses in the clause complex shown in the middle part. The left side shows the clause ID, and the right side is the clauses. The clauses can be related to each other in terms of taxis and logico-semantic relation under the boxes 1 to 7 from left to right in the middle.

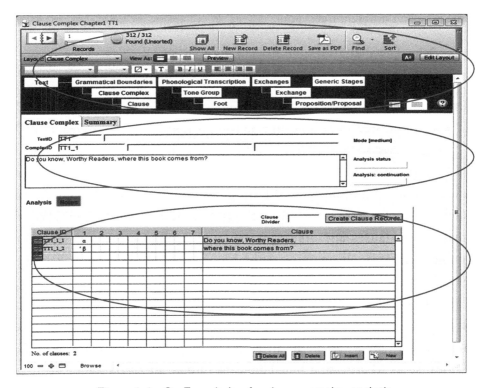

Figure 4-1　SysFan window for clause complex analysis

After analysing all the clauses in a text, SysFan can produce a summary of the results in terms of the two subsystems: taxis and logico-semantic relation. Each type and different combinations of the two subsystems are calculated in respect of number and frequency (see Figure 4-2). The nature of systemic functional grammar determines that "the probability of 'choosing' one thing rather than another" (Halliday, 1991: 42) is able to show the variation across the texts. Therefore, the data shown in the figure can be used for further analysis of the text to see how the different texts are lexicogrammatically realised in the logical metafunction.

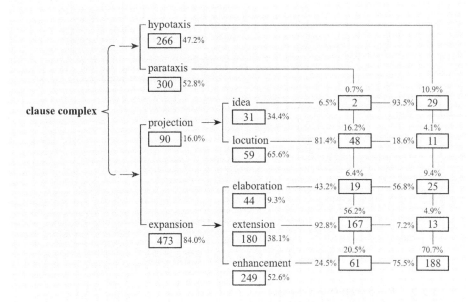

Figure 4-2   Summary of clause complex analysis in SysFan

4.2.1.2   SysConc

SysConc, also designed by Canzhong Wu, is a concordance tool used in data analysis. Apart from the lexicogrammatical realisation of the logical metafunction, the experiential realisation is also one factor in coherence patterns. Firstly, the ergative roles of the relevant tokens in the cohesive chains are annotated in an Excel document. Then, the ergative patterns of the chains are produced as output to be processed in SysConc. Figure 4-3 displays how SysConc is used in the frequency test of the patterns of cohesive chains in Chapter 7. The "word" patterns, counts and frequencies of the patterns are shown on the left. With these numbers and probabilities, the ergative patterns of the cohesive chains of each text become visible and measurable.

Figure 4-3　Frequency in SysConc

4.2.2　Research hypothesis

Based on the above analytical model, we expect to find similarities and differences across the Chinese source text and English target texts and also between the two English texts, in terms of the following aspects:

- the amount of the cohesive chains
- the proportion of clauses in cohesive chains
- the types of clause complexing in each text
- the ergative roles of the relevant tokens in the cohesive chains

For each aspect, the results can represent one facet of the coherence patterns of each text. The quantitative analysis of the data depicts an overview of the lexicogrammatical patterns of the realisation of coherence, while the qualitative analysis of the patterns evaluates the equivalence of the coherence patterns in translation.

4.3   Summary

This chapter has introduced the procedures for the analysis of the coherence patterns in the Chinese source text and English target texts. It has described how the cohesive chains from the textual metafunction and the clause with the relevant tokens from the ideational metafunction of both the ST and the TTs are analysed. The theoretical framework sets the description of both Chinese and English texts under the same framework, which is the basis for the comparative study and translation study. Torsello (1996: 88) claims that "grammar should be a part of the education of a translator, and in particular functional grammar since it is concerned with language in texts and with the role grammar plays, in combination with lexicon, in carrying out specific functions and realising specific types of meaning". The description of English grammar follows Halliday and Matthiessen (2004), while the systemic functional description of Chinese grammar follows Li (2003) and Halliday and McDonald (2004). The latter is generated on the same basis as the former description. Therefore, with the methodology presented in this chapter, the equivalence of the Chinese source text and English target texts in terms of coherence may make a contribution to the study of both translation studies and literary text analysis.

Chapter 5

Logical Metafunction in Building up Coherence

The logical metafunction is concerned with how units of a text are combined one with another and is an important factor in construing the coherence of a text, as has been identified in the literature review and theoretical framework: "The logical metafunction provides generalised resources for creating complexes at any rank — for expanding at any point in the development of a text" (Matthiessen, 1995: 90). It is expressed through the structure of these "unit complexes", such as clause complexes, group complexes, and morpheme complexes. Through the unit complexes, the text develops through logical interconnections: "Clause complexing is a resource for construing our experience of the 'flow of events' in the world as sequences of 'quanta of change'" (Matthiessen, 2002: 263). Through the connection between clauses, the logical development of a text is realised, as an indispensable element in the coherence of a text.

In this chapter, a comprehensive analysis of the logical relations in the Chinese source text and the two English target texts will be conducted. The chapter aims to identify what the structural patterns of the logically related clauses are, and how the logical metafunction works in the construction of a coherent text, both in the Chinese source text and English target texts. The analysis part of this chapter comprises two sections. In Section 5.1.1, clause complexity in each text is examined and compared to give an overview of the features of the development of clause complexes at the text level. Section 5.1.2 shows the patterns of clause nexus, with tables and graphs, to give a detailed view of what is typical in the ST and the TTs. Through the comparison and contrast between the source text and the target texts and also between the two target texts, an explanation is given of similarities and differences in the construal of the logical patterns in constructing coherence.

This chapter offers to answer four questions: What are the features of clause complexity in all the texts? What are the characteristics of the clause complexing types in all the texts? What are the similarities and differences in the clause complexes in the ST and the TTs? How are the previously identified features maintained and altered during the transference from the ST to the TTs?

It is not the purpose of this study to judge which translation is better in terms of coherence. Rather, the aim of the study is to explain how coherence is realized in the different translations in terms of logical metafunction, and how logical patterns contribute to the creation of coherence in both Chinese and English.

5.1 Implications of how the logical metafunction works in the present study

Clauses are connected with one another via a clause nexus to form the clause complex, which relation can recur. This connection is an open-ended structure, and can contain deepening layers of dependency (i.e. clauses that are dependent on dependent clauses, etc.). This interdependency relation realises complexing choices and forms a series or chain of clauses (Matthiessen, 1995: 128–129). The clause complex system generates clause complexes from two dimensions, vertical and horizontal. The vertical dimension is the linear progression of the clause complexes connected one by one; while the horizontal dimension is the internal layering within each clause complex (Matthiessen, 2002: 247). The deeper the vertical dimension goes, the more clauses for each clause complex. The wider the horizontal dimension reaches, the more extended a clause complex is.

Clause complexing is expressed through two systems. One is the degree of interdependency: TAXIS, in which the two different types of interdependency are hypotaxis (where the clauses connected are unequal in status) and parataxis (where the clauses connected are equal in status). The hypotatic relations between clauses are represented with Greek letters, α, β, γ, etc.; and the paratactic relations between clauses are represented with numbers, 1, 2, 3, etc. Hypotactic clause complexes are structured as α -> β -> γ -> δ, etc. Paratactic clause complexes are structured as 1-> 2-> 3 -> 4, etc. The other system of the clause complex unit is the LOGICO-SEMANTIC TYPE of projection and expansion. These two are the fundamental relations between the primary and secondary clauses, in other words, the inter-clausal relations. Projection is the relation that a locution or an idea is projected by another clause, with quoting or reporting. Locution is indicated by a double quote ", while an idea is indicated by a single quote '. Expansion means the secondary clause expands the primary one by elaboration (i.e. restating it in other words; indicated by "="), extension (i.e. adding a new element to it; indicated by "+") and enhancement (i.e. enhancing its meaning by specifying some circumstantial feature, such as time, place, cause, or condition; indicated by "×") (Halliday & Matthiessen, 2004: 367–482). Therefore, in the analysis, each set of logical relation is indicated with a union of these two systems. For example, "+ β" is used to indicate an extending hypotactic secondary clause.

The systems of TAXIS and LOGICO-SEMANTIC TYPE establish the relation between the clauses. Complexing creates dependency organisation rather than constituency organisation (Bateman, 1989: 265–266). The mutual effect of TAXIS and LOGICO-SEMANTIC TYPE shows the mode of expressing information in the text. The clause complex analysis provides the frequencies of different complexing types in realising information. Moreover, the dependency organisation of clauses reflects the method of realising logically related text. The logical relations between clauses can be expanded by the recursion of the combination of taxis and logico-semantic relations. Therefore, the lexicogrammatical patterns of coherence in the logical function in each text can be worked out through the complexing and development of the clause complexes. The analysis of clauses and clause complexes in the source and target texts is one way to examine how the logical metafunction is expressed, and therefore to examine the patterns of logical relations in creating a coherent text.

In this research, clause complex relations are investigated to the delicacy outlined in Figure 3–2. In the clause division, embedded clauses are not treated separately from the main clauses, because "the embedded clause is the nominalisation of a process" (Halliday and Matthiessen, 2004: 438). This grammatical distinction, between embedding and tactic relations, is clarified thus:

> Whereas parataxis and hypotaxis are relations between clauses (or other ranking elements), embedding is not. Embedding is a mechanism whereby a clause or phrase comes to function as a constituent within the structure of a group, which itself is a constituent clause (Halliday, 1985b: 219).

5.1.1　Clause complexity

The system of clause complexity decides whether to develop one free clause (clause simplex) or to expand the clause by introducing one or more clauses to form a clause complex (Matthiessen, 1995: 127). In linking clauses with each other, the logical function realises the semantic sequences of a text. Its role in building up a coherent text has been discussed by many scholars (Harabagiu, 1999; Huang, 1988; Wolf and Gibson, 2006). In addition, the clause complexity reveals characteristics of how a text is formed grammatically, whether a sentence has an intricate internal structure or not. The complexity of a text provides the grammatical foundation for the logically related text as a coherent whole. The features that clause complexity displays are important in showing the coherence patterns of a text.

5.1.1.1　Comparison of clause simplexes and clause complexes

In a narrative text, the flow of events is construed as a series of episodes, which are developed as sequences of figures. The semantic sequence of figures is realised by a series of clause complexes. Grammatically, the figures that make up the episodes are realised as clauses, which are combined as complexes:

> These clause complexes serve to construe **semantic sequences of figures**, not the whole episode, but local sequences in the flow of events that together make up the episode. Semantically, the effect of combining

clauses into a clause complex is one of **tighter integration in meaning**: the sequences that are realised grammatically in a clause complex are construed as being sub-sequences within the total sequence of events that make up a whole episode in a narrative (Halliday and Matthiessen, 2004: 364–365).

Clause complexes relate experiential events by virtue of combining clauses. The clause simplex is a clause complex with only one clause. In traditional grammar, this is a sentence made up of only one clause, termed a "simple sentence". Clause simplexes do not conform to the pattern of complexing at all. Therefore, grammatically, in clause simplexes the clause is not combined with another clause. Semantically, clause simplexes realise a semantic sequence by rhetorically complexing with other clause simplexes or complexes. In this process, clause complexes display a higher degree of integration than clause simplexes. The clause simplex is distinguished from the clause complex in this section only to see how the two different forms of clause combining construe meaning in different texts, and how grammatically intricate different texts show in realising semantic sequences.

The number and ratio of clause simplexes and clause complexes in the text (see Table 5–1) indicate the mode of the two languages in realising the sequences of experiential events, and also the strategies and styles of different translators in dealing with the sentence boundaries.

Table 5–1　Clause complexity in the ST and the TTs

		ST	TT1	TT2
clause simplex	Number	93	335	371
	Percentage	12.65%	36.22%	36.66%
clause complex	Number	642	590	641
	Percentage	87.35%	63.78%	63.34%
grammatical sentences	Number	735	925	1,012
	Percentage	100%	100%	100%

Table 5-1 exhibits the use of clause simplexes and clause complexes in the three texts analysed. The results show that the ST tends to use more complicated grammatical structures than the two TTs, with 87.35% clause complexes in the ST and less than 70% in the TTs. Accordingly, the Chinese source text uses far fewer simple sentences than the two English target texts. The use of clause simplexes in the ST is only 12.65%, but around 37% in the two TTs. The two TTs display a similar percentage of clause simplexes and clause complexes, around 37% and 63%, respectively. The ratio of clause simplexes and clause complexes in the three texts reveals a key difference between Chinese and English versions of this text. Chinese is more grammatically intricate than English, with more internal layering; while English tends to use more simple sentences. In translation, both of the two translators have simplified some of the clause complexes into clause simplexes, according to the characteristic of English. Take the following excerpt from ch2 of the novel as an example (see Text 5-1).

Text 5-1   An excerpt of clause complexity from ch2

Complex ID	Clause ID	Clause	Logical relations
ST			
ST-ch2-1	ST-ch2-1-1	子兴　　笑　　道： Zixing　laugh　say	1
	ST-ch2-1-2	"说着　别人家的　闲话， saying　other's　gossip	" 2 x β　　β
	ST-ch2-1-3	正好　　下酒， just right　with wine	= α
	ST-ch2-1-4	即　多吃　　几杯　　何妨！" If　have a few　more cups　why not	α
ST-ch2-2	ST-ch2-2-1	雨村　　向窗外看　　道： Yucun　look out of the window　say	1
	ST-ch2-2-2	"天　也　晚了， It is　also　late	" 2 x β
ST-ch2-2	ST-ch2-2-3	仔细　关了　　城！ careful　closed　the city gate	α

(continued)

Complex ID	Clause ID	Clause	Logical relations
ST-ch2-3	ST-ch2-3-1	我们　慢慢的　　进城　　　再谈 we　slowly　go into the city　and talk 未为不可。" is not impossible	
TT1			
TT1-ch2-1	TT1-ch2-1-1	"Gossip goes well with wine.	
TT1-ch2-1	TT1-ch2-1-1	Why not drink some more?"	
TT1-ch2-2	TT1-ch2-2-1	Yucun looked out of the window.	
TT1-ch2-3	TT1-ch2-3-1	"It's growing late.	
TT1-ch2-4	TT1-ch2-4-1	They'll soon be closing the city gates.	
TT1-ch2-5	TT1-ch2-5-1	Let's stroll back	1
	TT1-ch2-5-2	and continue our conversation in town."	x　2
TT2			
TT2-ch2-1	TT2-ch2-1-1	Zi-xing laughed.	
TT2-ch2-2	TT2-ch2-2-1	"There's nothing like a good gossip about other people's affairs for making the wine go down!	
TT2-ch2-3	TT2-ch2-3-1	I'm sure an extra cup or two won't do us any harm."	
TT2-ch2-4	TT2-ch2-4-1	Yu-cun glanced out of the window.	
TT2-ch2-5	TT2-ch2-5-1	"It's getting late.	

(continued)

Complex ID	Clause ID	Clause	Logical relations
TT2–ch2–5	TT2–ch2–5–1	We must be careful we don't get shut out of the city.	
TT2–ch2–6	TT2–ch2–6–1	Why not continue the conversation on our way back?	
TT2–ch2–7	TT2–ch2–7–1	Then we can take our time."	

The above excerpt exemplifies how the Chinese source text uses grammatically intricate sentences while the two English target texts adopt simpler sentences. There are 2 clause complexes and 1 clause simplex in the ST–ch2, enclosing 8 clauses; which are transformed into 5 clause simplexes and 1 clause complex with two clauses in the TT1–ch1, and 8 clause simplexes in the TT2–ch2. The two translators both chose to chunk the original clause complexes into clause simplexes in translation.

According to Lv (2008: 29), there are two ways to complicate the sentence in Chinese: either connecting clauses together; or expanding one element in a clause. In connecting clauses together, it is more common to find parataxis in the connection of clauses in Chinese than in other languages. In Chinese, the connections between clauses are realised by the semantic relations, instead of the syntagmatic means used in English (Lian, 1993; Liu, 1991). It is common not to use conjunctives between clauses, but rather the juxtaposition of clauses, in Chinese (Wang, 1945: 90). In the translation of Chinese into English, the juxtaposition of clauses is transferred into simple sentences. The clause simplexes are not closely connected to each other via syntagmatic relations, but through semantic relations. Therefore, considering the relationship among the clauses, the two translators' strategy of using clause simplexes is characteristic of English.

5.1.1.2   The nature of the data: words, clauses, and clause complexes

Table 5–2 is a preliminary comparison of clauses and clause complexes in the three texts in the different chapters. It shows the general features of the use of clauses and clause complexes in the texts from different aspects: the number of clause complexes; the number of clauses; the number of characters in the Chinese source text and words in the English target texts; the average number of clauses in a clause complex; and the average number of words in a clause.

Table 5-2　Comparison of clauses and clause complexes in different chapters

	ST-ch1	TT1-ch1	TT2-ch1
No. of clause complexes	253	310	309
No. of clauses	813	695	754
No. of words or characters	6,925	5,476	6,944
No. of clauses in a clause complex	3.21	2.24	2.44
No. of words/characters in a clause	8.52	7.88	9.21
	ST-ch2	**TT1-ch2**	**TT2-ch2**
No. of clause complexes	216	277	298
No. of clauses	644	529	613
No. of words or characters	5,990	4,366	5,973
No. of clauses in a clause complex	2.98	1.91	2.06
No. of words/characters in a clause	9.30	8.25	9.74
	ST-ch3	**TT1-ch3**	**TT2-ch3**
No. of clause complexes	266	338	405
No. of clauses	749	691	877
No. of words or characters	6,219	4,395	6,274
No. of clauses in a clause complex	2.82	2.04	2.17
No. of words/characters in a clause	8.30	6.36	7.15

The table above depicts an overview of the numbers of clauses and clause complexes in the texts in the three different chapters. These chapters are taken from different parts of the novel. Chapter 1 and Chapter 2 of the novel are the opening of the story. They provide the background on how the story begins, and also introduce the main characters who appear in the coming chapters of the story. These two chapters are mainly written as narration to set up a framework for what is going to happen later. In most chapters of the novel, the content is a replication of the living scenes of the characters' lives, with some conversations among them, such as in Chapter 39 (ch3). More than 20 characters appear in ch3, including almost all the important persons in the novel. Unlike ch1 and ch2, the plot in ch3 moves forward through conversations among those characters, rather than through the narrative of the introduction. Chapter 39 frames a setting of events as one of many in the plot of the novel. These three chapters are chosen as a representative case study of the novel to infer the patterns of the whole novel.

Even though there are some differences across the parameters across the different chapters, such as the number of clauses and clause complexes, the statistics in Table 5–2 show a trend in the three chapters in terms of the average clause length and clause complex length. Therefore, the three chapters are not distinguished from each other in the later analysis, since they are from the same novel, and do not display variation in register.

Table 5–3 gives an overview of the overall numbers of the clause complexes, clauses, and the average clause complex length, and clause length in the ST and the two TTs.

Table 5–3   An overall comparison of clauses and clause complexes of
the ST and the TTs in all the chapters

	ST	TT1	TT2
No. of clause complexes	735	927	1,012
No. of clauses	2,213	1,915	2,244
No. of words or characters	19,134	14,157	19,191
No. of clauses in a clause complex	3.01	2.07	2.22
No. of words/characters in a clause	8.65	7.40	8.55

The use of clauses and clause complexes can show differences between Chinese and English; and also differences between the two groups of translators.

The clause complex, on average, tends to have more clauses in Chinese than in English (Wu and Fang, 2007: 570). The ST has the least number of clause complexes, but each clause complex in the ST contains 3.01 clauses on average, more than the 2.07 and 2.22 in the TT1 and TT2, respectively. This indicates that the Chinese source text contains more clause nexuses in one clause complex than the English target texts. Within each clause complex, the recursion of the clause nexuses develops more grammatical intricacy in the ST than in the TTs. Therefore, the difference between the ST and the TTs is in the dimension of nexus connections. The ST has more internal layers of nexuses in one clause complex, which tends to horizontal development; whereas the TTs develop more clause complexes vertically in linear progression. In realising the logical metafunction, the two TTs show less intricate connections between clauses in a clause complex than the ST. Both of the translators choose to use more clause complexes, but fewer clauses in one clause complex, than in the ST.

However, the clauses in Chinese do not reveal a preference for using more words than in English. The difference between Chinese and English at the word rank is due to the different ranks of characters and words. The ST and the TTs are not aligned at the word rank, and there is no equivalence between Chinese characters and English words. The average number of words in a clause indicates the lexical density at the clause level. When a clause packs a larger number of words than another clause, it is lexically denser than the other (Halliday and Matthiessen, 2004: 654). Therefore, the different lexical density in these two TTs shows that the TT2 is denser and more intricate, at both clause and clause complex ranks, than the TT1. The TT1 incorporates 7.40 words in each clause, while the TT2 contains 8.55 words per clause. With more words in each clause and more clauses in each clause complex, the TT2 is much longer than the TT1.

The different translators' choices are manifested in terms of the number of words, clauses, and clause complexes. The TT1 is less explicit than the TT2 in terms of number of clauses, clause complexes, and also word counts.

Yang chooses to use shorter clauses, and therefore displays less lexical density than Hawkes. Yang's version also has simpler clause complexes — to put it in traditional grammar terms, sentences — than Hawkes' version. In general, the TT1 has fewer clause complexes, and simpler internal nesting within clause complexes than the TT2. Therefore, in respect of the two dimensions of clause complex development, the TT1 is both shorter vertically and narrower horizontally than the TT2. Yang prefers to use fewer words and shorter sentences to express the same content as Hawkes does.

The following Text 5–2 presents excerpts from the ST–ch1 and its equivalent translations in the TT1–ch1 and TT2–ch1 texts. They display the features of the number and average number of clauses in a clause complex, and average number of words in a clause, found in the above table, in a more specific way.

Text 5–2　An excerpt from ch1

Complex ID	Clause ID	Clause
ST		
ST–ch1–1	ST–ch1–1–1	看官，　　你道 readers　 you say
	ST–ch1–1–2	此书　　从何　　而起? this book　 where　 to begin
ST–ch1–2	ST–ch1–2–1	说来　　虽　　　近荒唐， talk　 even though　 ridiculous
	ST–ch1–2–2	细玩　　颇有　　趣味。 think over　 quite　 interesting
ST–ch1–3	ST–ch1–3–1	待　在下　将此来历　　注明， wait for　me　have this story　 explain
	ST–ch1–3–2	方使　　阅者　　了然不惑。 make　 the readers　 understand
ST–ch1–4	ST–ch1–4–1	原来　　　女娲氏　　　炼石　　　补天 originally　 the Goddess Nvwa　 melted stone　 repaired the sky 之时， the time

(continued)

Complex ID	Clause ID	Clause
ST-ch1-4	ST-ch1-4-2	于大荒山　　　　无稽崖　　　炼成 In the Great Waste Mountain　　Baseless Cliff　　melted 高经十二丈，方经二十四丈顽石 a hundred and twenty feet high and two hundred and forty feet square stone 三万六千五百零一块。 thirty-six thousand five hundred and one blocks of stone
ST-ch1-5	ST-ch1-5-1	那娲皇氏　　　只　用了　　　三万六千五百块， the Goddess Nvwa　only　used　thirty-six thousand five hundred blocks
	ST-ch1-5-2	单单　剩下　一块　未用， only　left　one block　unused
	ST-ch1-5-3	弃　　　　在青埂峰下。 threw　at the foot of Blue Ridge Peak
ST-ch1-6	ST-ch1-6-1	谁知　　此石　　自经　　　煅炼 who would expect　this stone　went through　melting and molding 之后， after
	ST-ch1-6-2	灵性　已通， spirituality　got
	ST-ch1-6-3	因　见　　　众石　　　俱得补天， because　seeing　other blocks of stone　repair the sky
	ST-ch1-6-4	独　自己　无材　不堪入选， only　itself　incapable　not chosen
	ST-ch1-6-5	遂　　自怨　　　自叹， thus　complained by itself　sighed by itself
	ST-ch1-6-6	日夜　悲号　惭愧。 day and night　cried　in shame
TT1		
TT1-ch1-1	TT1-ch1-1-1	Do you know, Worthy Readers,
	TT1-ch1-1-2	where this book comes from?

(continued)

Complex ID	Clause ID	Clause
TT1–ch1–2	TT1–ch1–2–1	The answer may sound fantastic,
	TT1–ch1–2–2	yet carefully considered
	TT1–ch1–2–3	is of great interest.
TT1–ch1–3	TT1–ch1–3–1	Let me explain,
	TT1–ch1–3–2	so that there will be no doubt left in your minds.
TT1–ch1–4	TT1–ch1–4–1	When the goddess Nu Wa melted down rocks
	TT1–ch1–4–2	to repair the sky,
	TT1–ch1–4–3	at Baseless Cliff in the Great Waste Mountain she made thirty-six thousand five hundred and one blocks of stone,
	TT1–ch1–4–4	each a hundred and twenty feet high and two hundred and forty feet square.
TT1–ch1–5	TT1–ch1–5–1	She used only thirty-six thousand five hundred of these
	TT1–ch1–5–2	and threw the remaining block down at the foot of Blue Ridge Peak.
TT1–ch1–6	TT1–ch1–6–1	Strange to relate, this block of stone [[after tempering]] had acquired spiritual understanding.
TT1–ch1–7	TT1–ch1–7–1	Because all its fellow blocks had been chosen
	TT1–ch1–7–2	to mend the sky
	TT1–ch1–7–3	and it alone rejected,

(continued)

Complex ID	Clause ID	Clause
TT1-ch1-7	TT1-ch1-7-4	it lamented day and night in distress and shame.
TT2		
TT2-ch1-1	TT2-ch1-1-1	Gental reader, what, <<TT2-1-2>> was the origin of this book?
	TT2-ch1-1-2	you may ask,
TT2-ch1-2	TT2-ch1-2-1	Though the answer to this question may at first seem to border on the absurd,
	TT2-ch1-2-2	reflection will show
	TT2-ch1-2-3	that there is a good deal more in it than meets the eye.
TT2-ch1-3	TT2-ch1-3-1	Long ago, when the goddess Nu-wa was repairing the sky,
	TT2-ch1-3-2	she melted down a great quantity of rock
	TT2-ch1-3-3	and, on the Incredible Crags of the Great Fable Mountains, moulded the amalgam into thirty-six thousand, five hundred and one large building blocks,
	TT2-ch1-3-4	each measuring seventy-two feet by a hundred and forty-four feet square.
TT2-ch1-4	TT2-ch1-4-1	She used thirty-six thousand five hundred of these blocks in the course of her building operations,
	TT2-ch1-4-2	leaving a single odd block unused,
	TT2-ch1-4-3	which lay, all on its own, at the foot of Greensickness Peak in the aforementioned mountains.
TT2-ch1-5	TT2-ch1-5-1	Now this block of stone, <TT2-ch1-5-2> possessed magic powers.

(continued)

Complex ID	Clause ID	Clause
TT2–ch1–5	TT2–ch1–5–2	having undergone the melting and moulding of a goddess,
TT2–ch1–6	TT2–ch1–6–1	It could move about at will
	TT2–ch1–6–2	and could grow
	TT2–ch1–6–3	or shrink to any size it wanted.
TT2–ch1–7	TT2–ch1–7–1	Observing that [[all the other blocks had been used for celestial repairs || and that it was the only one to have been rejected as unworthy.]]
	TT2–ch1–7–2	it became filled with shame and resentment
	TT2–ch1–7–3	and passed its days in sorrow and lamentation.

Table 5–4 summarises the features of the above texts.

Table 5–4   A comparison of clauses and clause complexes in the snapshot

	ST–ch1	TT1–ch1	TT2–ch1
No. of clause complexes	6	7	7
No. of clauses	17	17	20
No. of words/characters	176	141	206
No. of clauses in a clause complex	2.83	2.43	2.86
No. of words/characters in a clause	10.35	8.30	10.30

On one hand, in the two TTs, both of the translators use one more clause complex than in the ST. The ST has 6 clause complexes, while in translation these 6 clause complexes are transferred into 7 in both of the two TTs. The clause complex "ST–ch1–6" has 6 clauses, and it is divided into two clause complexes in the TT1 (TT1-ch1-6 and TT1-ch1-7), and three clause complexes in the TT2 (TT2-ch1-5, TT2-ch1-6 and TT2-ch1-7). The average number of clauses in each clause complex shows that the TT2 is more intricate than the TT1, 2.86 against 2.43 on average. To be specific, the TT1-ch1-6 and TT1-ch1-7 have 1 and 4 clauses, respectively, while the TT2-ch1-5, TT2-ch1-6 and TT2-ch1-7 have 2, 3 and 3 clauses, respectively. Thus, Yang's translation is simpler in grammatical complexity than Hawkes'.

On the other hand, Yang uses fewer clauses and words than Hawkes. There are 17 clauses in the TT1, but 20 clauses in the TT2. As to the average number of words in a clause, the TT1 has 8.30, while the TT2 has 10.30. Yang's version thus shows less lexical density than Hawkes'. For example, in TT1-ch1-6-1, "Strange to relate, this block of stone [[after tempering]] had acquired spiritual understanding." only has two words in the embedded clause, while in TT2-ch1-7-1, "Observing that [[all the other blocks had been used for celestial repairs || and that it was the only one to have been rejected as unworthy,]]", uses two embedded clauses with 23 words.

This example also shows that Chinese has more internal layering in clause complexing, and it is more grammatically intricate than the two English target texts. Therefore, Chinese text is more likely to express meaning through more intersections of clauses, while the English target texts tend to express meaning with a linear progression of clauses with more clause complexes. Within the two translations, the translators, Yang and Hawkes, have displayed their own personal preference of choice in the reproduction of the source text, in the use of clauses and clause complexes. It can be inferred that Yang uses a comparatively implicit style, while Hawkes uses a comparatively explicit method in translation.

5.1.2 Types of clause nexus in the ST and the TTs

As the clause complexity varies in the source and target texts, there should also be some differences in the manner of the combination of one clause and another: to be specific, in the clause nexus types in the texts.

The results of the clause complexing analysis, conducted using the tool SysFan and the methodology outlined in Chapter 4, will be presented in this section. In each text, clause complexes and clauses are endowed with IDs, with which clauses are grouped under the corresponding clause complex box within the relevant text, as shown in Figure 5-1. Each clause within the clause complex is listed, one by one, vertically. From left to right, the numbers 1, 2, 3 ... 7 represent the internal layers within the clause complex of the listed clauses. Level 1 is the most local clause nexuses, and level 7 is the most global ones. Each number (i.e. each level) comprises two parts, LOGICO-SEMANTIC TYPE, and TAXIS. The clauses within each clause complex can be combined together manually from left to right, in accordance with these levels. With SysFan, the analysis process can be very efficient, and the results can be further processed.

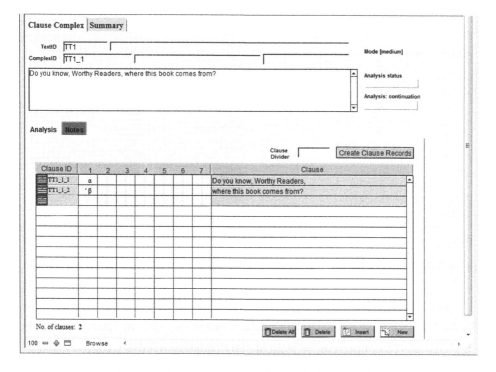

Figure 5-1   Clause complexing analysis in SysFan

The results of the clause complexing analysis can be shown in different forms in SysFan, such as a clause complex summary, and clause logical relations summary. Each format can be used for different purposes for further analysis of the data.

Figure 5-2 is a summary of the clause nexuses in all the source and target texts, as shown using the SysFan interface. Each type of clause nexus is listed in categories of the two subsystems of the clause complex, taxis and logical-semantic type. The number and percentage of each nexus and every possible combination of taxis and logical semantic relation in the text are also shown in Figure 5-2. With the categorised results, further processing can be conducted about the features of clause combining in different texts.

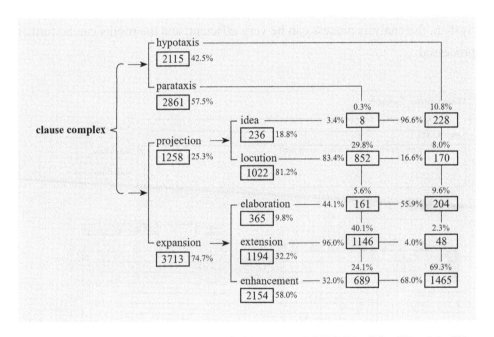

Figure 5-2   Frequencies of TAXIS and LOGICO-SEMANTIC TYPE in all the ST and the TTs

Each cell in the above figure reveals the probability that the nexus has in the text: "The systemic probabilities associated with the options and the combinations of options can be estimated by counting relative frequency in text" (Matthiessen, 2002: 249). Systemic functional grammar is a choice grammar, as a set of possibilities of each system: a potential for meaning creation (Halliday, 1991; Nesbitt and Plum, 1988): "Frequency in a text is the instantiation of probability in the system" (Halliday, 1991: 42). The frequencies of certain types of clause nexuses in the text represent the probabilities of choosing these clause nexuses rather than other types in the text. The probabilities assigned to the features in a system describe the pattern of choices (Nesbitt and Plum, 1988: 8). From the clause complex system, different combinations of TAXIS and LOGICO-SEMANTIC TYPE are realised through the frequencies they show in the text. These different frequencies form the patterns of the clause nexuses, which enable us to explain the features of different texts in realising logical meaning. The patterns of logical choices displayed by each text reveal the variation of the different languages and translators in realising semantic sequences. A clip of clause logical relations summary is shown in Figure 5–3.

ComplexID	ClauseID	7	6	5	4	3	2	1		Words
2TT1_1	2TT1_1_1	1							A verse says:	3
2TT1_1	2TT1_1_2	"2							Who can guess the outcome of a game of chess?	10
2TT1_1	2TT1_1_3								Incense burned out, tea drunk - it's still in doubt.	9
2TT1_1	2TT1_1_4	xβ							To interpret the signs of prosperity or decline	8
2TT1_1	2TT1_1_5	α							An impartial onlooker must be sought out.	7
2TT1_2	2TT1_2_1	xβ							Rearing the hubbub at his gate,	6
2TT1_2	2TT1_2_2	α	α						Feng Su hurried out	4
2TT1_2	2TT1_2_3		xβ						to see what the messengers wanted.	6
2TT1_3	2TT1_3_1	"1							"Ask Mr. Zhen to come out,"	6
2TT1_4	2TT1_4_1								"Be quick about it."	4
2TT1_5	2TT1_5_1	"1							"My name is Feng, not Zhen,"	6
2TT1_5	2TT1_5_2	2							he answered with an ingratiating smile.	6
2TT1_6	2TT1_6_1	1							"My son-in-law's name is Zhen,	7
2TT1_6	2TT1_6_2	+2	α						but he left home a year or two ago	9
2TT1_6	2TT1_6_3		xβ						to become a priest.	4
2TT1_7	2TT1_7_1								Is he the man you want?"	6
2TT1_8	2TT1_8_1								"How would we know?	4
2TT1_9	2TT1_9_1								We're here on the prefect's orders.	6
2TT1_10	2TT1_10_	xβ							If you're his father-in-law,	6
2TT1_10	2TT1_10_	α	α	1					you must come	3
2TT1_10	2TT1_10_			+2					and clear this up with His Honour	7
2TT1_10	2TT1_10_	xβ							to save us another trip."	5
2TT1_11	2TT1_11	+0							Giving Feng Su no chance to protest	7
									Total:	35,567
									Average:	6.0

Figure 5–3   A clip of Clause logical relations summary

Aside from the frequencies shown in Figure 5–2, Figure 5–3 is the results of clause logical relations in clause complex analysis, as shown in SysFan. The logical relation that each clause has is clearly shown in Figure 5–3. These results were outputted in Excel for further analysis, presented in the following subsections and in Chapter 7.

In order to see the results clearly and what the results can tell us, the features of clause complex are presented in bar charts in the following subsections.

5.1.2.1 TAXIS in the ST and the TTs

TAXIS, concerning with the interdependency between the clauses, shows how clauses are combined in terms of whether they enjoy an equal or unequal status.

Figure 5-4 presents the number and percentage of the two features of taxis in the Chinese ST and its two English TTs. In general, the skewed distribution of parataxis to hypotaxis shows the largest difference in the ST; while it tends to be more evenly balanced in the TT2. On one hand, it is obvious that the ST uses the most parataxis, while the TT2 uses the most hypotaxis among the three texts. On the other hand, the percentages of the two types of taxis provide more information about the usage of them in the three texts. Parataxis has the highest percentage in the ST (64.04%) among the three texts, and its percentage decreases in the two target texts, 53.99% (TT1) and 49.80% (TT2), respectively. Accordingly, the percentage of hypotaxis is lowest in the ST and highest in the TT2. The TT2 displays its distinction, where hypotaxis is slightly more favoured than parataxis, from the others, whereas in the ST and the TT1 parataxis has higher percentages. The TT1 percentage is in between that of the other two texts, but shows a similar trend of using more parataxis than hypotaxis as compared with the ST.

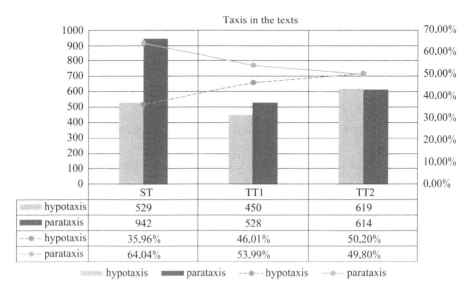

Figure 5-4 Comparison of taxis in the ST and the TTs

In translation, even though the ST shows the use of much more parataxis than hypotaxis, the two TTs do not show such a marked difference in the use of parataxis over hypotaxis. That is because in Chinese there are two ways of forming complex sentences: more than one clause can form a compound sentence; or one element in a clause develops to more than one clause. The Chinese clauses can combine with each other with or without conjunctions (Lv, 2008: 27–29), which allows Chinese clauses with equal status to develop complicated clause complexes. Hopper and Traugott (2003: 180) recognise that, in many languages, parataxis is the normal way of forming complex sentences. In Chinese in particular, paratactic clauses function as separate major clauses, which in other languages are often overtly marked as adverbial clause plus main clause. It is normal for Chinese sentences to use paratactic clauses, but not as common for English sentences to use them (Wang, 1945: 89). In the Chinese text, the higher percentage of parataxis is attributed to the features of the language itself.

The different probabilities of hypotaxis and parataxis in the source and target texts show the main difference between the two languages and also the two translators: Chinese tends to use more parataxis, while English tends to use more hypotaxis. Within the two TTs, the probabilities the two types of taxis display also show some differences. The TT1 tends to use more parataxis than the TT2. Yang, as a native speaker of Chinese, tries to keep the structure of the taxis of the source text to a greater extent than Hawkes when translating it into English. We can thus see the influence of Chinese as Yang's native language in his translation. This is propobaly the reason why the TT1 is in between the ST and the TT2 in terms of the use of taxis.

The following example, Text 5–3 exemplifies the above point in detail.

Text 5–3　An excerpt from ch2

Clause ID	Clause	Logical relations
ST		
ST–ch2–189–1	雨村　　　拍案　　　笑　　道： Yucun　strike the table　laugh　say	1

(continued)

Clause ID	Clause	Logical relations
ST-ch2-189-2	"怪道 这 女学生 读至 书, No wonder this female student read to book	" 2 1 x β α
ST-ch2-189-3	凡 中 有 '敏'字, All in have 'min' character	x β
ST-ch2-189-4	她 皆 念作 '密'字, she all read as 'mi' character	α
ST-ch2-189-5	每每 如 是; everytime like this	+ 2
ST-ch2-189-6	写字 遇着 '敏'字, write come across 'min' character	+ 3 x β
ST-ch2-189-7	又 减 一二 笔, again miss one or two stroke	α
ST-ch2-189-8	我 心中 就 有些 疑惑。" I in mind thus have doubt	x 4
TT1		
TT1-ch2-236-1	Yucun pounded the table with a laugh.	
TT1-ch2-237-1	"No wonder my pupil always pronounces min as mi	1
TT1-ch2-237-2	and writes it with one or two strokes missing.	+ 2
TT1-ch2-238-1	That puzzled me,	1
TT1-ch2-238-2	but now you've explained the reason."	+ 2
TT2		
TT2-ch2-253-1	Yu-cun clapped his hands with a laugh.	
TT2-ch2-254-1	"Of course! I have often wondered	α
TT2-ch2-254-2	why it is that my pupil Dai-yu always pronounces 'min' as 'mi' when she is reading and,	x β 1
TT2-ch2-254-3	if she has to write it,	x 2 x β
TT2-ch2-254-4	always makes the character with one or two strokes missing.	α
TT2-ch2-255-1	Now I understand."	

128

Text 5–3 displays details of how the paratactic clauses in the source text are maintained or transferred into hypotactic clauses in the two English target texts. The ST–ch2 is one multi-layered clause complex. It uses a paratactic structure in the two main clauses, ST–ch2–189–1 and ST–ch2–189–2, at the most local level; four paratactic clauses at the second level; two of which are further developed into hypotactic clauses at the third and fourth levels. Similarly, the TT1–ch2 consists of one clause simplex, TT1–ch2–236–1; and two clause complexes, TT1–ch2–237 and TT1–ch2–238. Both of the clause complexes consist of two paratactic clauses. All the clauses only develop one level of clause complex, and each of the clauses is in an equal status with the other. However, the TT2–ch2 is different in structure. It has two clause simplexes, TT2–ch2–253–1 and TT2–ch2–255–1; and one clause complex, TT2–ch2–254. The clause complex consists of four clauses: two of which are combined in a hypotactic way at the first level; and the secondary level consists of two paratactic clauses, one of which further develops into a hypotactic structure at the third level. The different choices of paratactic and hypotactic clauses in the two English texts verify the translators' preference: Yang keeps the paratactic structure; while Hawkes chooses to use more hypotactic structures.

Text 5–4 also shows that the TT1–ch2 keeps the original structure of the ST–ch2; and that a different structure is used in the TT2–ch2. The ST–ch2 uses three paratactic clauses, ST–ch2–73–1, 2, 3, in one clause complex. The TT1–ch2 preserves the tactic structure of the ST–ch2, with two paratactic clauses TT1–ch2–91–1 and TT1–ch2–91–2. However, the TT2–ch2 keeps the paratactic structure at the first level, with clauses TT2–ch2–87–1 and TT2–ch2–87–3; but develops two hypotactic clauses, from TT2–ch2–87–1, to the second level.

Text 5–4　An excerpt from ch2

Clause ID	Clause	Logical relations
ST		
ST–ch2–73–1	一面　说， while　say	1

(continued)

Clause ID	Clause	Logical relations	
ST–ch2–73–2	一面　让　雨村　　同席　坐了， while　ask　Yucun　same table　sat	x	2
ST–ch2–73–3	另　整上　　酒肴　　来。 other　order　wine and food　come	x	3
TT1			
TT1–ch2–91–1	He made Yucun sit down at his table	1	
TT1–ch2–91–2	and ordered more food and wine.	x	2
TT2			
TT2–ch2–87–1	Zi-xing conducted Yu-cun to his table	1	α
TT2–ch2–87–2	as he spoke	x	β
TT2–ch2–87–3	and ordered more wine and some fresh dishes to be brought.	x	2

The two translators use a different (set of) tactic relations in their translations. Yang uses a literal method in clause combination. He keeps the main paratactic structure and does not use dependent clauses in these examples. For Hawkes, his translation expresses the meaning of the original content without considering the way in which clauses combine with each other in the source text. That is why his version shows a distinctive difference in using taxis from the ST and the TT1.

5.1.2.2　Logico-semantic relations in the ST and the TTs

Logico-semantic relations are the relations holding between two clauses in a nexus. They can be divided into two types: projection, and expansion. "Projection" means that the secondary clause is projected through the primary clause; and it can be further divided into two subtypes: idea, and locution. Projection type is decided by the "directness" of the projected clause, and the content projected is within the linguistic content plane, which is semantics and lexicogrammar. "Idea" is the indirect projection of meaning, which is at the semantic level; "locution" is the direct projection of wording, which is at the lexicogrammatical level (Matthiessen, 1995: 142–143). "Expansion" means the secondary clause expands the primary clause; and it can be divided into "elaboration" "extension", and "enhancement" (Halliday and Matthiessen, 2004: 377). Details of clause complexing with logic-semantic relations are shown in Figure 5–1, in Section 5.1.

Figure 5–5 presents the details of the usage of the LOGICO-SEMANTIC TYPE in the three texts. The ST contains the most clauses that are connected to others with a logico-semantic relation, while the two TTs contain fewer of these clauses. All three texts show a similar preference for expansion rather than projection. Expansion is more than 75%, against the less than 25% projection across the three texts. From the ST to the TTs, the percentage of projection increases from 20% to 25%. Accordingly, expansion drops from 80% in the ST to 75% in the TT2. The two TTs are very close to each other in the probabilities of the two logico-semantic types. The increase of projection and decrease of expansion in the two TTs show that English tends to use more projecting clauses than Chinese, and that both of the translators choose to put similar emphasis on projecting clauses.

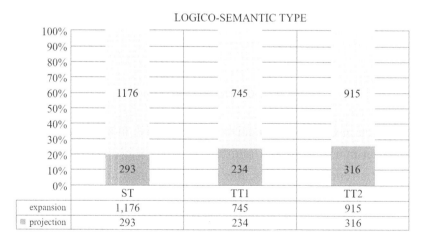

Figure 5–5   LOGICO-SEMANTIC TYPE in the texts

Figure 5–6 depicts the use of projecting clauses in the three texts. Within projection, the percentage of idea and locution exhibits an increasing and decreasing trend, respectively, from the ST to the TT2. The percentage of idea increases from 17% to 28% in the TT2, while locution decreases from 83% to 72% in the TT2; and the TT1 is in between of the ST and the TT2, with 22%

idea and 78% locution. Compared with the TT1, the TT2 uses larger numbers of both idea and locution, and has a higher ratio of idea. It can be inferred that Hawkes is more explicit than Yang in transferring projecting clauses, especially when he comes to the translation of indirect projection of meaning. The use of idea and locution in the three texts also reveals the features of different languages and translators in construing meaning through projection. In general, idea has a higher percentage in English target texts than in the Chinese text.

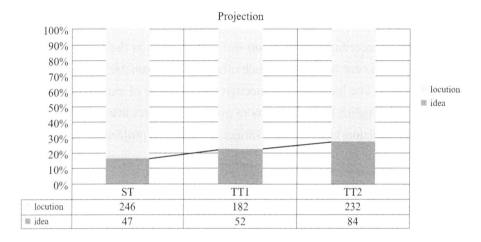

Figure 5-6　Projection in the texts

Projection in Chinese distinguishes from English in a few features. Firstly, the quotation marks are often omitted in Chinese projection. Secondly, in the hypotactic reporting clauses, there is no conjunction in Chinese. Thirdly, sometimes the reporting and reported clauses do not form a clause complex, but two clause simplexes (Zeng, 2000: 171). In Chinese, mental activities do not necessarily need to go with a sensing verb, but may be construed via a range of forms of expression. However, in English, mental activities are more often construed through a person and a sensing verb. The two translators choose to make the projected clauses explicit with syntactic variation and quotation marks. They follow the English habit of using projection, especially idea. The use of locution and idea in the TT1 reflects features in between those of the ST and the TT2 texts.

The three texts reveal diverse preferences for the subtypes of expansion, as shown in Figure 5-7. The ST has the most clauses connected with each other with an expanding relation, while the TT1 has the least. Within the expanding clauses, the probabilities for the three subtypes of expansion show features of each text. The ST and the TT2 show a high similarity in the percentage of the enhancing, extending and elaborating clauses; while the TT1 displays some differences. Enhancing clauses make up 60% of the ST and the TT2 texts, and 54% of the TT1. Elaborating clauses have no more than 1% difference across the three texts, all around 10%. As for extending clauses, the percentages in the ST and the TT2 show a high degree of conformity, about 31%; whereas in the TT1, it is 5% more than in the other two. This distinctive feature of the TT1, in the higher percentage of extending clauses, shows that Yang prefers to expand a clause by adding new elements, giving an exception or offering an alternative to the source.

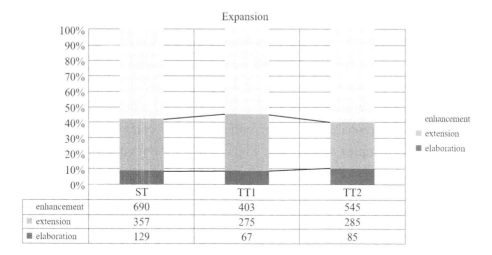

Figure 5-7   Expansion in the texts

Overall, the ST and the TTs display various features in the use of logico-semantic relations. All the texts on the whole use more expansion than projection. The two translators choose different ways of expressing the projecting and expanding relations in the different texts. The TT1 is in between the ST and the TT2 in respect of the incidence of projecting clauses; but the other two texts show similar percentages in the use of expanding clauses.

In order to explore the characteristics of clause complexing in the ST and the TTs, a further elaboration on the probabilistic patterns formed by the combination of taxis and logico-semantic type is needed: i.e. the intersection of the features in the clause complex system, in a probabilistic analysis of the text.

5.1.2.3　Intersection of taxis and logico-semantic type

The systems of taxis and logico-semantic type are simultaneous and intersect to define the serial structure of clause complex (Matthiessen, 2002: 249). The intersection of these two systems leads to the recursion of clause complexing; and as the recursion goes on with the development of the text, it brings out different instantiations of this intersection. The systems of taxis and logico-semantic type are independent of each other grammatically: the choice of any feature in one system does not affect the possible choice of feature in the other system (Nesbitt and Plum, 1988: 20). However, the choice of the features in the two systems is not entirely independent of each other in the text. Some features of the two systems are more likely to appear together, while some feature combinations are less likely favoured. The combinations of the features in each system can be used to measure the relation between taxis and logico-semantic relations, and thus giving a probabilistic profile of the text. The probabilities of the options and the combination of options in the clause complex system (see Figure 3-2) are not equally instantiated and can be estimated by the counts of relative frequency in a text. Therefore, the combinations of the two systems, taxis and logico-semantic type, display different percentages of usage, with some being favoured over others (Matthiessen, 2002: 249). The patterns displayed by the frequencies of different combination of options can indicate the patterns of the different texts in realising logical meaning.

With the frequencies and percentages of the frequencies of the features in the clause complex system, we can describe the ultimate distribution of the choices in a text.

Figure 5-8 presents the actual frequency of occurrences of the combination of taxis with logico-semantic type in the ST. The probabilities of the features are also calculated on the basis of the frequencies. The probabilities are meant to model the patterns of the features in the text. In the previous analysis of taxis, the use of parataxis and hypotaxis in the ST was shown to be not balanced, with around 30% more parataxis than hypotaxis. The texts also show skewed distribution in the combinations with logico-semantic relations, which indicates the association of taxis and logico-semantic relations with quantitative probabilities.

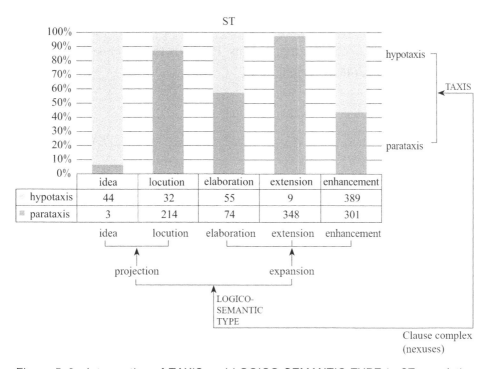

	idea	locution	elaboration	extension	enhancement
hypotaxis	44	32	55	9	389
parataxis	3	214	74	348	301

Figure 5-8   Intersection of TAXIS and LOGICO-SEMANTIC TYPE in ST — relative frequencies (total 1,469 clause nexuses)

Within projection, hypotaxis is more associated with idea, while parataxis is more likely with locution. The percentage occurrence of hypotactic idea is 93.62%; while for paratactic idea it is only 6.38%. Conversely, locution combines more with parataxis, which combination occurs 86.99% of the text. The probabilities and frequencies together are expressive in revealing the preference for options in the text. The most preferred pattern is thus paratactic locution, which has 214 occurrences in total. The least used pattern is paratactic idea, which appears only 3 times in the ST. The Chinese source text tends to use hypotactic idea and paratactic idea when the taxis is combined with projection.

Within expansion, paratactic extension is the most favoured combination. For elaboration, parataxis and hypotaxis are close in percentage of distribution, 57.36% and 42.64%, respectively. Enhancement, which shows the most frequency of all the logico-semantic relations, is expressed more with hypotaxis (56.38%) than with parataxis (43.62%).

The frequencies of various combinations of taxis and logico-semantic relations in the TT1, as shown in Figure 5-9, also display the different preferences in clause complexing patterns. Parataxis (53.99%) is slightly more used than hypotaxis (46.01%) in the TT1.

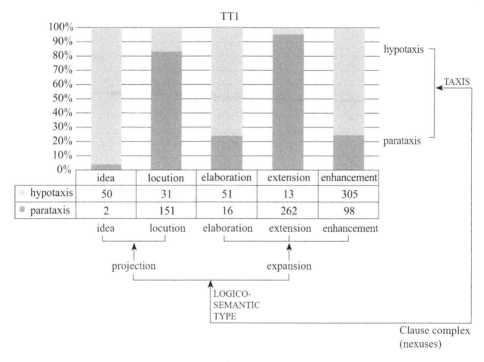

	idea	locution	elaboration	extension	enhancement
hypotaxis	50	31	51	13	305
parataxis	2	151	16	262	98

Figure 5-9　Intersection of TAXIS and LOGICO-SEMANTIC TYPE in the TT1 — relative frequencies (total 979 clause nexuses)

For projection, the TT1 displays the same preference as the ST in the use of more hypotactic idea than paratactic idea, and paratactic locution than hypotactic locution. There are only 2 paratactic ideas, or 3.85%. The

136

use of hypotactic locution is 17.03%; while the use of paratactic locution is 82.97%.

Within expansion, extension combines much more with parataxis (95.27%) than with hypotaxis (4.73%). Elaboration and enhancement both have a similar skewing, of over 75%, toward a preference for hypotaxis rather than for parataxis.

With reference to the statistics shown in Section 5.1.2.1, hypotaxis (50.20%) and parataxis (49.82%) are almost evenly distributed in the TT2 (see Figure 5-10), which is the only text with more hypotaxis than parataxis. However, the co-selections of taxis and logico-semantic relations show uneven preferences. For projection, hypotactic idea (96.43%) and paratactic locution (77.59) are more favoured than paratactic idea (3.57%) and hypotactic locution (22.41%). For expansion, paratactic extension is overwhelmingly preferred over hypotaxis, 92.98% against 7.02%, respectively. Hypotaxis also combines more with elaboration and enhancement than parataxis does.

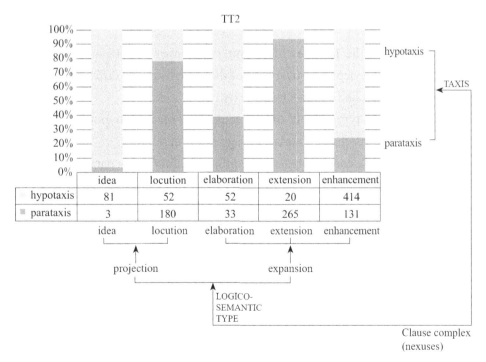

	idea	locution	elaboration	extension	enhancement
hypotaxis	81	52	52	20	414
parataxis	3	180	33	265	131

Figure 5-10　Intersection of TAXIS and LOGICO-SEMANTIC TYPE in the TT2 — relative frequencies (total 1231 clause nexuses)

The frequencies and probabilities of the combinations of the two systems in the three texts not only show their own patterns in the realisation of logical relations, but also the preferences of the author of the Chinese source text and the translators of the English target texts. If we compare the probabilities of different combinations of the two systems in the three texts, we find they show similarities and differences in terms of instantiation of the options.

The similarities they show are: ① the three texts display similar preferences for favouring hypotactic idea and paratactic locution; ② and paratactic extension takes up more than 90% of extension in all the three texts.

The differences are: ① hypotaxis is less combined with elaboration than parataxis is in the ST, but is more so in the two TTs — paratactic elaboration in the ST is 57.36%, but is only 23.88% and 38.92% in the TT1 and the TT2; ② the combination of taxis with enhancement shows a similar trend as that of elaboration. In all the three texts, there is more hypotactic enhancement than paratactic enhancement, but the distribution of these two types is different: in the ST, hypotaxis is 56.38%; but in the two TTs, it is 75.68% and 75.96%, respectively.

In summary, the features of the intersection of TAXIS and LOGICO-SEMANTIC TYPE depict an overview of the patterns of the different texts: the Chinese source text and English target texts.

(1) The more typical way of projecting an "idea" is hypotaxis through indirect report, rather than parataxis through direct quoting.

(2) "Locution", conversely, is more projected directly by parataxis through quote. Compared to ideas, locutions are much more likely to be offered as direct speech because they are closer to the final manifestation of the content. Conversely, ideas are much more likely to be presented as indirect thought because they are farther from the final realisation of the content (Matthiessen, 1995: 146). The combinations of paratactic locution and hypotactic idea are more likely to be found in both Chinese and English texts.

(3) The Chinese source text shows a preference for paratactic elaboration, while the English target texts show a preference for hypotactic elaboration.

(4) Extension is more likely to combine with parataxis in all the texts. This doesn't reflect a difference between languages or translators. Since extending is

basically additive, adversative or varying of the primary clause with a secondary clause, and parataxis is the juxtaposition of two clauses, the combination of extension and parataxis is more easily understood semantically than hypotactic extension.

(5) The ST uses more paratactic enhancement than the two TTs, even though in all the texts hypotaxis is more favoured in combination with enhancement. This indicates that in the transference of paratactic enhancement, both of the translators choose to change some of the combinations to hypotactic enhancement. The two TTs show a similar preference for the combination of taxis with enhancement. It is possible that English is a more hypotaxis-inclined language, while Chinese tends more towards parataxis in meaning realisation.

The profile of the combination of the features in the clause complex system, in the ST and the TTs, provides an overview of how the two languages construe meanings of logically related clauses. In the development of clause complexes, the probabilities of the taxis and logico-semantic relations reveal how the semantic sequence is formed and realised in lexicogrammar. Furthermore, the profile also depicts a map of the patterns of clause complexing in different texts in terms of frequencies. They are indicative in revealing the characteristics of the logical development of both Chinese and English literary texts. The comparisons of the English target texts with the Chinese source text, and between the two target texts, are important for translation studies of the construing logical semantic sequences with certain patterns that are representative in the specific language or for specific translation purposes.

5.2   Summary

In realising coherence, the logical metafunction role was elaborated in this chapter.

In respect of clause complexity, the Chinese source text emphasises the inner logical relations between clauses by using more intricate clause complexes. In translation, both of the two English target texts use less complicated clauses and clause complexes in realising logical meaning.

The clause complex analysis in this chapter is applicable to the whole novel. A corpus of 30 pieces of dialogues between the two main characters, Baoyu and Daiyu, across 80 chapters in the novel and its two English translations is analysed. In a literary text, dialogues between the characters are important in making the story coherent. In turns of the dialogues, a coherent structure is established by the progression of the story. This underlying logical structure in a coherent text directs the reader through it (Neubert and Shreve, 1992: 94). The analysis of clause complexes of dialogues in the ST and the TTs reflects how the logical metafunction functions in the realisation of coherence in a literary text. The analysis also reveals how the different translators deal with clause complex in recreating a coherent text in the target language.

The quantitative analysis of clause nexuses makes it possible to detect the patterns of combination of the two systems in terms of probabilities in the text. The skewed or balanced distributions of features shown by each text are the product of the choices of the text producer. These choices form the patterns of the novel in the realisation of logical metafunction at the lexicogrammatical level. The preferences of each text can be attributed to typological differences and the translators' styles. In addition, the probabilities of features in the clause complex systems set a basis for further analysis of the patterns of coherence when integrated with analyses of other metafunctions. These patterns can be related to and analysed from the perspective of other choices at the clause rank and at the lexicogrammatical level.

Chapter 6

Cohesive Chains in Forming the Patterns of Coherence

This chapter elaborates, from the perspective of the textual metafunction, how cohesive chains work in the creation of coherence in the Chinese source text and the English target texts. The textual metafunction is relevant to the creation of texture, which is taken to be coherence in a reader or listener's perception (Halliday and Hasan, 1976). Cohesion is considered as "the aspect of texture which upholds textuality by making a sequence of sentences hang together as a coherent text" (Hatim and Mason, 1990: 210). The texture of a text is manifested by certain patterns of semantic relations between the units of text [Halliday and Hasan, 1985 (1989): 71]. The nature of those relations and lexico-grammatical patterns is realised by cohesive ties and cohesive chains. Therefore, cohesive chains are taken as the threads of semantic sequences of the text; and contribute to the creation of coherence.

Cohesive chains are investigated in terms of how they are formed and how similar and different between the source and target texts, to reveal the choices of the translators in maintaining the texture of the source text. This chapter comprises two main parts. In Section 6.1, the features of the grammatical and lexical cohesion are examined, and thus cohesive chains in the ST and the TTs are calibrated in terms of number and type. In Section 6.3, the results of the analysis in 6.1 are evaluated from the perspective of translation equivalence, to depict an overview of the role that cohesive chains play in the recreation of a coherent text for different translation purposes.

This chapter aims to answer the following questions: What are the characteristics of the cohesive chains in the Chinese source text and the two English target texts? What are the similarities and differences of the cohesive chains in the ST and the TTs? How do the cohesive chains contribute to the patterns of coherence in the text? How are these patterns dealt with in translation?

6.1　Cohesive Chains in the ST and the TTs

Cohesive chains are formed out of cohesive devices, the ways of which connect to each other reflect the coherence of the text. As stated in Chapter 3, this research focuses on two types of non-structural cohesion only, to be specific, grammatical and lexical devices of componential relations (see Table 3-5). The connection among the grammatical and lexical cohesive devices is the basis for making cohesive ties and chains. The cohesive chains in a text are the threads linking the different parts of the text grammatically and lexically. They form the cohesive patterns that reflect and reinforce the interplay of localised and generalised imagery, and add to something complex, both abstract and intangible, and concrete and very tangible (Halliday and Hasan, 1976: 345). They realise the semantic continuity of the text. In a literary text, the analysis of cohesive chains describes the connections between clauses, and relates the cohesive chains to the topic of the text, so as to obtain the strings of events and characters, and the development of these entities in the text. Thus, cohesive chains indicate the patterns of coherence in the text, and how they are dealt with in translation.

"Cohesion refers to the range of possibilities that exist for linking something with what has gone before" (Halliday and Hasan, 1976: 10), and it is created through the use of the grammatical and lexical devices in any of the categories in Table 3-5. When one cohesive device is interpreted by reference to some items in the text, or the two items form a semantic relation such as synonymy, antonymy and hyponymy, cohesive ties are established, and cohesion is created via the ties. According to the semantic relation between the two items, the relation of the tie can be identified as either co-referentiality, co-classification or co-extension. The study of cohesion is actually the study of the cohesive ties. However, the ties alone cannot make a text coherent. "The coherence arises from the imposition of a grid upon sensory precepts; the categories of cohesion are the lexicogrammatical indication of the details of such a grid" (Hasan, 1984: 210). Therefore, the study of coherence calls for a longer semantic relation among the devices than the cohesive tie, i.e., the cohesive chain.

This research has illustrated and analysed the use of cohesive devices in the ST and the TTs. Every cohesive device used in each clause is noted in the text along with its interpretive sources. The relationship between the cohesive devices and their interpretative sources allows us to identify the cohesive ties and chains. The presentation of the cohesive devices in the form of chains contributes to the texture of the text. Since "in any coherent discourse, threads of semantic continuity are created through the construction of cohesive chains" (Hasan, 1984: 138), the development of the semantic sequence of both the ST and the TTs can be visualised with numbers and patterns through the analysis of cohesive chains.

6.1.1　Cohesive chains

A cohesive chain "is formed by a set of items, each of which is related to the others by the semantic relations of co-reference, co-classification and/or co-extension" [Halliday and Hasan, 1985 (1989): 84]. Considering the principles for chain formation, Hasan (1984) recognises two major categories of cohesive chains: the "identity chains", and the "similarity chains". An identity chain is formed out of the relations of co-reference between the members. In an identity chain, every member refers to the same thing, and it is text-bound. For example, in the present data, there are identity chains referring to certain characters through the narration of the story. These identity chains are only applicable in the specific text, not anywhere else. A similarity chain is formed out of the relations of either co-classification or co-extension between the members. It refers to the things or events in the same category or class, but not the identical items, and it is not text-bound. For example, a group of synonymous words, "cry, sob, lament", can form a similarity chain not only in the text analysed here but also in any other text.

Identity chains are text specific, while similarity chains are genre specific.

Identity chains can trace the topical unity of a text. In contrast, similarity chains are formed out the semantic relations not only in one specific text but in the language. There is often overlapping of similarity chains in the same contextual configuration. Therefore, the collaboration of these two types of cohesive chains can build the semantic threads in the text and also in the context of culture, which are important in the perception of coherence.

With the interweaving of identity and similarity chains, the unity of the text can be ascertained within the text and also in relation to the context. Therefore, the perception of the text can be framed as a grid, which can be seen as the patterns contributing to the coherence of a text. The patterns in both the ST and the TTs are expected to reveal similarities and differences in the ways texture is realised, so as to manifest the strategies of different translators in maintaining the coherence of the source text in the transference of texture from Chinese to English.

The use of cohesive chains in each text is then summarised in terms of numbers of each type of chain.

6.1.1.1   Grammatical cohesion

Grammatical chains construct the "topical" unity of a text through pronominal reference. The "topical" unity displays part of the semantic coherence of a text.

The following excerpt Text 6-1 and its translations are from ch1. The ST-ch1 consists of 11 clauses; while the TT1-ch1 and the TT2-ch1 has 9 and 14 clauses, respectively. They are shown here to demonstrate how the cohesive chains in the text are created.

Text 6-1   An excerpt from ch1

ST-ch1	
1	原来女娲氏炼石补天之时， When the Goddess Nvwa was repairing the sky,
2	于大荒山无稽崖炼成高经十二丈、方经二十四丈顽石三万六千五百零一块。 at the Baseless cliff of The Great Waste Mountain, she tempered thirty six thousand five hundred and one blocks of stone, each one hundred third feet high and two hundred sixty feet square.

(continued)

3	娲皇氏只用了三万六千五百块， The Goddess Nvwa only used thirty six thousand five hundred blocks,
4	单单剩了一块未用， leaving only one block unused,
5	弃在青埂峰下。 and threw it at the foot of the Blue Ridge Peak.
6	谁知此石自经煅炼之后， Who would have known that this stone after being tempered,
7	灵性已通。 has possessed magical power.
8	因见众石俱得补天， Seeing that all the other blocks of stone are used to repair the sky,
9	独自己无材不堪入选， only itself was rejected,
10	遂自怨自叹， it grumbled and sighed,
11	日夜悲号惭愧。 lamenting day and night. [My own translation]

TT1–ch1

1	When the goddess Nu Wa melted down rocks
2	to repair the sky,
3	at Baseless Cliff in the Great Waste Mountain she made thirty-six thousand five hundred and one blocks of stone, each a hundred and twenty feet high and two hundred and forty feet square.
4	She used only thirty-six thousand five hundred of these
5	and threw the remaining block down at the foot of Blue Ridge Peak.
6	Strange to relate, this block of stone after tempering had acquired spiritual understanding.
7	Because all its fellow blocks had been chosen to mend the sky

145

(continued)

8	and it alone rejected,
9	it lamented day and night in distress and shame.
TT2–ch1	
1	Long ago, when the goddess Nu-wa was repairing the sky,
2	she melted down a great quantity of rock
3	and, on the Incredible Crags of the Great Fable Mountains, moulded the amalgam into thirty-six thousand, five hundred and one large building blocks,
4	each measuring seventy-two feet by a hundred and forty-four feet square.
5	She used thirty-six thousand five hundred of these blocks in the course of her building operations,
6	leaving a single odd block unused,
7	which lay, all on its own, at the foot of Greensickness Peak in the aforementioned mountains.
8	Now this block of stone, <9> possessed magic powers.
9	having undergone the melting and moulding of a goddess,
10	It could move about at will
11	and could grow or shrink to any size it wanted.
12	Observing that all the other blocks had been used for celestial repairs and that it was the only one to have been rejected as unworthy,
13	it became filled with shame and resentment
14	and passed its days in sorrow and lamentation.

Table 6-1 shows the process and results of the cohesion analysis of the excerpt in Text 6-1. The first column lists the cohesive devices in the text with the clause ID in each row; and the interpretative source correlates the cohesive devices with the referred items in the text with the corresponding clause ID. The cohesive devices and the interpretative source make ties, the status of which is presented in the third column. When the tie is exophoric, the interpretative source is not to be found within the text, and it is labelled with a blank "—". Only when the tie is anaphoric or cataphoric is the interpretative source to be found in the text. When the interpretative source is ambiguous, a question mark is placed to indicate the possible interpretative source or the uncertainty of interpretation. The last column specifies the chain formation.

For example, in the ST–ch1, the chain "11e–8e–6–4s–3–2" represents the interrelationship from the omitted subject in clause 11 to the same omission in clause 8, to clause 6 "此石 (this stone)" and to "一块 (one stone)" in clause 4, to "三万六千五百块 (thirty-six thousand five hundred blocks of stone)" in clause 3, and to "顽石 (the stone)" in clause 2. All the cohesive devices in these clauses form an identity chain, referring to "顽石 (the block of stone)" in the text. In the two TTs, the process of identifying the cohesive chains is presented in the last column with the growth of these chains. The shaded chains are the final chains developed from the unshaded chains, clause by clause, in the text. This is how the grammatical chains are formed with the cohesive devices and their interpretative sources. To make the cohesive devices easily recognisable, the cohesive devices, especially the definite articles and personal references, are followed by brackets with the relevant nominal and verbal groups next to them.

Table 6-1 Cohesive chains analysis of the excerpt from ch1

ST–ch1			
Cohesive devices	**Interpretative sources**	**Tie status**	**Grammatical chains**
3. 三万六千五百块 thirty six thousand five hundred blocks	2. 顽石 stone	anaphoric	
4. 一块 one block	3. 顽石 stone	"	
5. 此 here	2. 大荒山 The Great Waste Mountain	"	
6. 此 here	4. 一块(顽石) one (block)	"	

(continued)

| 8. subject ellipsis | 6. 此石 <br> this stone | " | |
| 11. subject ellipsis | 8. 石 <br> stone | " | <u>11e-8e-6-4s-3-2顽石</u>
 <u>(the stone)</u> |

TT1–ch1

Cohesive devices	Interpretative sources	Tie status	Chains
1. the goddess	-	exophoric	
2. the sky	-	"	
3. the (Great) she each -substitution	- 1. the goddess 3. Stone	exophoric anaphoric "	
4. she these	3. she 3. each	" "	4-3-1 <u>4-3-3 blocks</u>
5. subject ellipsis the (remaining) the (foot)	4. She - -	" exophoric "	<u>5e-4-3-1 goddess</u>
6. this	5. the remaining	anaphoric	
7. its the sky	6. this 2. the sky	" "	7-6-5
8. it	7. its	"	8-7-6-5
9. it	8. it	"	<u>9-8-7-6-5 stone</u>

TT2–ch1

Cohesive devices	Interpretative sources	Tie status	Chains
1. the (goddess) the (sky)	- -	exophoric "	
2. she	1. the goddess	anaphoric	
3. the the (Great) subject ellipsis the (amalgam)	- - 2. she -	exophoric " anaphoric exophoric	3e-2-1

(continued)

4. each (stone)- substitution	3. blocks	anaphoric	
5. She (used) these (blocks) the (course) her (building)	3. subject 3. blocks - 5. she (goddess)	" " exophoric anaphoric	<u>5–3e–2–1 goddess</u> <u>5–5–3e–2–1 goddess</u>
7. its the (foot) the	6. block - -	anaphoric exophoric "	
8. this (block)	7. its	anaphoric	8–7–6
9. the (melting)	-	exophoric	
10. It (could)	8. this	anaphoric	10–8–7–6
11. subject ellipsis it (wanted)	10. It 11. subject	" "	11e–10–8–7–6 11–11e–10–8–7–6
12. other (blocks) 12. it the (only)	? 11. it -	anaphoric exophoric	12–11–11e–10–8–7–6
13. it	12. it	anaphoric	13–12–11–11e–10–8– 7–6
14. subject ellipsis its	13. it 14. subject	" "	14–14e–13–12–11– 11e–10–8–7–6 block 14–14e–13–12–11–11e– <u>10–8–7–6 block</u>

There are ambiguities in the cohesive chains above. In the TT2-ch1, the interpretative source of the reference "other" in the clause 12 is not identified. It is a comparative reference, compared with the subject, i.e. the stone, of clause 11. However, its referent is not to be found in the co-text, but lies in the semantic realisation of the reference and the co-text. Since the grammatical cohesive devices are mainly formed out of the pronominal definite article "the" and demonstratives, which all refer to the specific character, entity, event and so on alike in the text, the grammatical chains can be traced throughout the text. To keep the chains clear and traceable, the ambiguity is not taken into consideration of the chain formation in the analysis.

The "topical" unity of the text is achieved through the grammatical chains. In a narrative structure, Chatman (1980: 30) believes that the narrative existents (characters, items of setting) must remain the same from one event to the next, thus inferences can be made through the development of these existents. The referent and references form a cohesive chain referring to the same entity or character in the text, which indicates the development of the same existent throughout the text. Thus, through this kind of cohesive chain, the "topic" of the text can be inferred. In the ST–ch1, the grammatical chain "11e–8e–6–4s–3–2" means that "the stone" runs through the clauses 2, 3, 4, 6, 8 and 11. The "4s" stands for the substitution of the object "stone", and the "8e" and "11e" represent the subject ellipsis of "the stone". Similarly, in the TT1–ch1, the grammatical chains "4–3–1", "4–3–3" and "9–8–7–6–5" refer to the "goddess", the "blocks" and the "stone" in the text. In the TT2–ch2, the chains "5–3e–2–1" and "14–14e–13–12–11–11e–10–8–7–6" refer to the "goddess" and the "block" throughout the text. All these grammatical chains are text-bound; and they are the strings that concern an entity of the text. With these grammatical chains, the topical development of these entities can be traced in the text, achieving semantic unity.

With the process of cohesion analysis mentioned in the above table, all of the (Chinese source and English target) texts are examined, and the grammatical cohesion is identified.

6.1.1.2　Lexical cohesion

The analysis of lexical cohesion in the text is more complicated than that of grammatical cohesion, because the effect of lexical cohesion on a text is "subtle and difficult to estimate" (Halliday and Hasan, 1976: 288).

> With grammatical cohesion the effect is relatively clear: if one comes across the word he, for example, there is no doubt that some essential information is called for, and that the identity of the he must be recovered from somewhere. Reference items, substitutes and conjunctions all explicitly presuppose some elements other than themselves. In lexical cohesion,

however, it is not a case of there being particular lexical items which always have a cohesive function. EVERY lexical item MAY enter into a cohesive relation, but by itself it carries no indication whether it is functioning cohesively or not. That can be established only by reference to the text (Halliday and Hasan, 1976: 288).

Even though lexical cohesion is not as easily identified as grammatical cohesion, it is vital in creating the texture of a text. "However luxuriant the grammatical cohesion displayed by any piece of discourse, it will not form a text unless this is matched by cohesive patterning of a lexical kind" (Halliday and Hasan, 1976: 292). The lexical cohesive devices form lexical patterns in a text, which "serve to transform a series of unrelated structures into a unified, coherent whole" (Halliday and Hasan, 1976: 320).

1) TTR

TTR is often used to indicate the lexical density of a text. It is a measurement of the range and diversity of vocabulary used by a writer, or in a given corpus. It is the ratio of the different types of words to the overall number of words in a text or a corpus (Baker, 2000: 250). In different translations of the same source text, a higher ratio implies that the translator uses more types of words, or in other words, the translation has a wider range of vocabulary. The repetition of words in the lower ratio text is more than that in the higher ratio text. "A high TTR (i.e. a high degree of lexical diversity in a text) serves to increase the semantic precision and informational density of a written text" (Biber et al., 1999: 43). "It must be stressed, however, that both TTR and lexical density can only serve to provide a first quantitative indication of lexical cohesion and can only be interpreted in terms of repetition" (Hansen-Schirra et al., 2007: 261). The analysis of TTR and lexical density in the two target texts here aims to give a primitive description of the lexical cohesion in the two texts, and to explore the possible preferences that the two translators show in using lexical items.

The two target texts are translations of the same source text; but they are different in word counts. Since the numbers of sentences and clauses of the two texts differ, the TTR in the texts with different word counts may not be very reliable in calculating the lexical richness. Therefore, Standard Type-Token Ratio (STTR) is adopted in the comparison of different size texts. It calculates TTR on the basis of every 1,000 words. This research uses STTR to test the lexical complexity of each text. Table 6-2 shows the STTR of the two target texts in the overall data.

Table 6-2 STTR of the two TTs

	TT1	**TT2**	**discrepancy**
Tokens	14,193	19,105	−4,912
Types	3,113	3,753	−640
STTR	22%	20%	+2%

The STTR of the two TTs shows a difference in the lexical complexity of the two texts. Yang uses 4,912 fewer words than Hawkes in total. However, the STTR in the TT1 is 2% higher than that in the TT2, which indicates that the lexical density in the TT1 is higher than that in the TT2. Yang is thus richer in the range of vocabulary than Hawkes. Also, Hawkes uses more tokens than Yang, which suggests that he uses more repetition of words.

For example, the following excerpt, Text 6-2 from the two English target texts, shows the difference in lexical complexity. And Table 6-3 shows the STTR in Text 6-2.

Text 6-2 An excerpt from ch2

T1-ch2	
55-1	It so happened that Yucun had caught a chill which laid him up in his inn for a month and more.
56-1	Exhausted by his illness, and short of funds,
56-2	he was searching for somewhere to recuperate.
57-1	Fortunately he had two old friends here who knew that the Salt Commissioner was looking for a tutor.
58-1	Upon their recommendation Yucun was given the post,

(continued)

58-2	which provided the security he needed.
59-1	He was lucky, too, to have as pupil only one small girl accompanied by two maids.
60-1	Since the child was so delicate,
60-2	her lessons were irregular
60-3	and this meant that his duties were light.
TT2-ch2	
54-1	Now Jia Yu-cun had had the misfortune to catch a severe chill
54-2	while staying in his lodgings at Yangchow,
54-3	and after his recovery, found himself somewhat short of cash.
55-1	He was therefore already looking around for some more permanent haven where he could rest and recuperate,
55-2	when he chanced to run into two old friends who were acquainted with the new Salt Commissioner and who, knowing that the latter was looking for a suitable tutor for his daughter, took Yu-cun along to the yamen and introduced him, with the result that he was given the job.
56-1	Since Yu-cun's pupil was both very young and rather delicate,
56-2	there were no regular hours of instruction;
56-3	and as she had only a couple of little maids studying with her for company who stayed away when she did,
56-4	Yu-cun's employment was far from arduous
56-5	and left ample time for convalescence.

Table 6-3   STTR in Text 6-2

	TT1-ch2	TT2-ch2	discrepancy
Tokens	102	146	-44
Types	74	103	-29
STTR	73%	71%	2%

The two pieces exhibit how the STTR represents lexical complexity of the two TTs-ch2. The TT1-ch2 uses fewer tokens and types than the TT2-ch2, but it has a higher STTR. The tokens underlined in the excerpt refer to the same "person" in the texts. In the TT1-ch2, four types of four tokens "pupil, girl, child, her" are used; whereas in the TT2-ch2, four types out of five tokens — "daughter, pupil, she, her, she" — are used. The same token "Yu-cun" appears twice in the TT1-ch1, but four times in the TT2-ch2. There is more repetition of the same type in the TT2-ch2. It can be inferred that, in larger size samples, the TT1 uses more diverse words than the TT2; and that there is a higher rate of lexical repetition in the TT2.

In summary, the lexical density shows the personal style of the two translators: Hawkes uses more words than Yang, whereas Yang is richer in vocabulary because of the less repetition of words. For detailed interpretation of the lexical cohesion, more analytical processes need to be done; which are presented in the following sections.

2) Lexical cohesive chains

"Lexical semantic relations are the building blocks of lexical cohesion, cohesive harmony, and the concept of patterns of lexical affinity" (Morris and Hirst, 2006: 43). Lexical cohesion is divided into two types: general lexical relations, and instantial ones. The first are supratextual; while the latter are text-bound. Therefore, lexical cohesion can build up not only a text specific structure, but also establish the relationship between the text and the context.

Table 6-4 demonstrates the lexical cohesive devices in the same excerpt as the grammatical cohesion in Text 6-1. The numbers in the first column indicate the chain number; and the numbers in the right column show the tokens in the chain. The identification of the lexical cohesion is based on the classification of lexical cohesive devices, as shown in Table 3-5.

There are certain issues in the analysis that need to be clarified here. Firstly, "word" is taken as a token in the analysis, because in the formation of a lexical cohesive chain, the function of "word" and "token" is alike. Secondly, collocation is not under consideration here, because it has "proved problematic" in Hasan's (1984: 195) words; and it is too difficult to exhaust all the collocation of a word in the text. For example, in the TT2-ch1, the collocation of "blocks" in clause 3 and "building" in clause 5 may be problematic, since one analyst considers that they can appear together with a tie, while others may not. Thirdly, semantic relation is taken into consideration as part of the lexical cohesive chains. For instance, in the ST-ch1, "女娲氏" (the goddess Nvwa) in clause 1 and "娲皇氏" (the empress Nvwa) in clause 3 form an equivalent tie in referring to the same goddess. In summary, the instantial lexical cohesive devices only are part of the analysis. All possible efforts to avoid ambiguity caused by these problems in the analysis have been made.

Table 6-4　Lexical cohesive chains in Text 6-1: An excerpt from ch1

ST-ch1			tokens
1		女娲氏1.　　　　娲皇氏3. The Goddess Nvwa　The Goddess Nvwa	2
2		石1.　顽石2.　石6.　石8. stone　hard stone　stone　stone	4
3		补天1.　　　　补天8. to repair the sky　to repair the sky	2
4		大荒山2.　　　　山5. the Great Waste Mountain　mountain	2
TT1-ch1			tokens
1		rocks 1. blocks of stone 3. block 5. block 6. blocks 7.	5
2		the sky 2. the sky 7.	2
3		the Great Waste Mountain 3. Blue Ridge Peak 5.	2
TT2-ch2			tokens
1		goddess 1. goddess 9.	2
2		repairing 1. repairs 12.	2
3		rock 2. blocks3. blocks 5. block 6. block 8. blocks 12.	6
4		the Great Fable Mountains 3. mountains 7.	2
5		building 3. building 5.	2

As stated before, there are two main categories in the formation of lexical cohesive chains: general, and instantial. The general lexical cohesive devices are not text-bound, because repetition, synonymy, antonymy and meronymy relations of a group of items exist in any text. The instantial lexical cohesive devices are text-bound. The relations created by equivalence, naming and semblance only exist in the specific text. For example, the equivalent relation between "女娲氏" (the goddess Nvwa) and "娲皇氏" (the empress Nvwa) can only be identified via the co-text, but not in any other text. Both of the two categories of chain formation can connect the items within the same group so as to establish the semantic strings related to the development of the text. The chain connection patterns in texts are an expression of the development of the content of the text (Hasan, 1984: 199). The lexical chains, no matter whether general or instantial, also contribute to the topical development of the text, as do the grammatical cohesive devices.

6.1.1.3　Identity and similarity chains

Grammatical and lexical cohesion together make the text a semantic whole. For a further process out of the results of the analysis of the grammatical and lexical cohesion, conducted using the method outlined in 6.1.1.1 and 6.1.1.2, a different principle of the recognition from the grammatical and lexical chains needs to be applied. Based on the relationships between the items in a chain, cohesive chains are categorised into identity chains and similarity chains.

An identity chain is formed out of the relation of co-reference between grammatical cohesive devices and co-classification as well as between instantial lexical cohesive devices such as co-referentiality and equivalence. For example, in the excerpt TT1-ch1 in Table 6-1, the demonstrative "this" in clause 6, pronominal "its" in clause 7, and "it" in clauses 8 and 9, all refer to the same stone in clause 5. The lexical devices "rocks" in clasue 1, "blocks of stone" in clause 3, "block" in clauses 5 and 6, "Blocks" in clause 7 in the same text also refer to the same stone with an equivalent bond among them. Both co-referentiality of grammatical cohesion and equivalent lexical cohesion form identity chains. The items in an identity chain refer to the same entity within the text. The equivalence between the instantial cohesive devices is legitimated within the text: for example, "shiyin" in the text is also referred to as "master". This kind of relation is built from explicit declarations of equivalence in the wording of a specific text. The chain determined by the semantic relationships within the text captures metaphoric relations that are significant to the logical "skeleton" of meanings within a text (Butt et al., 2010: 273).

A similarity chain is formed out of the relation of co-classification or co-extension. In the excerpt of TT1–ch1, "the Blue Ridge Peak" is part of "the Great Waste Mountain", so they form a cohesive tie via meronymy. The simple repetition of "the sky" in clause 2 and "the sky" in clause 7, referring to the same sky in the excerpt, forms a co-reference relation between them. The relation of the co-classification and co-reference is applicable not only in this text but also in other texts.

Identity and similarity chains engage both grammatical and lexical cohesion in forming the cohesive structure of the text: "The revised conception of chains has the effect of integrating the lexical and grammatical cohesive patterns of the text, so that they are seen neither as just lexical nor as just grammatical, but have a status by reference to their potential function in the text" (Hasan, 1984: 211). The different functions of the two types of cohesive chain enable the items in the chains to form grammatically repeated unities, which can be used for further research on the degree of coherence of the text. Even though the previous literature has shown that chain interaction is a crucial tool in measuring the coherence of the text, the analysis of chain interaction is beyond the scope of the current research. Cohesive chains only are able to explain the patterns that are related to the creation of coherence. Chain interactions are used to evaluate how and to what extent the text is coherent. However, the degree of coherence of each text is not being examined here; instead, the assumption has already been made that all texts are coherent. It is the patterns of coherence realised at the lexicogrammatical level that are being investigated, not the specific model for measuring textual coherence. Only cohesive chains are listed and taken as the resources for making the text coherent. Therefore, chain interaction is not taken into consideration in the present research.

6.2 Cohesive chains in the texts

Given the above description of cohesive chains, all the grammatical and lexical cohesive devices in the ST and the TTs have been identified, and the identity chains and similarity chains formed out of those cohesive devices have been listed. It is assumed that coherence remains constant in translation from the ST to the TTs; but the ways in which the coherence is reflected on the text — the cohesion, i.e. the cohesive devices employed — show differences with variations of languages and texts (Hatim and Mason, 1990: 195). The use of cohesive chains in each text is presumed to provide evidence about the effect of the textual metafunction in the creation of coherence.

The number of each type of chain in the different texts reveals the different patterns of chain formation of different languages, and also of different translators.

Table 6-5 exhibits an obvious difference between the Chinese source text and the two English target texts. Firstly, the ST has the least number of cohesive chains: 671 in total, both identity chains and similarity chains. The two English target texts have more cohesive chains than the ST. With 803 and 968 cohesive chains in total, the TT1 and the TT2 exceed the ST by about 20% and 44%. Secondly, the three texts also show discrepancy in percentages of each type of cohesive chain. Identity chains have the least percentage in the ST, and the most in the TT1. Conversely, similarity chains are most used in the ST, and least in the TT1. The two TTs show only less than 1% discrepancy of the identity chains and similarity chains between them; but the discrepancy between these and the ST is more than 6%. The final figure is the difference between the Chinese and English in the use of cohesive chains.

Table 6-5　The use of cohesive chains in the texts

	ST		TT1		TT2	
Identity Chains	351	52.31%	474	59.03%	564	58.26%
Similarity Chains	320	47.69%	329	40.97%	404	41.74%
Total	671	100%	803	100%	968	100%

The numbers and percentages reveal the characteristics of Chinese and English, and also the different translators, in the construction of a text with cohesive chains. The Chinese source text is the most implicit one, while Hawkes's translation is the most explicit one in terms of the cohesive chain numbers. Yang's version is in between the ST and the TT2 in terms of explicitness, and therefore shows the features of both Chinese and English texts.

The identity chains include the use of substitutions and ellipses. In most cases, substitutions and ellipses in the texts are nominal substitutions and subject ellipses, and the interpretative sources of these are the pronominals and nouns. Therefore, substitutions and ellipses are taken as part of the identity chain referring to the same entity. Moreover, the Chinese source text contains more substitutions and ellipses in its identity chains than the two English target texts do. Even so, the identity chains in the ST are still far fewer than in the two English TTs. Therefore, in terms of linking the cohesive devices into a network, which sets the basis for the coherence of the text, the Chinese source text is looser in structure; while the two English target texts are tighter, with more threads of meaning concerning topical development.

There is a distinctive characteristic of the identity chains in the Chinese text. In the ST, the same character is not always referred to by personal pronouns, but instead is often referred to by name, title, or someone else's honorific title for him/her. However, in the TTs, the character is more often likely to be referred to by personal pronouns throughout a whole chapter. Meanwhile, there is no definite article "the" in Chinese, so the relation between the entity and nouns is not realised with "the" in identity chains in Chinese. However, in an identity chain in English, the tokens can refer to any one of the definite article "the", pronominal or noun. The definite article "the" can function to link the nouns and the pronouns. In this sense, there are fewer chain disjunctions in the English target texts than in the Chinese source text, and therefore, longer identity chains.

To take an excerpt from Chapter 3 as an example: Table 6–6 lists the formation of grammatical chains and lexical chains in the excerpt. The grammatical chains are labelled in grey shading. The lexical chains are listed in a separate table, and identified as identity chains and similarity chains. In the ST-ch3, the identity chain, "老太太" (the old lady), is formed with three relevant tokens in clauses 10, 11, and 12, of which two are subject-ellipses. The token, "老太太" (the old lady), is a noun in Chinese, and without any definite article before it. The lexical tokens, "老太太" (the old lady) in clauses 7, 10, 13, 17, 19 and 22, also form another identity chain as equivalent to each other. In the TT1-ch3, the referent, "the old lady", forms an identity chain with 6 relevant tokens, which are in the form of the noun "the old lady", and pronouns "she" and "her", in the clauses. In the TT2-ch3, the same identity chain is formed out of the equivalence of lexical cohesive device "Grandma", which refers to "the old lady". The identity chains in the three texts are formed via different ways, but they refer to the same person. Substitutions and ellipses are included in the identity chains, because they refer to the same referent.

In all the texts, this situation of chain disjunction is taken into consideration in analysis when counting the quantification of cohesive chains:

> When chain conjunction takes place, precisely the same principle applies in respect of the referent entities of the chains so connected. Nonetheless ... the option is open of introducing a differentiation of function between the separate entities. The point at which this option is taken is the point at which chain disjunction takes place (Hasan, 1984: 199).

Moreover, "chain disjunction is a possibility open to only complex chains" (Hasan, 1984: 199). In the TT1-ch3, "Baoyu" in clause 1 and "he" in clause 3 form a cohesive tie. "Baoyu" in clause 29 and the subject-ellipsis in clause 30 form another cohesive tie. These tokens cannot form a cohesive chain due to chain disjunction, which happens because "Baoyu" in clause 13 interrupts the chain formation. "Baoyu" is a noun, and can only link with other instances of "Baoyu" in clause 1 and clause 29, and form an identity chain based on the equivalence of the lexical devices; but not with the pronominals due to the differentiation of function. Given the size of the texts analysed, most of the chains are complex, and the pronominal referring to the same entity is sometimes interrupted by entity nouns. Consequently, chain disjunctions separate the tokens; and the tokens can only connect to another one, not a set of tokens, to form a chain.

Table 6-6　Cohesive chains formation in an excerpt from ch3

ST-ch3

ID	Clause	Cohesive devices	Interpretative sources	Tie status	Grammatical chains
1	宝玉 心中 只记挂着 捆柴的故事， Baoyu in heart only thinks of the sotry of firewood				
2	因 阿阿闷的 心中 穿画。 gloomy in heart plan therefore				
3	探春 因 问 他 Tanchun therefore asked him	3. 他	1. 宝玉	anaphoric	3-1
4	"昨日 扰了 史大妹妹， yesterday disturbed Cousin Shi				
5	咱们 回去 商议着 邀一社， we go back discuss have a meeting	5. 咱们	-	exophoric	
6	又 还了席， again give back the meeting				
7	也 请 老太太 赏菊花。 also invite the Old Lady appreciate the chrysan themum	7. subject-ellipsis	5. 咱们	anaphoric	7e-5
8	何如？" How about it				

(continued)

9	宝玉 笑 道： Baoyu smiled said				
10	"老太太 说了， the Old Lady said		10. 老太太		
11	还 要 摆酒 还史妹妹的席 作陪呢 also have to give a feast for Cousin Shi	11. subject-ellipsis	11. subject 7. subject	anaphoric	11–10
12	叫 咱们 作陪呢。 ask us as company	12. subject-ellipsis 咱们		; ;	12e–11e–10老太太 (The Old Lady) 12–7e–5
13	等着 吃了 老太太的， wait for having the Old Lady's				
14	咱们 再请 不迟。" We invite not late	14. 咱们	12. 咱们	;	14–12–7e–5
15	探春 道： Tanchun said				
16	"越住前去 越冷了， time goes colder				
17	老太太 未必 高兴。" The Old Lady may not be happy				

(continued)

18	宝玉　道： Baoyu　said				
19	"老太太　又喜欢　下雨　下雪的。 The Old Lady　likes　raining　snowing				
20	不如　咱们　等 better　we　wait	20. 咱们	14. 咱们	：：	20 14-12 7e-5
21	下　头场　雪， fall　first　snow				
22	请　老太太　赏　雪　岂不好？ invite　the Old Lady　enjoy　the snow　is it better				
23	咱们　雪下　吟诗， We　in the falling snow　recite poems	23. 咱们	20. 咱们	：：	23-20-14-12-7e-5
24	也　更有趣了。" also　more interesting				
25	林黛玉　忙　笑　道： Lin Daiyu　hastened　smiled　said				
26	"咱们　雪下　吟诗？ We　in the falling snow　recite poems	26. 咱们	23. 咱们	：：	26-23-20-14-12-7e-5 咱们(we)
27	依我说， According to me	27. 我	25. 林黛玉	：：	27-25

(continued)

No.	ST (text)				
28	还不如 弄 一捆柴火， It would be better to get a bundle of firewood				
29	雪下 抽 柴， In the falling snow pull out firewood				
30	还 更有趣儿呢。" also more fun				
31	说着， Saying this,				
32	宝钗等 都 笑了。 Baochai and others all laughed				
33	宝玉 瞅了他 一眼， Baoyu stared at him a glance	33. 他	27. 我	〃	33–27–25 林黛玉 (Lin Daiyu)
34	也 不 答话。 also didn't say anything	34. subject-ellipsis	33. 宝玉	〃	34e–33
ST	**Lexical chains**				
1	宝玉1; 宝玉9; 宝玉18; 宝玉33 Baoyu Baoyu Baoyu Baoyu				Identity chain
2	柴1; 柴火28; 柴29 firewood firewood firewood				Similarity chain

(continued)

ID	Clauses	Cohesive devices	Interpretative sources	Tie status	Grammatical chains
3	探春3; 探春15 Tanchun Tanchun				Identity chain
4	问3; 道9; 道15; 道18; 道25; 说27; 说着31 ask say say say say say saying				Similarity chain
5	笑9; 说10; 笑25; 笑32 laugh say laugh laugh				Similarity chain
6	赏7; 赏22 reward reward				Similarity chain
7	老太太7; 老太太10; 老太太13; 老太太17; 老太太19; 老太太22 the old lady the old lady the old lady the old lady the old lady the old lady				Identity chain
8	请7; 请14; 请22 invite invite invite				Similarity chain
9	下雪19; 雪21; 雪22; 雪23; 雪下26; 雪下29 snow snow snow snow snow snow				Similarity chain
10	吟诗23; 吟诗26 recite recite				Similarity chain

TT1-ch3

ID	Clauses	Cohesive devices	Interpretative sources	Tie status	Grammatical chains
1	Baoyu, however, was still trying to imagine				

(continued)

2	what could have become of the girl who took the firewood,	2. the / the (firewood)	- / -	exophoric / ..	- / -
3	when he was addressed by Tanchun.	3. he	1. Baoyu	anaphoric	3–1 Baoyu
4	"Yesterday Xiangyun treated us,"	4. us	-	exophoric	-
5	she said.	5. she	3. Tanchun	anaphoric	5–3 Tanchun
6	"When we go back	6. we	4. us	..	6–4
7	let's talk over our next meeting and how to ask her back.	7. us / our / her	6. we / 7. us / 4. Xiangyun	.. / ..	7–6–4 / 7–7–6–4 us / 7–4 Xiangyun
8	Suppose				
9	we invite The old lady to come and look at the chrysanthemums?"	9. we / the (old) / the	7. us / - / -	anaphoric / exophoric / ..	9–7–7–6–4 us
10	"The old lady says	10. The	9. the (old)	anaphoric	10–9
11	she means to give a party herself in return for Xiangyun's,	11. she	10. The	..	11–10–9
12	and we'll be invited too,"	12. we	9. we	..	12–9–7–7–6–4 us
13	replied Baoyu.				

166

(continued)

14	"So we'd better wait till after that."	14. we that	12. we 11. party	" "	14-12-9-7-7-6-4 us 14-11 party
15	"If we wait	15. we	14. we	"	15-14-12-9-7-7-6-4
16	until it's cold, though,				
17	The old lady may not like it."	17. the it	11. she	" "	17-11-10-9 17-(9)
18	"Why not?				
19	She enjoys rain and snow.	19. She	17. the	"	19-17-11-10-9
20	Better wait for the first fall of snow	20. subject-ellipsis better the	15. we comparative -	anaphoric ? exophoric	20-15-14-12-9-7-7-6-4
21	and then ask her to a snow party.	21. subject-ellipsis her	20. subject 19. she (old lady)	anaphoric "	21e-20-15-14-12-9-7-7-6-4 we 21-19-17-11-10-9 old lady
22	We'll have more fun ourselves too,	22. We more	21. subject comparative	anaphoric ?	22-21e-20e-15-14-12-9-7-7-6-4 we
23	writing poems in the snow."	23. the	20. snow	anaphoric	23-20

167

(continued)

24	"Writing poems in the snow?"	24. (snow)	23. the	"	24-23-20
25	put in Daiyu mockingly.				
26	"I don't think	26. I	25. Daiyu	"	26-25 Daiyu
27	that would be half as much fun as building a woodpile and having a campfire in the _snow_."	27. (snow)	24. the (snow)	"	27-24-23-20 the _snow_
28	Baochai and the others laughed,	28. the others	-	exophoric	
29	while Baoyu flashed a glance at Daiyu				
30	but said nothing.	30. subject-ellipsis	29. Baoyu	anaphoric	30-29 Baoyu
TT1	**Lexical chains**				
1	Baoyu 1; Baoyu 13; Baoyu 29				Identity chain
2	Xiangyun 4; Xiangyun 11				Identity chain
3	said 5; says 10; said 30; talk 7				Similarity chain
4	invite 9; invited 12				Similarity chain
5	old lady 9; old lady 17				Identity chain
6	party 11; party 21				Similarity chain

(continued)

ID						Chain type
7	wait 14; wait 15; wait 20					Similarity chain
8	snow 19; snow 20; snow 21; snow 23; snow 24; snow 27					Similarity chain
9	writing 23; writing 24					Similarity chain
10	poems 23; poems 24					Similarity chain
11	Daiyu 25; Daiyu 29					Identity chain
12	like 17; enjoys 19					Similarity chain
13	firewood 2; woodpile 27					Similarity chain

TT2–ch3

ID	Clauses	Cohesive devices	Interpretative sources	Tie status	Grammatical chains
1	But Bao-yu, <2> looked glum and preoccupied.				
2	whose thoughts were still on the beautiful pilferer of firewood,	2. the	-/previous	anaphoric	
3	His sister Tan-chun observed this	3. His this	1. Bao-yu 2. whole clause	" "	3–1 3–2
4	and sought to distract him.	4. subject-ellipsis him	3. Tan-chun 3. His	" "	4e-3 4-3

(continued)

5	"We've got to make some sort of return for Cousin Shi's party, Bao.	5. We	-?	exophoric	6–5
6	Why don't we go back now	6. we	5. we	anaphoric	7e–6–5
7	and discuss	7. subject-ellipsis	6. we	"	
8	when the next poetry meeting is to be?	8. the	-/previous	anaphoric	
9	We can have our party for Cousin Shi at the same time,	9. We our the same	7. subject 9. We comparative	" "	9–7e–6–5 9–9–7e–6–5
10	and Grandma will be able to come		10. Grandma -		
11	and look at the chrysanthemums."	11. subject-ellipsis the		anaphoric exophoric	11e–10
12	"Grandma's already promised to give a return party for Cousin Shi herself,"				
13	said Bao-yu,				
14	"and we are all invited.	14. we	9. our	anaphoric	14–9–9–7e–6–5
15	We'd better wait	15. We better	14. we comparative	"	15–14–9–7e–6–5
16	until that's over	16. that	12. a return party	"	16–12

(continued)

17	before putting on anything of our own."	17. our	15. We	"	17 – 15 – 14 – 9 – 9 – 7e – 6 – 5
18	"The longer we delay,	18. The longer we	comparative 17. our	"	18 – 17 – 15 – 14 – 9 – 9 – 7e – 6 – 5
19	the colder the weather will be,"	19. the colder the (weather)	comparative -	exophoric	
20	said Tan-chun.				
21	"It won't be much fun for Grandma	21. It	-?		
22	if it's too cold."	22. it	-	exophoric	
23	"But she loves parties	23. she	21. Grandma	anaphoric	23 - 21
24	when it's raining or snowing,"	25. it	22. it	anaphoric	25 - 22
25	said Bao-yu.				
26	"Why don't we wait	26. we	18. we	anaphoric	26 – 18 – 17 – 15 – 14 – 9 – 9 – 7e – 6 – 5
27	until the first snowfall	27. the (first)	-	exophoric	
28	and have it then?	28. subject-ellipsis it	26. we 9. party	anaphoric "	28e – 26 – 18 – 17 – 15 – 14 – 9 – 9 – 7e – 6 – 5 28 – 9

(continued)

					29-28-9 party
29	Call it a snow-viewing party.	29. it	28. it	"	
30	Think how romantic: chanting poems in the falling snow!"	30. the	-	exophoric	
31	"It would be more romantic still," <35>	31. It / more	? Comparative		
32	"if instead of chanting poems we had a big bundle of firewood	32. we	28. subject	anaphoric	32−28e−26−18−17−15−14−9−9−7e−6−5
33	and took it in turns to tiptoe through the snow	33. subject-ellipsis it / the (snow)	32. we / 32. firewood / 30. the (snow)	" / " / "	33e−32−28e−26−18−17−15−14−9−9−7e−6−5 / 33−32 / 33−30
34	and pull out sticks from it."	34. subject-ellipsis it	33. subject / 33. it	" / "	34e−33e−32−28e−26−18−17−15−14−9−9−7e−6−5 we / 34−3−32 firewood
35	said Dai-yu drily,				
36	Bao-chai and the other girls all laughed,	36. the other	-	exophoric	
37	but Bao-yu stared at Dai-yu rather crossly				

(continued)

		38. subject-ellipsis	37. Bao-yu	anaphoric	38e–37
38	and said nothing.	38. subject-ellipsis	37. Bao-yu	anaphoric	38e–37
TT2	**Lexical chains**				
1	Bao-yu 1; Bao 5; Bao-yu 13; Bao-yu 25; Bao-yu 37				Identity chain
2	firewood 2; firewood 32				Similarity chain
3	Tan-chun 3; Tan-chun 20				Identity chain
4	Cousin Shi 5; Cousin Shi 9; Cousin Shi 12				Identity chain
5	party 5; party 9; parties 23; party 29				Similarity chain
6	Grandma 10; Grandma 12; Grandma 21				Identity chain
7	said 13; said 20; said 25; said 35; said 38				Similarity chain
8	wait 15; wait 26				Similarity chain
9	snowing 24; snowfall 27; snow 30; snow 33				Similarity chain
10	romantic 30; romantic 31				Similarity chain
11	chanting 30; chanting 32				Similarity chain
12	poems 30; poems 32				Similarity chain
13	Dai-yu 35; Dai-yu 37				Identity chain

Similar to identity chains, similarity chains also show a trend of increasing explicitness from the Chinese source text to the English target texts. There are more general lexical cohesive devices in the two TTs than in the ST. The relations of repetition, synonymy, antonymy and meronymy in the TTs are more explicit than in the ST. Within the two TTs, the TT2 still has more similarity chains than the TT1. This implies that the general lexical devices in the TT2 form more co-classification and co-extention relations than those in the TT1. These lexical devices not only reflect the semantic relation among these items but also tie the text to its context of culture. In this sense, the ST shows the least semantic connection within the text and the context; and the TT2 shows the most. Comparatively, the perception of coherence in the Chinese source text relies more on the readers' knowledge; while in the English target texts it relies more on the structure of the cohesive devices and chains. In the translation, both of the translators adapt the usage of cohesive devices and chains to the target English norms.

6.3 Cohesive chains in translation

The cohesive chains form the patterns of cohesion in the texts, which contribute to the coherence of the text. In translation, the cohesive chains represent the different methods of dealing with patterns of cohesion in different languages and by different translators.

6.3.1 Cline of explicitation

Explicitness and explicitation are two different terms. Implicitness or explicitness is a property of lexicogrammatical or cohesive structures and configurations in one text. Explicitation is a process or a relationship between intralingual variants and (or) translationally related texts (Hansen-Schirra et al., 2007: 243). In other words, implicitness or explicitness is the expression of cohesive devices at the lexicogrammatical level, while explicitation is a translation strategy which can be evaluated by explicitness. Explicitation happens when the translated text displays more explicit lexicogrammatical and cohesive properties than the original text. The explicitation can be defined thus:

We assume explicitation if a translation (or, language-internally, one text in a pair of register-related texts) realizes meanings (not only ideational, but also interpersonal and textual) more explicitly than its source text — more precisely, meanings not realized in the less explicit source variant but implicitly present in a theoretically-motivated sense. The resulting text is more explicit than its counterpart (Hansen-Schirra et al., 2007: 243).

Only through the comparison of both the source text and target texts can we conclude whether or not there is explicitation in the process of translation.

By and large, the use of cohesive chains in the three texts shows a cline of explicitation from the Chinese ST to the English TT2. The ST displays the most implicit pattern of cohesion, while the TT2 exhibits the most explicit, and the TT1 is in between. If we put the three texts in a cline, which can reveal the trend of explicitation in the process of translation from Chinese into English, it can be visualised as in Figure 6-1.

Figure 6-1　Cline of explicitation

The cline of explicitation implies that Chinese and English display different preferences for using grammatical and lexical cohesive chains in the patterns of cohesion realisation and in creating a coherent text. Cohesive devices and chains are parameters of the realisation of semantic meaning within the textual metafunction. In translation, both of the translators choose to use more explicit cohesive devices and cohesive chains in reconstructing the semantic meaning of the original text and also the context of situation in the target language. Hence, English is more explicit in the expression of cohesion and meaning; so explicitation happens when translating from Chinese into English. For another, during the process of explicitation in translation, the two translators also generate their own styles of utilising cohesive devices. The ways that the translators make choices in using them reveal the characteristics of the target texts and of the translators. These are the choices that make the text the way it is. The translators' choice of cohesive devices and the grammatical and semantic relations among the devices generates their own styles in translation: "in the process of creating coherence, choices are made about what is relevant, about how entities and processes are worded and how they interrelate" (Lukin, 2013). That Hawkes' translation is more explicit than Yang's verifies that, from Chinese to English, more explicit cohesive devices and chains are required. However, being always in between the Chinese source text and Hawkes' English translation, Yang's translation implies that he was influenced by both the Chinese and English ways of realising cohesion and coherence with cohesive devices. The different choices in the cohesive chains in different texts can reveal how the choices are instantiated and structured in the ST and the TTs by different languages and translators; and thus providing guidance for the translation between the source language and the target language.

6.3.2 Translation equivalence

The equivalence of cohesive chains in the ST and the TTs is achieved at lexicogrammatical and semantic levels and throughout the text. The transference of these in translation maps the lexicogrammatical structure and semantic meaning from the Chinese ST to the English TTs. Matthiessen (2001) sets up the environments of translation in the SFL framework from different dimensions, such as stratification, rank, and axis. The variation in these aspects results in the free and literal translations. The higher the stratum or rank the equivalence happens at, the freer the translation is. Given the patterns of cohesion, Hawkes' version is freer, while Yang's is comparatively more literal. This is because while both the translations take place at the lexicogrammatical level in realising the same semantic meaning, the structures of these translations differ with different numbers of cohesive chains, and their percentage varies, so that the one more congruent to the ST is more literal. In addition, the way in which the two TTs maintain the cohesive patterns of the ST reveals the extent to which the TTs are in accordance with the lexicogrammar and semantics of the ST. The TT2 is more explicit than the ST and the TT1. Therefore, the TT2 is freer in translation than the TT1.

The reasons causing these differences are ascribed mainly to the different contextual configurations of the ST and the TTs. The tenor in the three contextual configurations matters the most in the two translations. They are targeting different readers. The readers of the novel also differ significantly. For the original Chinese text, the readers range from the 19th century to now, and from almost every class of the society. For the two English translations, both are targeted at English speakers. The readers of the translated versions are far in distance and time from the original readers. In addition to the linguistic and cultural distance of the writer and audience, there is also temporal distance between the audience of the original text and the audience of the translated texts. Moreover, the two translators have different translation purposes. The targeted audience of the two translations are also slightly different. Yang's version is for those who already know Chinese culture and want to explore further into the novel. Hawkes' version is more for the English speaking public, and its target readers cover a wider range in general.

6.4　Summary

"Meaning in literary works is not simply a function of the signification that linguistic items have as code elements but a function of the relationship between this signification and the value these items take on as elements in a pattern created in the context" [Widdowson, 1983 (2014): 46]. In the literary text, one of the most important characteristics is "its recurrent linguistic patterning, or 'cohesion'" (Traugott, 2008: 41). Through the exploration of the cohesive chains in the texts, this chapter has revealed patterns of realisation of textual meaning in the Chinese source text and the English target texts. The patterns that literary texts display are indicative of the habits of the language users and thus the cultures of the languages.

In the realisation of coherence within the textual metafunction, the ST and the TTs show different preferences. The ST is the most implicit in the usage of cohesive chains, while the TT2 is the most explicit, and the TT1 is in between. In the translation from the ST to the TT2, explicitation occurs. The extent of explicitation in the translation can reveal the different styles of the translators.

Kieras (1980) claims that highly cohesive texts are easier to process. The evidence that the TT2 displays the highest extent of cohesion shows that it is easier for the readers of the TT2 to perceive the text and its meaning via the cohesive chains than the TT1. The different extent of explicitation in the two translations can also be attributed to the different translation purposes of the two target texts.

Chapter 7

The Patterns of Coherence from the Experiential, Logical and Textual Meanings

As stated in the previous chapters, the construction of coherence is related to the experiential, logical and textual meanings of a text. The experiential meaning connects the text with the experiential world, while the logical relations between clauses determine the logical development of a text; and the clauses with cohesive devices in cohesive chains make the overall texture of a text recognisable. The outline of the cohesive chains establishes the structure of cohesion upon which the textual coherence arises; and the cohesive devices that make these cohesive chains are important in forming the grid of a cohesion structure. Hence, in the construction of textual coherence, the clauses with those cohesive devices are more significant than those clauses without them. Accordingly, the transitivity and clause complexity of the clauses with those cohesive devices are also important in identifying the lexicogrammatical structure involved in the experiential and logical development of a text. Therefore, the clauses containing relevant tokens are the focus of this chapter. The relevant tokens are those in the cohesive chains; and those not in the cohesive chains are peripheral tokens. Since cohesive chains are the threads of semantic continuity in the text, the relevant tokens in the chains show how the meanings are connected in the text, and how coherence is achieved by the presupposition relationship between the clauses with relevant tokens.

The lexicogrammatical patterns of clause complexes realise semantic sequences of processes, such as temporal or causal sequences, making the connection between clauses possible in developing the logical sequence of the text. The clauses that embed cohesive devices are the environment in which cohesive chains function. Matthiessen (1995) clarifies the relationship between the clause complex and the textual cohesion of ellipsis and substitution as follows:

> The clause complex is one environment in which the textual clause system ELLIPSIS/SUBSTITUTION operates: One clause displays ellipsis or substitution and another clause contains the presupposed wording. The effect is one of making continuous information non-prominent and contrastive information prominent (Matthiessen, 1995: 158).

Given that coherence is a multi-functional concept, the lexicogrammatical realisation of the clauses with relevant tokens from the experiential and logical functions contributes to the overall patterns of coherence. In translation, the patterns are preserved or shifted to some extent due to different reasons. It is necessary to explore the possibility that a literary translator might consistently show a preference for using specific lexical items, syntactic patterns, and cohesive devices (Baker, 2000: 248). Therefore, the study of coherence patterns is not only instructive in the two different languages but also in the translation of literary texts.

This chapter aims to answer the following questions: How are the cohesive chains manifested in clauses? How do the logical and textual metafunctions together contribute to the coherence patterns of the text? How do the experiential and textual metafunctions together contribute to the coherence patterns of the text? What features of clause complexing and ergative organisation show in a coherent text? What do these features mean in the literary text?

7.1　The logical functional environment of cohesive chains

The logical metafunction is concerned with the logical semantic development of the text. The clause complexity displayed by the clauses involved in the construction of cohesive chains forms the logical metafunctional environment of those chains. The realisation of both logical and textual functions has been analysed at the lexicogrammatical level in the previous chapters, in terms of clause complexes and cohesive chains, respectively. This chapter presents an investigation of how clause complexes and cohesive chains interact with each other and how they together form the patterns of coherence in the text. It will focus on the lexicogrammatical realisation of the clauses involved in cohesive chains from both logical and textual meanings, which is taken as one of the main features contributing to the coherence of the text in this research.

7.1.1   The clauses in cohesive chains

Cohesive chains are the threads of semantic continuity (Hasan, 1984). The identity and similarity chains together in a text reflect the development of the text. They are important in delivering a message or information about the content of the story, and in building up the foundation of coherence in the textual metafunction. The coherence of a text is achieved by the presupposition relationship between the clauses with relevant tokens.

The different types of tokens take different responsibilities in the creation of a coherent text: "Relevant tokens are related to each other through cohesion, and ... they are related to the topical development of the text" (Hasan, 1984: 211). They are more important than peripheral tokens in the creation of textual coherence.

The clauses with relevant tokens are more important in the development of textual coherence than other clauses since they take more responsibility for linking with other clauses than the ones without relevant tokens do. From the logical metafunctional perspective, the clauses are not separated from but connected with one another to form clause complexes. The organisation of the clause complex concerns whether clauses are combined or not combined with each other, and how they are combined: specifically, the taxis and logico-semantic relations of clauses in connection with each other. The clause complexity patterns of the clauses with relevant tokens show how the logical and textual functions together contribute to the creation of textual coherence, and how these patterns are dealt with in translation.

Table 7-1   An excerpt from the TT2-ch3

Clause ID	Clause	Cohesive devices	Interpretative sources	Tie status	Identity chains	Similarity chains
1	PATIENCE, <2> had just returned to the party.	1. the (party)	-/in previous chapters	anaphoric	Patience1; Patience 7	asked 4; said 8
2	you will recall,	2. you	-	exophoric		
3	"What's happened to your mistress?"	3. your	1. PATIENCE	anaphoric		
4	the others asked her.	4. the (others) / her	- / 3. mistress	exophoric / anaphoric	4–3–1 Patience	
5	"Why doesn't she come back	5. she	3. mistress	"		
6	(subject) and join us?"	6. subject-ellipsis / us	5. she / 4. others	" / "	6e–5–3	
7	"She hasn't got time,"	7. She	6. subject	"	7–6e–5–3 mistress	
8	said Patience,					
9	laughing.					

Table 7-1 is an excerpt from the TT2-ch3. It lists the identity and similarity chains in the text, and illustrates how to identify the clauses with relevant tokens, which are labelled in shading. The excerpt consists of 9 clauses, which are numbered and listed in two left-most columns. The cohesive devices in the clauses, and the interpretative sources of the devices, are listed in left third and fourth columns, and then the cohesive chains are identified and listed in the right-hand two columns. The subject-ellipsis in clause 6 is taken as part of the identity chain, because it refers to the same entity of the chain "7-6e-5-3", referring to "the mistress". There are two identity chains and one similarity chain in this excerpt. The cohesive chains are also shaded and shown in the right-hand two columns. The relevant tokens in the chains can be found in 7 clauses; only clause 2 and clause 9 do not contain any relevant token; so the number of clauses with relevant tokens is 7. Thus, the proportion of clauses in the cohesive chains is 77.78% (7 out of 9). With the analysis in the excerpt, all the clauses with relevant tokens in the ST and the TTs are identified, and the results shown in number and ratio in tables.

The texts are from three different chapters of the novel; each is different in narrative mode. Ch1 and ch2 are mostly narrative, while ch3 is mainly with conversations. It is assumed that there are some significant stylistic differences in the use of clauses involved in cohesive chains, as the narrative mode differs in each text. Table 7-2 depicts an outline of the numbers of clauses and clauses involved in the cohesive chains, and the percentage of all the clauses in the text that are in the chains in each text.

Table 7-2   Clauses with the cohesive chains in different chapters

	ST–ch1	TT1–ch1	TT2–ch1
Clauses	815	695	752
Clauses in the chains	487	518	566
percentage	59.8%	74.5%	75.3%
	ST–ch2	TT1–ch2	TT2–ch2
Clauses	644	529	613

(continued)

Clauses in the chains	445	438	521
percentage	69.10%	82.80%	84.99%
	ST–ch3	**TT1–ch3**	**TT2–ch3**
Clauses	741	684	877
Clauses in the chains	584	562	762
percentage	78.81%	82.16%	86.89%

Table 7–2 shows a similar trend of the ratio of clauses in cohesive chains to clauses as a whole in both Chinese and English. All the three STs are the lowest in percentage of clauses in chains, while the TT2s have the highest percentage, and the TT1s are in between. The three texts thus display an increasing trend, from the ST to the TT2, of clauses being in cohesive chains. As the initial analysis of each chapter above does not exhibit stylistic differences due to the different narrative modes, the following section does not treat the chapters separately, but as a whole.

Table 7–3 shows the numbers and percentages of clauses in cohesive chains in the source text and two target texts. There is a clear distinction between Chinese and English texts in terms of percentages of clauses in the chains. The ST displays the lowest percentage of clauses entering into cohesive chains, while the two TTs show close percentage figures. Both of the TTs contain a greater percentage of clauses with cohesive chains than the ST does, with 79.82% and 82.39% as against 69.27%, respectively. Compared with Chinese, more clauses in English texts are involved in the construction of cohesive chains, and therefore in the structure of coherence. As a result, the English texts are more explicit than Chinese in the construction of texture, because in the English TTs more clauses take part in realising the coherence of the text. To be more specific, around 70% clauses in the ST link with each other in setting up a grammatically and semantically related net that is taken as the foundation of coherence; whereas almost 80% clauses in the English TTs are connected to each other. The higher proportion of clauses in the English texts reveals that the coherence of the two TTs is realised through more involvement of the clauses than in the ST.

Table 7–3   Clauses in the cohesive chains in the ST and the TTs

	ST	TT1	TT2
Clauses	2,213	1,915	2,244
Clauses in the chains	1,516	1,518	1,849
percentage	69.24%	79.82%	82.39%

It can be inferred that, in the Chinese source text, the degree of involvement of clauses in the construction of semantic sequences in the text is lower than that in the English target texts. In other words, in building up the structure that realises the coherence of the text, the ST is comparatively implicit while the two TTs are relatively explicit. As mentioned in Chapter 6, we assume explicitation if a translation realises meanings more explicitly than its source text, and the resulting texts are more explicit than its counterpart (Hansen-Schirra et al., 2007: 243). Thus, explicitation happens during translation from the ST to the TTs. In literary translation, explicitation is "a stylistic translation technique which consists of making explicit in the target language what remains implicit in the source language because it is apparent from either the context or the situation" (Vinay and Darbelnet, 1995: 342). In translation, both of the translators choose to explicitate some implicit elements in the ST, with more relevant tokens in cohesive chains, to adjust to the target texts' audiences and cultures. This is because what was implicit in the source text is no longer apparent in the context of the target texts.

Between the two English TTs, the difference in the percentage of clauses with relevant tokens is not significant, being only 2.57%. Even though the explicitation is mainly due to typological difference from Chinese to English, translators' personal choices are also reflected. Given the slight difference of the clauses with relevant tokens in the TT1 and the TT2, 79.82% and 82.39%, respectively, Hawkes' version is more explicit than Yang's in the construction of structure that realises the coherence of the text. In addition, the TT1 exhibits features in between those of the ST and the TT2. Despite the fact that the TT1 is closer to the TT2, we can infer that the TT1 is still affected by the translator's mother tongue, Chinese. It is probable that the differences between the two TTs are also caused by the different translation purposes and different target audiences.

In the explicitation hypothesis, Blum-Kulka (2000) proposes that the process of translation entails explicitation both in textual and discoursal relationships. Explicitation of cohesion at the level of the text is mainly attributed to different stylistic preferences for cohesive markers in different languages. Explicitation at the discourse level is caused by two conditions: reader-focused shifts, and text-focused shifts. Culturally different audiences and the translation process per se are both reasons for shifts of coherence in translation. In the present research, explicitation occurs due to the comprehensive reasons of typological differences, translators' different orientations, and translation purposes.

A literary text is coherent in nature. It can be assumed that both of the English TTs are as coherent as the Chinese source text. Even though the ST and the TTs display different degrees of explicitness in realising coherence, the implicit aspects lie in the readers' understanding of the text and the context.

7.1.2 The logical relational features of the clauses in cohesive chains

In the summary of *Coherence and Cohesive Harmony* (1984), Hasan points out that "there yet remains the problem of integrating the cohesive analysis of the interpersonal meaning relations. In addition, and closely related to it, is the problem of the calibration of cohesive harmony with the analysis of logical relations between clauses" (1984: 219). The significance of cohesive harmony intrigues further research on the integration of cohesive harmony with the interpersonal and logical metafunctions. As stated before, the collaborative effect of the textual and logical functions can be probed through the logical relations of clauses with relevant tokens. This section describes in detail the differences in the clauses with relevant tokens in both the ST and the TTs.

The clause complexity of clauses represents the logical development of a text. It is important in configuring the inter-clausal relations. Both clause simplex and clause complex can represent the status of clause combinations, as either combined with another clause or not. If combined, each clause in a clause complex is a two-dimensional expression of the taxis and logical-semantic type. Take the following sentence as an example: "In the fields just north of our village there stands a small shrine," she said. In the clause complex, clause 1 "In the fields just north of our village there stands a small shrine," and clause 2 "she said" are in an equal status; and they are indicated with Arabic letters 1 and 2 in terms of taxis. In terms of logico-semantic relation, clause 1 is projected by clause 2; and clause 1 is indicated by "1" and clause 2 is indicated by "2". An example of the results of the logical relations analysis is shown as below in Table 7-4. Clause simplex is labelled as null in terms of logical relations.

Table 7-4   Clause complex analysis of an excerpt from the TT1-ch3

ID	Clause	Logical relations					
3TT1-30-1	It's as I always say:	α					
3TT1-30-2	When Monk Tripitaka was searching for Buddhist scriptures,	"	β		1	x	β
3TT1-30-3	a white horse turned up to carry him;						α
3TT1-30-4	when Liu Zhiyuan was fighting for the empire,			+	2	x	β
3TT1-30-5	a melon spirit appeared to give him armour.						α
3TT1-31-1	In the same way, Xifeng has you.						

Apart from the clause complexity of the clauses with relevant tokens, the study of the calibration of cohesive chains with other functions is foregrounded in this analysis. Through the cohesive chains, both identity and similarity, the plot is continuous, with the strings of events and characters under a certain context, in narrative texts. The combination of cohesive chains and the logical relations demonstrates how the semantic continuity of the text is realised grammatically via the progression of the clauses. The coherence of the text can be expressed by the lexico-grammatical patterns of the combination of the logical and the textual.

The example in Table 7-5 is an excerpt from the TT2-ch2. There is an identity chain referring to "Lucky, the maid" throughout the text, and this chain is labelled as "9-8-6-5-4-3-2-1"; only clause 7 is not involved in the cohesive chain. The shaded words are the relevant tokens in the cohesive chain. From the excerpt, one clause simplex, eight hypotactic clauses, and three paratactic clauses are in the cohesive chain. In terms of logico-semantic relation, one idea and two enhancing clauses are in the cohesive chain. Thus, the proportions of each type of clause in the chains can be calculated. With this method exemplified, all the texts are investigated in respect of clause types involved in the cohesive chains.

Table 7-5 Clause complex analysis of an excerpt from the TT2-ch2

Clause ID		Clause	Logical relations		
2TT2-26-1	1	Lucky was, of course, the maid who had once turned back to look at Yu-cun when they were living at the house in Soochow.			
2TT2-27-1	2	She could scarcely have foreseen at the time	α		
2TT2-27-2	3	what singular good fortune that one glance would procure for her.	' β		
2TT2-28-1	4	But she was destined to be doubly fortunate.			
2TT2-29-1	5	She had not been with Yu-cun more than a year	1	α	
2TT2-29-2	6	when she gave birth to a son;		x β	
2TT2-29-3	7	and a mere six months later Yu-cun's first wife died,	x 2	α	
2TT2-29-4	8	whereupon Lucky was promoted to fill her place		x β	1
2TT2-26-1	9	and (subject-ellipsis) became Her Ladyship.		+	2

The clauses with relevant tokens show the lexico-grammatical patterns of the text in construing coherence. The ratio of each logical relation can show the role that these clauses play, and how they are used in the construction of the Chinese source text and the English target texts.

7.1.2.1   The clause types in the cohesive chains in the texts

The clauses entering into the cohesive chains can be considered as contributing to the formation of cohesion, and also to the texture of the text, in terms of their complexity, taxis, and also logico-semantic relations. The features these clauses display show the lexicogrammatical realisation patterns of the logical and textual metafunctions together in a coherent text.

Figure 7-1 shows the numbers and percentages of clause simplexes and clause complexes with relevant tokens of the ST and the two TTs. In general, the two TTs show a similar inclination for involving the different types of clauses in the cohesive chains. Firstly, the numbers and percentages of clause simplexes involved in the cohesive chains in the three texts differ significantly, especially between the Chinese ST and the two English TTs. The ST contains the least clause simplexes in the cohesive chains: 81 clause simplexes only form about 4.01% of all the clauses in the chains. In the two TTs, both the number and proportion of clause simplexes are more than those in the ST: 282 makes 15.55% and 321 makes 14.29%, for the TT1 and the TT2, respectively, of all the clauses in the chains in each text. Secondly, clause complexes take a higher percentage than simplexes in the cohesive chains. In terms of the taxis of those clause complexes, the Chinese source text is also distinguished from the two English target texts: the ST uses the most paratactic clauses in the cohesive chains, with 1,176 paratactic clauses making about 61% of all the clauses with relevant tokens; however, in the two TTs, the numbers are 840 and 962 for the TT1 and the TT2, making around 46.31% and 42.83% in all the clauses in the cohesive chains, respectively. Accordingly, the hypotactic clauses in the cohesive chains show a similar trend to that of the paratactic clauses: the ST and the TT1 are closer to each other in terms of the percentage of hypotactic clauses with relevant tokens, with 35.01% and 38.15%, respectively; while the TT2 has the most hypotactic clauses in cohesive chains, 963, making 42.88% of the total.

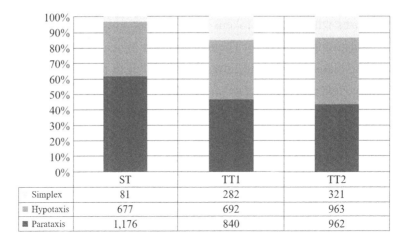

	ST	TT1	TT2
Simplex	81	282	321
■ Hypotaxis	677	692	963
■ Parataxis	1,176	840	962

Figure 7-1   Clause types in the chains in the three texts

The different numbers and percentages of each type of clause with relevant tokens show the trends of the Chinese text and the two English texts in using different kinds of clause in the construction of the cohesive chains, and therefore, in building up the threads of coherence in the text. The percentages of the clause simplexes and the taxis types of clause complexes with relevant tokens reveal that Chinese source text relies more on clause complexes, and especially on paratactic clauses in the construction of cohesive chains and that the two English target texts show more preference for clause simplexes than the ST. Despite there being more clause simplexes in the TT1, the TT1 displays features more alike to the ST than to the TT2.

The two translators have their own preferences for using different types of taxis in the construction of cohesive chains; and the analysis of their use of taxis reveals the different degrees of involvement of taxis in building up the semantic threads of the text.

7.1.2.2   The LOGICO-SEMANTIC TYPE in the cohesive chains in the three texts

In addition to TAXIS, LOGICO-SEMANTIC TYPE also needs to be probed in terms of involvement in cohesive chains.

Figure 7-2 displays the composition of both the Chinese ST and the two English TTs in respect of projecting and expanding clauses. In all the three texts, expanding clauses show an increasing trend from the ST to the TT2; while the projecting clauses accordingly show a decreasing trend. Expansion makes up 80% of the ST, and decreases to 76% and 75% in the TT1 and the TT2, respectively. Conversely, projection increases from 20% in the ST to 24% and 25% in the TT1 and the TT2, respectively. The TT1 and the TT2 display a conformable trend in their use of expansion and projection, with only about 1% discrepancy between the two texts.

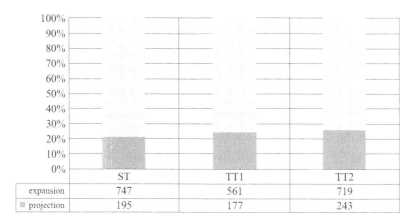

	ST	TT1	TT2
expansion	747	561	719
projection	195	177	243

Figure 7-2   Number of clauses in the chains in terms of LOGICO-SEMANTIC TYPE in the three texts

In translation, projecting clauses with relevant tokens in the TTs have a higher ratio than in the ST, even though the numbers of those clauses in the three texts vary. The two translators display a similar trend of making projecting clauses more explicit in the TTs than in the ST.

To see the use of the subtypes of LOGICO-SEMANTIC TYPE in detail, more data analyses are shown in Table 7-6 and Table 7-8 in terms of projection and expansion.

Table 7-6   Comparison of types of projection

	ST		TT1		TT2	
Locution	168	86.15%	135	76.27%	187	73.91%
Idea	27	13.85%	42	23.73%	66	26.09%

Table 7-6 lists the two types of projection in the three texts. The ST distinguishes itself from the two TTs by using much more locution and less of idea. It uses the least percentage of idea (13.85%), and accordingly the most locution (86.15%). The results of Figure 7-2 show that the TT1 makes the projecting clauses more implicit, while the TT2 makes them more explicit, in the cohesive chains, compared to the ST. However, within these projecting clauses, the two TTs show a similar trend, of 23.73% and 26.09% (the TT1 and the TT2, respectively) for idea and 76.27% and 73.91% for locution, in each text.

In translation, the transference of idea in the target texts is made more explicit than in the ST. Hence, it can be inferred that, in the translation of the TT2, Hawkes makes the projecting clauses more explicit, in addressing the semantic sequence of the text; and he also appears to have added certain referencing items in the clauses to indicate the projection.

In Table 7-7, the ST does not contain an identity chain for "you", referring to Patience in the text. However, in the TT2, the identity chain is made explicit: only clause 3TT2-12-2 is not involved in the chain. Within the clauses with the relevant token, "you", clause 3TT2-13-3 is projected by an "idea". In translation, the projection is made explicit.

Table 7-7　Clause complex and cohesive chain analysis of an excerpt from ch3

Clause ID	Clause	Logical relations		
3ST-11-1	李纨　　道： Li Wan　said	1		
3ST-11-2	"偏不许　你　去。 Won't let　you　go	"　2		
3ST-12-1	显见得　只有　凤丫头， obviously　only　Feng	x　β		
3ST-12-2	就不听了。"　我的　话 don't listen to　my　words	α		
Clause ID	**Clause**	**Logical relations**		
3TT2-12-1	"I won't let you go!"	"　1		
3TT2-12-2	said Li Wan.	2		
3TT2-13-1	"The only person you ever take any notice of is that precious Feng of yours;	1		
3TT2-13-2	you think	+	2	α

(continued)

Clause ID	Clause	Logical relations
3TT2-13-3	you don't need to obey me;	'　β
3TT2-13-4	but you shall."	+　3

Aside from the projection, the three texts also display differences in expansion, which consists of three subcategories, elaboration, extension and enhancement. Table 7-8 shows the results of the three subcategories of expansion in the three texts.

Table 7-8　Comparison of expansion in the three texts

	ST		TT1		TT2	
Enhancement	456	61.04%	301	53.65%	427	59.39%
Extension	216	28.92%	215	38.32%	237	32.96%
Elaboration	75	10.04%	45	8.02%	55	7.65%

In general, the ST and the TTs show both similarities and differences. Firstly, the most distinctive feature is that extending clauses are in the highest percentage in the TT1: about 38.32% in the TT1, which is much more than the 32.96% and 28.92%, in the TT2 and the ST, respectively. Secondly, the ST uses the most "elaboration", with 75 elaborating clauses making about 10.04% of the total. This percentage decreases to 8.02% and 7.65% in the TT1 and the TT2, respectively. Thirdly, the ST and the TT2 show similar preferences for using enhancing clauses in the chains, with about 60% for both.

In the translation of expansion, the percentages in the TT1 and the TT2 indicate that the two translators choose different approaches to dealing with "enhancement" and "extension": Yang prefers to use more "extension" than Hawkes. In addition, extending clauses have more importance in shaping the cohesive structure of the TT1. In general, Hawkes use similar proportions of each subtype of expanding clauses in the cohesive chains in comparison to the source text.

7.2　The experiential functional environment of the cohesive chains

The other main perspective of identifying the lexico-grammatical coherence patterns of the clauses in the cohesive chains is from the experiential functional point of view. Since the clause is a mode of reflection, for imposing order on the endless variation and flow of events (Halliday and Matthiessen, 2004: 170), the different flows of the nominal, verbal and other types of groups reflect the patterns of how the clause is organised to construe experiential meaning. The roles that these different groups play imply the ways of realising coherent information. In this section, the cohesive devices in each text are analysed from the perspective of their ergative roles in the clauses. The output of the experiential and textual metafunctions is interwoven, on the grounds that "the output of the textual function is the chains and the interactions; the output of the experiential function at the rank of clause and group is what the interaction is built upon" [Halliday and Hasan, 1985 (1989): 94]. All textual choices are mapped onto choices in other metafunctions.

7.2.1 Ergative profile of the cohesive devices

The transitive model and ergative model complement each another, and two models together make the general system of transitivity (Halliday and Matthiessen, 2004: 285). "While a transitive model is oriented to the extension of a process (i.e. from an Actor through Process to a Goal), the ergative model emphasises what brought the process about (Medium/Process + Agent)" (Butt, 1983: 41). As mentioned in Chapter 3, the ergative roles of the cohesive devices fall into the following categories: Medium, Agent, Beneficiary and Range. Minor clauses contain several cohesive devices as well. These cohesive devices nonetheless contribute to the construction of cohesive chains even though they do not play the same ergative roles in minor clauses as they do in the main clause. This kind of cohesive device is labelled as "N/A" in the analysis. Apart from the ergative roles of the participants, some cohesive devices that function as Process or Circumstance in the clause are also taken into consideration in the analysis.

Table 7-9 shows the cohesive chains in an excerpt from the TT2. There are 6 cohesive chains in the text. All the relevant tokens in the coheive chains are in shades. Table 7-10 lists all the cohesive chains and annotates each chain with an ergative role of the relevant tokens. By doing so, the cohesive chains in Table 7-9 can be labeled as their ergative roles. For example, the chain "6-4-1" refers

Table 7-9 Ergative roles of the cohesive chains in an excerpt from the TT2

	Clause	Cohesive devices	Interpretative sources	Tie status	Cohesive chains
1	"The wording is commonplace to a degree,"	1.The	-	exophoric	Wording 1; inscription 6
2	Yu-cun reflected,				Yu-cun 2; Yu-cun 10
3	"yet the sentiment is quite profound.	3. the	-	exophoric	
4	In all the famous temples and monasteries I have visited, I cannot recollect having ever seen anything quite like it.	4. the I I it	2. Yu-cun 4. I 1. The wording	anaphoric " " "	
5	I shouldn't be surprised to find	5. I	4. I	"	
6	that some story of spectacular downfall and dramatic conversion lay behind this inscription.	6. this	4. it	"	6-4-1 (wording)
7	It might be worth going in and inquiring."	7. It	6. this	"	
8	But when he went inside	8. he	5. I	"	
9	and (he) looked around,	9. subject-ellipsis	8. he	"	
10	he saw only an ancient, wizened monk cooking some gruel [[who paid no attention whatsoever to his greetings and who proved, when Yu-cun went up to him and asked him a few questions, to be both deaf and partially blind.]]	10. he his him him	9. subject 10. monk 10. his 10. him	" " " "	10-9e-8-5-4-4-2 (Yu-cun)
11	His toothless replies were all but unintelligible,	11. His	10. him	"	11-10-10-10-10(monk)
12	and in any case bore no relation to the questions.	12. the	-	exophoric	

Table 7–10   Ergative roles of the cohesive chains in an excerpt from the TT2

	Wording						
1	The wording	Medium					
2			Yu-cun	Medium			Yu-cun	Medium
3								
4	like it	Range	I	Agent				
5			I	Medium				
6			I	Medium				
7	behind this inscription	Circumstance			inscription	Circumstance		
8			he	Medium				
9			subject-ellipsis	Medium				
10	monk	Range	he	Medium			Yu-cun	Medium
	to his greetings	Beneficiary						
	to him	Beneficiary						
	asked him	Beneficiary						
11	His toothless replies	Medium						
12								

to "the wording" with the cohesive devices "the wording, it, this" in clauses 1, 4, 6 respectively. The ergative roles of these devices in the correspondent clauses are "Medium" "Range", and "Circumstance" respectively. Therefore, the chain "6–4–1" can be labled as "MRC" for short.

With this method, all the relevant tokens in the cohesive chains in the ST and the TTs are annotated with ergative roles, and the overall number of each role in each text can be caculated for further analysis.

Table 7–11 exhibits the number of the cohesive devices functioning as ergative roles of Participants, Process and Circumstance in the different texts. The data analysis depicts an overview of cohesive devices as different roles in the different texts. In general, all the texts show a similar trend in using these roles as cohesive devices. Except for Process, the ST uses the least number of cohesive devices as ergative roles in each text, while the TT2 uses the most, and the TT1 is in between in number. The three different chapters do not differ significantly in the use of the ergative roles; and in order to view the use of these ergative and transitive functions more clearly, their use in the separate texts in each chapter is not compared, but only the ST and the TTs. The data will be further analyzed from two perspectives: horizontally, in terms of how the different roles are distributed in different texts; vertically, in terms of what the proportions are of the roles in each text.

Table 7–11   Number of the transitivity and ergative functions of all the texts

	ST–ch1	TT1–ch1	TT2–ch1	ST–ch2	TT1–ch2	TT2–ch2	ST–ch3	TT1–ch3	TT2–ch3
Medium	458	577	674	357	453	588	540	592	759
Agent	71	135	128	50	98	91	52	108	123
Beneficiary	17	39	57	14	31	51	31	65	89
Range	102	144	171	97	132	162	78	113	194
N/A	4	13	8	7	9	11	6	28	34
Process	160	109	104	148	55	80	344	100	264
Circumstance	42	112	191	47	106	146	42	86	133

Horizontally, Figure 7-3 shows the numbers of different ergative roles in the three texts. All the ergative roles, Medium, Agent, Beneficiary and Range, show an increasing trend from the ST to the TT2. It is not surprising that Medium has the most number in the source text and the target texts, since "Medium is obligatory in all processes; and it is the only element that is, other than the process itself" (Halliday and Matthiessen, 2004: 289). Medium is verified as the most important role in expressing the nucleus information of the clause, by taking the greatest number of cohesive devices in all the texts. From the ST to the TT2, the number of Medium increases from 1,355 to 2,021; while the TT1 is in between, with 1,622 devices acting as Medium in the clause. As for other cohesive devices acting as Process and Circumstance in the clauses, the bars in Figure 7-4 show quite different trends. The use of Circumstance is in accordance with the use of the other types of ergative roles, exhibiting an increasing trend from the ST to the TT2. However, the use of Process is very distinctive from that of the other ergative roles. The ST has 652 relevant tokens as Process in the clauses, which is the highest number in the three texts. The two English target texts use Process much less than the source text: in particular, the TT1 uses only 264 relevant tokens as Process, around 40% of the total of those in the ST; while the TT2 has 448 devices as Process, making 69% of those in the ST.

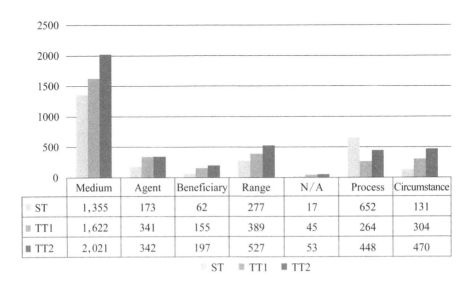

	Medium	Agent	Beneficiary	Range	N/A	Process	Circumstance
ST	1,355	173	62	277	17	652	131
TT1	1,622	341	155	389	45	264	304
TT2	2,021	342	197	527	53	448	470

ST ■ TT1 ■ TT2

Figure 7-3　Number of the ergative roles in the three texts

From these statistics, we can also tell that the use of cohesive devices in the two English target texts is higher than that in the source text. This reflects the explicitation in translation from Chinese into English. The ST is the most implicit text; and in the process of translation, the TT1 shows explicitation to some extent by using more cohesive devices in the cohesive chains; while the TT2 shows a higher degree of explicitation than the TT1 does. Unlike the other types of ergative roles, the translation of Process shows a trend of implicitation. We can infer that in the Chinese source text, Process plays a more important role in making the text coherent than in the English target texts.

Vertically, Figure 7-4 illustrates the outline of the ergative roles in the three texts. Firstly, in the nucleus of the clause, Medium takes the highest proportion in all the texts, with 51% in the ST, 53% in the TT1, and 50% in the TT2. Secondly, for the elements in the inner ring of the clause, the three texts also show more similarities than differences. Agent and Beneficiary are the most used roles in the TT1, while Range is the most used in the TT2. The difference in the percentage is no more than 2% across the three texts. This indicates that the translation of the Chinese source text into the English target texts preserves the roles of the relevant tokens in realising coherence. The use of Process and Circumstance displays more differences than the use of ergative roles in the three texts. The ST uses the highest percentage of Process, about 25%, in the cohesive chains; whereas the two English target texts, the TT1 and the TT2, use only 9% and 11%, respectively. This percentage reduction in translation shows that the interpretation of coherence in the English target texts relies less on Process than in the Chinese source text. The use of Circumstance in the three texts shows a distinctive difference between the ST and the two TTs: there are around 5% Circumstance in the cohesive devices in the ST; while this percentage doubles in the two English target texts. It can be inferred that, in the Chinese source text, the nucleus of the clause, Process + Medium, has the highest proportion of the cohesive devices in the formation of cohesive chains, altogether around 75% of the total. In the two TTs, the proportion of the nucleus is less than that in the ST; but the proportion of the inner ring, Agent, Beneficiary and Range, and the outer ring, Circumstance, is more than that in the ST. Figure 7-5 summarises these trends in translation.

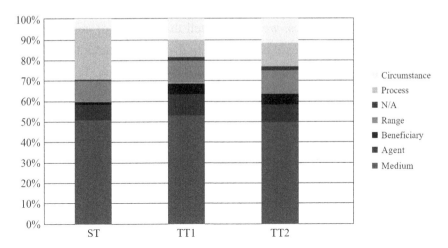

Figure 7-4　The proportion of the transitivity and ergative function in each text

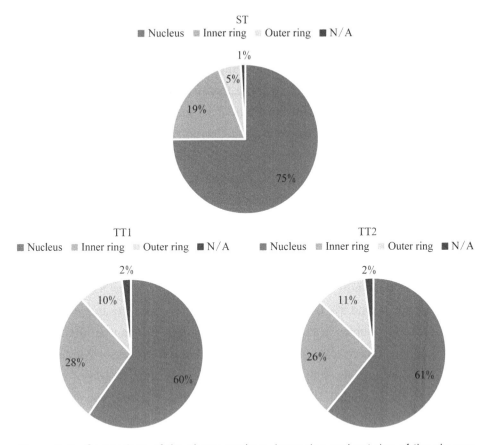

Figure 7-5　Comparison of the clause nucleus, inner ring and out ring of the clauses across the three texts

Figure 7–5 shows the difference between the ST and the TTs in respect of clause nucleus configuration of Process + Medium, inner ring roles of Agent, Beneficiary and Range, and outer ring role of Circumstance. The two TTs are similar to each other in the use of these elements in the cohesive chains. In translation to English, the function of the Nucleus is weakened; while the functions of the inner ring elements and outer ring Circumstance are strengthened.

7.2.2   Ergative patterns of the cohesive chains

After tagging all the relevant tokens with the ergative roles they play in the clauses, the cohesive chains are listed as the chains of ergative roles. Thus, the ergative patterns of the cohesive chains reflect the coherence patterns from the experiential and textual metafunctions. The repetition of certain patterns shows the coherence style of each text. Table 7–12 exhibits the most frequent 30 patterns of cohesive chains as the ergative role chains in the three texts. The capital letters are the initials of the roles: "M" stands for "Medium"; "P" for "Process"; "R" for "Range"; "A" for "Agent"; "B" for "Beneficiary"; and "C" for "Circumstance".

Table 7–12   The most frequent 30 patterns of cohesive chains in the three texts

	ST1			TT1			TT2		
	Chain	Count	%	Chain	Count	%	Chain	Count	%
1	MMM	67	9.91	PP	47	5.76	PP	54	5.55
2	PP	56	8.28	MMM	45	5.51	MM	44	4.52
3	MM	51	7.54	MM	42	5.14	MMMM	28	2.88
4	MMMM	26	3.85	CC	29	3.55	CC	28	2.88
5	PPP	24	3.55	MR	22	2.69	MMM	27	2.77
6	MR	19	2.81	RM	21	2.57	RM	22	2.26
7	PPPP	17	2.51	RR	17	2.08	PPP	20	2.06
8	RM	13	1.92	MMMM	14	1.71	RR	20	2.06

(continued)

	ST1			TT1			TT2		
	Chain	**Count**	**%**	**Chain**	**Count**	**%**	**Chain**	**Count**	**%**
9	RR	12	1.78	MC	13	1.59	MR	19	1.95
10	MMMMM	11	1.63	PPP	11	1.35	MRM	14	1.44
			43.78			**31.95**			**28.37**
11	PPPPP	11	1.63	RC	9	1.10	MC	13	1.34
12	MAM	9	1.33	MA	9	1.10	MMR	11	1.13
13	MMMMM	9	1.33	PPPP	8	0.98	PPPPP	11	1.13
14	MMA	8	1.18	M	8	0.98	RC	10	1.03
15	CC	8	1.18	CR	8	0.98	RMMM	10	1.03
16	PPPPP	7	1.04	MMR	8	0.98	MA	9	0.92
17	RMM	7	1.04	RMM	8	0.98	CMC	9	0.92
18	CR	6	0.89	MRM	8	0.98	MMC	9	0.92
19	RC	6	0.89	AM	7	0.86	CR	9	0.92
20	PPPPPPP	6	0.89	MMA	7	0.86	MMMMM	8	0.82
			11.40			**9.80**			**10.16**
21	MMRM	5	0.74	MAM	7	0.86	MMMMM	8	0.82
22	CM	5	0.74	MMMMM	7	0.86	MAM	7	0.72
23	CRR	5	0.74	BM	7	0.86	PPPP	7	0.72
24	PPPPPP	5	0.74	MCC	7	0.86	MCM	7	0.72
25	RRR	5	0.74	RA	6	0.73	CM	6	0.62
26	MAA	5	0.74	MMC	6	0.73	CCC	6	0.62
27	MMAM	5	0.74	PC	6	0.73	PM	6	0.62
28	AMM	4	0.59	CM	5	0.61	M2	5	0.51

(continued)

	ST1			TT1			TT2		
	Chain	Count	%	Chain	Count	%	Chain	Count	%
29	MAMM	4	0.59	MMMR	5	0.61	RA	5	0.51
30	MRM	4	0.59	AMM	5	0.61	MMA M	5	0.51
			6.95			**7.46**			**6.37**

In the transference of the cohesive chains from the ST to the two TTs, the ergative roles of the relevant tokens in the two TTs show consistency to a certain extent, especially in the top 10 frequent cohesive chains. The total percentage of the top 10 patterns also displays a distinctive difference between the ST and the TTs. However, this trend is not obvious in the percentages of the top 20 and 30 patterns. This implies that the ergative roles of the relevant tokens in the ST are more centralised to some patterns; whereas, in translation, these patterns are dispersed in the two TTs, with more diverse types of patterns.

The top 10, top 20, and top 30 patterns also display certain features; particularly the top 10 patterns. In the ST, the most frequent pattern is "MMM", which forms 9.91% of all the cohesive chains; while in the two TTs, the most frequent pattern is "PP", which also has a similar percentage in the two texts, 5.76% and 5.55% for the TT1 and the TT2, respectively. Longer chains — to be specific, chains with more than 5 relevant tokens in the two TTs — are not as frequent as in the ST. For example, "MMMMMM" ranks the 10th in the ST, while "MMMMM" appears as the 22nd in the TT1, and "MMMMMM" as the 20th in the TT2.

If we look at the "MMM" chain in the ST and the TT1 and "MM" in the TT2 for more detail, we can find that they show some interesting patterns. The most frequent chains are "MMM" and "MM" in the ST and the TT1, and "MM" and "MMMM" in the TT2.

Table 7–13 shows the use of the two most frequent ergative patterns in the three texts. As the cohesive chains are classified into two types, the identity chains and the similarity chains, the top two types of cohesive chains expressed with ergative roles of the relevant tokens can also be compared in terms of the identity chains and similarity chains. It is apparent that the ST and the TT1 display a high degree of consistency; while the TT2 shows a difference in percentage of the two types of cohesive chain. It can be inferred that, in the use of cohesive chains, Yang's translation is closer to the original text, while Hawkes' version shows its own uniqueness in this respect.

Table 7-13　The two most frequent ergative patterns in the three texts

1	ST	MMM	TT1	MMM	TT2	MM
Identity chains	60	89.55%	41	89.13%	27	61.36%
Similarity chains	7	10.45%	5	10.87%	17	38.64%
2	ST	MM	TT1	MM	TT2	MMMM
Identity chains	31	62%	25	60.98%	25	89.29%
Similarity chains	19	38%	16	39.02%	28	10.71%

7.3　Summary

The experiential and logical environments of the cohesive chains are manifested by the clause complexity and taxis and logico-semantic relations in clause complexes, and the ergative roles of the cohesive devices, revealing not only the coherence patterns of the ST and the TTs but also the different translators' styles. Style is a matter of patterning, as "it involves describing preferred or recurring patterns of linguistic behaviour, rather than individual or one-off instances of intervention" (Baker, 2000: 245). The percentage of each clause type exhibits the patterns of choice of different text producers. These patterns of choice (whether conscious or subconscious), rather than individual choice in isolation (Baker, 2000: 246), can reflect the styles of text producers and also the reasons behind the choices.

The patterns in the ST and the TTs in this research reflect the characteristics of the translators, and the cultural and ideological influences that shape both the original and target texts in predicatable patterns. To better understand the patterns of the experiential, logical and textual metafunctions in the construction of a coherent text, the interweaving of clause and cohesive chains at the lexico-grammatical level in the above analysis can be summarized, to give a general view. In general terms, the clauses in the cohesive chains in the Chinese source text and the two English target texts display some similarities as well as differences.

From the logical metafunctional perspective, the similarities of the clauses in the cohesive chains among the ST, the TT1 and the TT2 are mainly in TAXIS:

(1) More paratactic clauses contain relevant tokens than hypotactic clauses do in the ST and the TT1; whereas the amount of hypotaxis outweighs parataxis in the TT2. Chapter 5 shows that the Chinese source text prefers parataxis over hypotaxis; and this preference is maintained when the clauses are allocated to cohesive chains. On one hand, the clauses with relevant tokens reflect the features of the language itself; on the other hand, in translation, the translators are also affected by the features of their first language in construing the texture of the text.

(2) The percentage of both hypotactic and paratactic clauses involved in the cohesive chains in the TT1 is in between those of the ST and the TT2. This shows that the TT1 exhibits characteristics of both the Chinese and English languages.

(3) Compared with the results in Chapter 5, the ratio of paratactic and hypotactic clauses in the cohesive chains is similar to the ratio of their overall use in the texts. This means that the contribution of taxis to the construction of the cohesive chains and semantic sequences of the text is reflected in the use of parataxis and hypotaxis in the text. In the ST, more paratactic clauses are involved in the cohesive chains; while in the TT2, more hypotactic clauses are used with relevant tokens; and the TT1 is in between the ST and the TT2 amounts.

There is no specific pattern in the use of clauses in the cohesive chains from the perspective of LOGICO-SEMANTIC TYPE. Each text has shown its unique trend and characteristics with regard to "projection" and "expansion" are as follows:

(1) In the English target texts, there are more instances of "idea" than those in the Chinese source text; thus, conversely, fewer "locution".

(2) For the expanding clauses in the cohesive chains, elaborating clauses are the least favoured, while enhancing clauses are the most favoured. The TT2 is closer to the ST than the TT1 to the ST in this respect.

From the experiential metafunctional perspective, the ST displays a distinctive difference from the two TTs in respect of the nucleus, inner ring, and outer ring of the elements of the clause. It puts more emphasis on the nucleus and less on the inner ring elements and outer ring Circumstance in realising coherence than do the two TTs.

The probabilities and the patterns displayed above reveal the characteristics of literary text with a probabilistic model, because:

> Probabilistic model of lexicogrammar ... enables us to explain register variation. Register variation can be defined as the skewing of (some of) these overall probabilities, in the environment of some specific configuration of field, tenor, and mode. It is variation in the tendency to select certain meanings rather than others realising variation in the situation type (Halliday, 1991: 57).

The patterns in the texts reflect the purpose of the author and the translators of the literary text. The writer of the Chinese novel builds up a coherent text with comparatively implicit ways of realising coherence; while the translators create more explicit English target texts in the manifestation of coherence patterns. One possible reason for this difference is that the Chinese readers do not need as much explicit coherence patterning to understand the context of the text; while the English readers need much more explicit expression of the connections of the segments of the text to build up the cultural context of the texts. Another reason for this difference might be that the distance between the text and the reader for the ST and the TTs is different. The Chinese readers are within the same context of culture as the source text; whereas the English readers are within a different context of culture. Therefore, the differences and distances reflected in the texts are shown via the similarities and differences of the coherence patterns, as revealed in the analyses presented in this chapter.

Chapter 8

Conclusion

This study examines coherence patterns in the Chinese novel *Hong Lou Meng* and its two English translations. It provides a practical model for analyzing coherence in literary texts and translations. Systemic functional linguistics forms the basis for analysing both source and target texts. As a semantic concept, coherence is realized through lexicogrammatical patterns which create meaning. Clause complexes and cohesive chains are explored to show how coherence is realized, as ideational meaning and textual meaning mutually shape coherence. This research demonstrates how systemic functional linguistics aids investigating coherence and how lexicogrammatical coherence patterns differ across source and target texts.

8.1 Overview

This research aims to examine the patterns of coherence in translation, and to build up a descriptive and analytical model within the SFL framework for the reproduction of coherence in Chinese-English translation. It has described the classic Chinese novel *HLM* and its two English translated versions with respect to the lexicogrammatical patterns the texts display in realising coherence. As one of the most dynamic and created areas of literary studies (Traugott, 2008: 39), linguistic analysis of a literary text makes its translation studies more objective, profound and scientific, which in turn broadens the application of linguistic studies. The translation process involves both comprehending the source text and recontextualising it as a target text (Neubert and Shreve, 1992:

10). In translation, linguistic analysis can provide a solid support to the fully comprehension of the source and target texts. This study has deepened the understanding of texts in translation, and thus contributing to translation studies from the systemic functional linguistic perspective.

In translation, the translator's task is to recreate the author's coherence into another language and culture for the target readers (Nord, 1997: 23). As a semantic concept, coherence is realised at the lexicogrammatical level, which is "the powerhouse where meanings are created" [Halliday 1985 (1994): 15]. In this level, "the clause is the central processing unit", and different kinds of meanings are "mapped into an integrated grammatical structure" (Halliday and Matthiessen, 2004: 10). The previous chapters have given detailed analysis of lexicogrammatical patterning of coherence from the ideational and textual metafunctions, with the ultimate goal of investigating the patterns of coherence in translation from Chinese to English.

Focusing on the lexicogrammatical realisation of coherence, this research has provided a fundamental and practical model for the analysis of coherence patterns in a literary text and translation. Chapter 2 reviewed research related to coherence, with an emphasis on the systemic functional linguistic view of coherence, providing a solid foundation for the current study within the scope of coherence. Chapter 3 placed this research within the systemic functional linguistic framework, and made the analysis of both Chinese and English texts plausible with the use of the same criteria. Chapter 4 introduced the methodological procedures and analytical tools used in the study. Chapter 5 explored the modes of clause complexes and their effect on the construction of a coherent text. Chapter 6 focused on the cohesive chains in the texts, which show the textual metafunctional realisation of coherence. Chapter 7 investigated the mutual effect that ideational meaning and textual meaning have on the realisation of coherence.

In general, this research has shown how SFL works in the investigation of coherence, and how the lexicogrammatical patterns that realise coherence are expressed in the Chinese source text and the English target texts.

8.2 The findings of the study

Cohesion has always seemed to be the most practical aspect of discourse analysis or text linguistics that may be applied to translation (Newmark, 1987: 295). Taking into consideration of the relationship between cohesion and coherence, exploring coherence is relevant with the nature of translation. In the translation of Chinese into English, the coherence of both the source text and the target texts is closely related to their cultures. Hence, SFL, with a special emphasis on context, can play a role in translation studies.

This study has also contributed to the application of SFL in the analysis of a literary text. Through the investigation of the lexicogrammatical realisation of the ideational and textual metafunctions in the construction of coherence, this research has answered the questions proposed in Chapter 1.

(1) How are the patterns of coherence realised in the text by the mutual effect of the ideational and textual metafunctions?

The ideational and textual metafunctions together contribute to coherence in a text. The logical meaning is construed through the logically related semantic relations via the clause complex. The textual meaning is engendered through the threads of semantic sequences via the cohesive chains. The clause complex shows the inner logical relations between clauses; while the cohesive chains show the development of the semantic meaning throughout the text. They complement each other in realising the coherence of a text.

The clauses with cohesive devices in the cohesive chains are considered as taking a more important role than the other clauses in the construction of coherence. On one hand, the clause complex types of the clauses in the cohesive chains implement the logical development of the text. The frequencies and probabilities of each type of clause complexing in terms of TAXIS and LOGICO-SEMANTIC TYPE are the logical manifestation of the patterns of coherence. On the other hand, exploring the roles that the cohesive devices play through experiential meaning reflects how the clauses construe the experiential world. The ergative roles of the relevant tokens form the patterns of experiential meaning in realising a coherent text.

(2) What are the similarities and differences in the realisation of coherence in the Chinese source text and the English translated texts?

The lexicogrammatical patterns realising coherence display features that are both language specific and translator specific. The features are closely related to the social-cultural motivations of both Chinese and English.

> Systemic Functional Linguistics concerns itself with how language works, how it is organized and what social functions it serves. It is a social-linguistically and contextually-oriented framework, where language is viewed as being embedded in culture, and where meanings can be properly understood only with reference to the cultural environment in which they are realized (Manfredi, 2008: 37).

Considering the different translators and readerships, the lexicogrammatical patterns each text diaplay can be summarised thus:

The ST uses the least percentage of clause simplexes in the cohesive chains. The two TTs show similar percentage of both clause simplexes and clause complexes. Within the clause complexes, the ST prefers to use more paratactic clauses than the two TTs do; while the latter two again show slightly different percentages in their use of parataxis and hypotaxis.

In terms of the logico-semantic relations of the clauses in the cohesive chains, the percentage usage in the TT1 of expansion and projection is in between that of the ST and the TT2. Within projection, the ST uses the least idea and the most locution; whereas the two TTs use a greater percentage of idea but less locution than the ST does; while they show a similar preference for the two subtypes of projection. Within expansion, the three texts show a similar trend in using elaboration the least and enhancement the most. As to the specific percentages of the three subtypes of expansion: the ST and the TT2 show analogous preference in using each subtype; while the TT1 shows a distinctive feature in using more extension than the other two texts.

With respect to the patterns of the ergative roles of the relevant tokens, the usage of Medium, Agent, Beneficiary, Range and Circumstance displays an increasing trend from the ST to the TT2. Process is used the most in the ST and the least in the TT1. In respect of the proportion these roles take in each text: there is a clear difference between the ST and the TTs; while the two TTs show very close percentages in their usage of the nucleus, inner ring and outer ring elements. The nucleus elements, Process and Medium, make up 75% of the ST and 60% and 61% of the TT1 and the TT2, respectively. The inner ring elements, Agent, Range and Beneficiary, make up 19% of the ST and 28% and 26% of the TT1 and the TT2, respectively. The outer ring, Circumstance, in the ST is 5% but is double in the TT1 and the TT2, with 10% and 11%, respectively.

The similarities and differences in the lexicogrammatical patterns from the ideational and textual metafunctions reveal the patterns of different languages and different translators in the realisation of coherence. Firstly, Chinese is paratactic while English is hypotactic; and the translators follow the rule of the target language. Secondly, the use of logico-semantic relations in the ST and the TTs shows the difference both in Chinese and English and the two translators. The translators' personal preferences is decided by both their mother tounges and the target langauge readers' cultural backgrounds. Thirdly, the ergative roles of the relevant tokens indicate the habits of the two languages in expressing information carrying coherent features.

(3) How are the patterns of coherence kept and transferred in translation from Chinese into English?

Given the similarities and differences of the three texts in realising coherence, some features of the translation strategy can be determined. From the ST to the TT2, the use of cohesive chains exhibits a trend of explicitation. This means that, in translation, the two TTs display more explicit lexicogrammatical and cohesive properties than the ST does.

From the analysis of the logical and experiential meanings through which the coherence is realised, the similarities and differences the three texts display, shown in Chapter 5 and Chapter 7, reveal that the TT1 is closer to the ST than the TT2. In logical realisation, the TT1 displays features in between those the ST and the TT2, in the use of TAXIS and LOGICO-SEMANTIC TYPE; except for the subtypes of expansion. In experiential realisation, the ergative patterns in the three texts show an increasing frequency, from the ST through the TT1 to the TT2. The results also show that the TT1 displays a higher level of consistency with the ST than with the TT2.

Therefore, in the translation of the Chinese ST to the English TT1 and TT2, the two TTs display features that are distinctive in English, such as the explicitation of cohesion, and the higher proportion of hypotaxis and idea than those in the Chinese ST. Within the two TTs, they are different in the extent of the above-mentioned aspects, with the TT2 always showing a higher level of difference with the ST than with the TT1.

(4) How do the patterns of coherence in the two TTs indicate the translators' styles?

The features displayed in the two TTs indicate the translators' styles. In translation, the study of a translator's style focuses on the manner of expression that is typical of a translator (Baker, 2000: 245). Firstly, in terms of clause complexity, the TT1 uses simpler clause complexes and fewer words in each clause than the TT2 does. The translator of the TT2, Hawkes, consistently shows a preference for using more grammatically intricate clause complexes in translation than the translator of the TT1, Yang. This means that Hawkes is lexically denser than Yang in translation. However, in terms of the STTR of the two TTs, the TT1 is slightly higher than the TT2, which means that Yang uses a richer range of vocabulary than Hawkes does. Secondly, from the clause complexing point of view, in the clauses with cohesive devices, Yang uses a greater percentage of clause simplexes and parataxis, and less projection but more expansion, than Hawkes does. Thirdly, Yang is more implicit while Hawkes is more explicit in the use of cohesive chains. Yang uses slightly more identity chains but fewer similarity chains in realising the semantic sequence of the text than Hawkes does. This means that Yang leaves the conception of coherence to the readers to a larger extent, while Hawkes chooses to use explicit devices and chains to create a coherent text. These linguistic choices are seen as the translators' personal imprints, which implies their social and cultural understanding of the source text and the source text producer. In the translation of a literary text then, understanding the translators' styles play a crucial role in translation studies.

(5) What does the variation in coherence patterns between the two translations suggest?

The variations in the different coherence patterns are considered to have a guiding effect on the translation studies of a literary text. The backgrounds and the translation purposes of the two translators vary, which makes the translation of the same source text different in the realisation of coherence. Meanwhile, the different patterns in the two translations in turn imply the social cultural contexts of the two translators.

The translation patterns indicate the translator's style. "A study of a translator's style must focus on the manner of expression that is typical of a translator, rather than simply instances of open intervention. It must attempt to capture the translator's characteristic use of language, his or her individual profile of linguistic habits, compared to other translators" (Baker, 2000: 245). The linguistic habits and stylistic patterns are meaningful when they indicate some cultural and ideological positioning of the translator, or of translators in general, or about the cognitive processes and mechanisms that contribute to shaping our translational behaviour (Baker, 2000: 258). The variation in the two translations forms a contrast between the styles of the two translators, which implies some hidden assumptions about the translator and the translating process, because the linguistic patterns in the translation are important in conveying information about the context that the translator establishes through the text to the readers. Hasan (1985: 100) relates patterning in the style of genres to the community's notions about knowledge and knowledgeable persons. Therefore, the translation variation can reflect the notions of the target community about Chinese literature through the choices of the different translators with different translation purposes.

8.3　The implications of the study

The findings of this study contribute to the study of coherence, the application of SFL in translation studies, the stylistic analysis of *HLM*, and literary translation from Chinese to English.

Firstly, the focus of this study is on patterns of coherence, contributing to the understanding of coherence in text analysis. This study describes the patterns of coherence within the framework of SFL with both quantitative and qualitative approaches. The quantitative analysis depicts the basic structures realising coherence in the different texts. The qualitative analysis provides an explanation of the similarities and differences in the patterns of coherence in the different texts. This study provides a model for the analysis of coherence for further research.

Secondly, while SFL in translation studies is not a new perspective, the large-scale analysis of a literary text in Chinese to English translation study is relatively rare. This study therefore enlarges the application of SFL in translation studies by analyzing the lexicogrammatical realisation of coherence in a literary text and its translation.

Thirdly, language is important to verbal art because it functions as the translator's point of departure, and the reader's point of entry (Hasan, 1985: 99); and meanwhile, it involves the writer's point of departure and the translator's point of entry. The linguistic analysis of the translation of a literary text involves the interpretation of the points of view of the original writer, the translator and the reader. In the analysis of a literary text, it is necessary to conduct detailed linguistic analysis of the text, otherwise, "it is meaningless to talk about evaluation, for what we are evaluating in the absence of such careful analysis is more likely to be our inexplicit impressions against our equally accidental preconceptions of what an artist should or should not do" (Hasan, 1985: 106). The stylistic analysis of the classic novel *HLM* has provided insights into the study of this novel not only for the field of literary criticism but also for translation studies from a linguistic point of view. Therefore, this study has implications for both the stylistic study of Chinese and English and for the study of translation from Chinese to English.

In summary, the model described and applied in this study has implications for different fields of study; and the examination of the patterns of coherence presented here can be applied to different texts in the same genre and also in different genres.

8.4　The limitations of the study

This research has certain limitations due to the limited size of the corpus. Although the texts in this study have covered the features that are representative of the coherence of a text, a larger corpus with all the chapters in the novel and their two translation versions would give the findings a more solid evidential basis.

The analysis in this research is conducted at the lexicogrammatical stratum of the experiential, logical and textual metafunctions. The textual realisation is carried out in terms of the investigation of cohesive chains. However, theme, which is also considered to contribute to the coherence of a text, is not included in the research. Moreover, the interpersonal metafunction also plays a role in the construction of a coherent text. Thus, the study would be more representative of the patterns of coherence if it had included the lexicogrammatical analysis of mood and theme.

The data is only from one classic Chinese novel, and the patterns worked out are only applicable for this specific text, and thus are not sufficient to represent the study of literary texts in general. Accordingly, the results in this research are also not sufficient to be considered representative of the patterns of coherence in this genre.

The translation of a literary text is wide in scope. The linguistic analysis of *HLM* provides an entry point to the translation of this novel within the framework of SFL only; and the interpretation of the patterns of coherence in translation mainly focuses on the explicitation in translation and translators' styles. For more detailed and comprehensive evaluation of the translation, more translation theories could be drawn upon in the qualitative analysis of the texts.

8.5   Suggestions for future study

Despite the limitations outlined in the previous section, this study provides insights and directions for future research. Studies that go further than the present research may raise further questions about the study of coherence, the application of SFL in translation, and about different aspects of translation; and not only between Chinese and English, but also between other languages.

The methodology adopted in Chapter 5 has been applied to the clause complex analysis of 30 pieces of dialogue between the two main characters, Baoyu and Daiyu, across 80 chapters of the whole novel, in a journal article by the author of the present research. The results verify the findings in Chapter 5 of the role that the logical metafunction plays in the construction of a coherent text. That paper also further develops the application of clause complex analysis in the interpretation of different characters in the literary text to distinguish the styles of the characters. The analysis and results in the paper imply that the model presented in the current study can be applied to the whole novel and its translations.

To deepen the research on coherence within SFL, the exploration of coherence in this research could be extended to include the analysis at other ranks and of systems of all the metafunctions.

The analysis regime established in this research within a systemic functional linguistic framework may be developed to include more texts in the same genre, and also texts of other genres. Larger corpora could be established, either with an increased number of excerpts from the same novel, with other literary texts in the same genre, or with texts in other genres. The corpus tools and methodology used in the present research can be adopted in the analysis of such larger corpora to investigate the patterns of coherence more thoroughly.

With the features identified in this study, corpus tools can be adopted for tagging the clauses. The tagged clauses make it possible to work out the patterns of coherence in larger corpora.

For comparative study, this study has conducted initial research on a Chinese source text and two English target texts, which suggests potential comparative research between different languages.

Overall, it is hoped that the present study can serve as an inspiration for future research concerned with the nexus of coherence, stylistics and translation.

References

[1] ANDRIESSEN J, DE SMEDT K, ZOCK M. Discourse planning: Experimental and modeling approaches [J]. Computational Psycholinguistics: Symbolic and Network Models of Language Processing, 1996: 247–278.

[2] ARMSTRONG E M. The potential of cohesion analysis in the analysis and treatment of aphasic discourse [J]. Clinical Linguistics & Phonetics, 1991, 5(1): 39–51.

[3] BAKER M. Corpus linguistics and translation studies: Implications and applications [J]. Text and Technology: In Honour of John Sinclair, 1993: 233–250.

[4] BAKER M. In Other Words: A Coursebook on Translation [M]. London and New York: Routledge, 1997.

[5] BAKER M. Towards a methodology for investigating the style of a literary translator [J]. Target, 2000, 12(2): 241–266.

[6] BATEMAN J A. Dynamic Systemic-Functional Grammar: a New frontier [J]. Word, 1989, 40(1–2): 263–286.

[7] BATEMAN J A. From Systemic-Functional Grammar to Systemic-Functional Text Generation: Escalating the Exchange [M]. Los Angeles: University of Southern California Marina Del Rey Information Sciences Inst, 1990.

[8] BEAUGRANDE R D, DRESSLER W. Introduction to Text Linguistics [M]. New York: Longman Inc, 1981.

[9] BEAUGRANDE R D. Text, Discourse, and Process: Toward a Multidisciplinary Science of Texts [M]. Norwood, NJ: Ablex, 1980.

[10] BELL R T. Translation and Translating (Vol. 56) [M]. London: Longman, 1991.

[11] BIBER D, JOHANSSON S, LEECH G, CONRAD S. Longman Grammar of Spoken and Written English (Vol. 2) [M]. London: Longman, 1999.

[12] BIBER D. Representativeness in corpus design [J]. Literary and Linguistic Computing, 1993, 8(4): 243−257.

[13] BLUM-KULKA S. Shifts of Cohesion and Coherence in Translation [M]// VENUTI L. The Translation Studies Reader. London and New York: Routledge, 2000: 298.

[14] BROWN G, YULE G. Discourse Analysis [M]. Cambridge: Cambridge University Press, 1983.

[15] BUTT D G, MOORE A R, HENDERSON-BROOKS C, et al. Dissociation, Relatedness, and "Cohesive Harmony" : A linguistic measure of degrees of "fragmentation" ? [J]. Linguistics and the Human Sciences, 2010, 3(3): 263−293.

[16] BUTT D G. Semantic drift in verbal art [J]. Australian Review of Applied Linguistics, 1983, 6(1): 38−48.

[17] BYSTROVA-MCINTYRE T. Cohesion in Translation: A Corpus Study of Human-translated, Machine-translated, and Non-translated Texts (Russian into English) [D]// Kent: Kent State University, 2012.

[18] CAMPBELL K S. Coherence, Continuity, and Cohesion: Theoretical Foundations for Document Design [M]. London and New York: Routledge, 1995.

[19] CAO X. Hong Lou Meng [A Dream of Red Mansions] [M]. Beijing: Foreign Languages Press, 2008.

[20] CARRELL P L. Cohesion is not coherence [J]. TESOL Quarterly, 1982, 16(4): 479−488.

[21] CATFORD J C. A Linguistic Theory of Translation: An Essay in Applied Linguistics [M]. Oxford: Oxford University Press, 1965.

[22] CHATMAN S B. Story and Discourse: Narrative Structure in Fiction and Film [M]. New York: Cornell University Press, 1980.

[23] CHOMSKY N. Syntactic structures [J]. Language, 1957, 33(3): 375−408.

[24] COULTHARD M. Advances in Written Text Analysis [M]. London: Routledge, 1994.

[25] CUI S. A Comparison of English and Chinese Expository Rhetorical

Structures [D]// Los Angeles: University of California, 1986.

[26] DANES F. Functional sentence perspective and the organization of the text [J]. Papers on Functional Sentence Perspective, 1974: 106–128.

[27] EGGINS S. An Introduction to Systemic Functional Grammar [M]. London: Pinter, 1994.

[28] ENKVIST N E. Coherence, Pseudo-Coherence, and Non-Coherence [G]// OSTMAN I O. Cohesion and semantics. Abo: Abo Akademi Foundation, 1978.

[29] FAIS L. Inferable centers, centering transitions, and the notion of coherence [J]. Computational Linguistics, 2004, 30(2): 119–150.

[30] FANG J, SONG Z, WU C. What may be hidden behind a translator's choices: A comparative analysis of two translations of The Art of War [J]. Odense Working Papers in Language and Communication, 2008, 29: 283–306.

[31] FANG Y, MCDONALD E, MUSHENG C. On theme in Chinese: From clause to discourse [J]. Amsterdam Studies in the Theory and History of Linguistic Science Series, 1995, 4: 235–274.

[32] FANG Y. A Systemic Functional Perspective on the Growth of Chinese [C]// Current Issues in Systemic Functional Linguistics-Papers from the 8th Chinese Systemic Week, 2008: 74–90.

[33] 冯庆华.母语文化下的译者风格:《红楼梦》霍克斯与闵福德译本研究[M].上海:上海外语教育出版社,2008.

[34] FIRTH J R. The technique of semantics[J]. Transactions of the Philological Society, 1935, 34(1): 36–73.

[35] FRIES P H. Some aspects of coherence in a conversation [G]// D. LOCKWOOD, P. FRIES, W. SPRUIELL, M. CUMMINGS. Relations and Functions within and around Language. London: A&C Black, 2002: 346.

[36] FRIES P H. What makes a text coherent? Text and texture [C]// Systemic Functional Viewpoints on the Nature and Structure of Text. Paris: L'Harmattan, 2004.

[37] FRIES, P H. On the Status of Theme in English: Argument from Discourse From Texts[M]. Hamburg: Helmut Buske Verlage, 1981.

[38] GARROD S, DOHERTY G. Special determinants of coherence in spoken dialogue [C]// RICKHEIT G, HABEL C. Focus and Coherence in Discourse Processing. Berlin and New York: Walter de Gruyter,1995: 97−114.

[39] GIORA R. Notes towards a theory of text coherence [J]. Poetics Today, 1985, 6(4): 699−715.

[40] GIVÓN T. Coherence in text vs. coherence in mind [G]// GERNSBACHER M A, GIVÓN T. Coherence in Spontaneous Text. Amsterdam: John Benjamins Publishing 1995, 31: 59−115.

[41] GRIMES J E. The Thread of Discourse (Vol. 207) [M]. Berlin and New York: Walter de Gruyter, 1975.

[42] HALLIDAY M A K, HASAN R. Cohesion in English [M]. Beijing: Foreign Language Teaching and Research Press, 1976.

[43] HALLIDAY M A K, HASAN R. Language, Context, and Text: Aspects of Language in a Social-semiotic Perspective [M]. Oxford: Oxford University Press, 1985 [1989].

[44] HALLIDAY M A K, MATTHIESSEN C M. An Introduction to Functional Grammar [M]. London: Edward Arnold, 2004.

[45] HALLIDAY M A K, MATTHIESSEN C, YANG X. Construing Experience through Meaning: A Language-based Approach to Cognition [M]. Philadelphia: MIT Press, 1999.

[46] HALLIDAY M A K, MCDONALD E. Metafunctional profile of the grammar of Chinese [G]// CAFFAREL A, MARTIN J R, MATTHIESSEN C M. Language Typology: A Functional Perspective. Amsterdam: John Benjamins Publishing, 2004: 305−396.

[47] HALLIDAY M A K, MCINTOSH, STREVENS P. The Linguistic Sciences and Language Teaching [M]. London: Longman, 1964.

[48] HALLIDAY M A K, WEBSTER J. On Grammar in the Collected Works of MAK Halliday (Vol. 1) [M]. London: Continuum, 2002.

[49] HALLIDAY M A K. An Introduction to Functional Grammar [M]. London: Edward Arnold, 1985b.

[50] HALLIDAY M A K. Dimensions of discourse analysis: Grammar [G]// Handbook of Discourse Analysis. London: Academic Press, 1985a.

[51] HALLIDAY M A K. Functional Grammar [M]. London: Edward Arnold,

1994.

［52］ HALLIDAY M A K. Grammar, Society and the Noun [G]// HALLIDAY M A K. On language and linguistics (Vol. 3). London: Continuum, 1967.

［53］ HALLIDAY M A K. Grammatical categories of modern Chinese [J]. Transactions of the Philological Society, 1956, 55(1): 177-224.

［54］ HALLIDAY M A K. Language as a Social Semiotic: The Social Interpretation of Langauge and Meaning [M]. London: Edward Arnold, 1978.

［55］ HALLIDAY M A K. Language as code and language as behaviour: A systemic-functional interpretation of the nature and ontogenesis of dialogue [J]. The Semiotics of Culture and Language, 1984, 1: 3-35.

［56］ HALLIDAY M A K. Language theory and translation practice [J]. Rivista internazionale di tecnica della traduzione, 1992: 15-25.

［57］ HALLIDAY M A K. Learning How to Mean — Explorations in the Development of Language [M]. London: Edward Arnold,1975.

［58］ HALLIDAY M A K. Modes of meaning and modes of expression: Types of grammatical structure, and their determination by different semantic functions [G]// HAAS W, ALLERTON D J, CARNEY E, HOLDCROFT D. Function and Context in Linguistic Analysis: A Festschrift for William Haas. Berlin: Walter de Gruyter, 1979: 57-79.

［59］ HALLIDAY M A K. Notes on transitivity and theme in English: Part 1 [J]. Journal of Linguistics, 1967, 3: 37-81.

［60］ HALLIDAY M A K. Notes on transitivity and theme in English: Part 3 [J]. Journal of Linguistics, 1968, 4(02): 179-215.

［61］ HALLIDAY M A K. On the "architecture" of human language [G]// M A K. HALLIDAY & J. WEBSTER. On Language and Linguistics. London and New York: Equinox, 2003, 3: 15-16.

［62］ HALLIDAY M A K. Systemic Background [G] // BENSON J D, GREAVES W S. Systemic Perspectives on Discourse (Vol. 1). Noorwood: Ablex Publishing Company, 1985c.

［63］ HALLIDAY M A K. Text as semantic choice in social contexts [C]// Grammars and Descriptions. Berlin: Walter de Gruyter, 1977: 50-73.

［64］ HALLIDAY M A K. Towards a theory of good translation [G]// E. STEINER & C. YALLOP. Exploring Translation and Multilingual Text

Production: Beyond Content. Berlin: Walter de Gruyter, 2001, 3: 13.

［65］HALLIDAY M A K. Towards probabilistic interpretations [J]. Functional and Systemic Linguistics, 1991: 39–61.

［66］HANSEN-SCHIRRA S, NEUMANN S, STEINER E. Cohesive explicitness and explicitation in an English-German translation corpus [J]. Languages in Contrast, 2007, 7(2): 241–266.

［67］HARABAGIU S M. From lexical cohesion to textual coherence: A data driven perspective [J]. International Journal of Pattern Recognition and Artificial Intelligence, 1999, 13(02): 247–265.

［68］HASAN R, CLORAN C B, WILLIAMS G, et al. Semantic networks: The description of linguistic meaning in SFL [G]// HASAN R, MATTHIESSEN C, WEBSTER J. Continuing Discourse on Language: A Functional Perspective. London and Oakville: Equinox Publishing Ltd, 2005, 2: 697–738.

［69］HASAN R, MATTHIESSEN C, WEBSTER J. Continuing Discourse on Language: A Functional Perspective [M]. London and Oakville: Equinox Publishing Ltd, 2005.

［70］HASAN R. Coherence and cohesive harmony [G]// J. FLOOD. Understanding Reading Comprehension: Cognition, Language and the Structure of Prose, 1984:181–219.

［71］HASAN R. Linguistics, Language and Verbal Art [M]. Geelong: Deakin University Press, 1985.

［72］HASAN R. Situation and the definition of genres [G]// A. D. GRIMSHAW, What's Going on Here? : Complementary Studies of Professional Talk. Norwood, NJ: Ablex Publishing Corporation, 1994: 27–172.

［73］HASAN R. Text in the systemic-functional model [G]// DRESSLER W. Current Trends in Text Linguistics. Berlin: Walter de Gruyter, 1978, 2: 229–245.

［74］HATIM B, MASON I. Discourse and the Translator [M]. London and New York: Longman, 1990.

［75］HATIM B, MUNDAY J. Translation: An Advanced Resource Book [M]. London: Psychology Press, 2004.

[76] HAWKES D. The Story of the Stone: The Crab-Flower Club (Vol. 2) [M]. Great Britain: Penguin Group, 1977.

[77] HAWKES D. The Story of the Stone: The Golden Days (Vol. 1) [M]. Great Britain: Penguin Group, 1973.

[78] HOBBS J R. Coherence and coreference [J]. Cognitive Science, 1979, 3(1): 67–90.

[79] HOEY M. On the Surface of Discourse [M]. London: Allen & Unwin, 1983.

[80] HOPPER, P. J., TRAUGOTT, E. C. Grammaticalization [M]. Cambridge: Cambridge University Press, 2003.

[81] HOU Y. Nominalization in the translation of literary prose from Chinese into English: Based on the three English versions of Hong Lou Meng [D]. Sydney: Macquarie University, 2011.

[82] HOU Y.候羽.《红楼梦》英译研究的新阶段: 读《〈红楼梦〉中英文语料库的创建及应用研究》有感[J].英语广场: 学术研究, 2012,（1）: 28529.

[83] HOUSE J. Translation Quality Assessment: A Model Revisited [M]. Tübingen: Gunter Narr Verlag, 1997.

[84] HOVY E H. Approaches to the Planning of Coherent Text [M]. Berlin: Springer, 1990.

[85] HOVY E H. Planning coherent multisentential text [C]// Proceedings of the 26th Annual Meeting on Association for Computational Linguistics, 1988.

[86] HU Z. Discourse Cohesion and Coherence [M]. Shanghai: Shanghai Foreign Language Education Press, 1994.

[87] HUANG G.黄国文.杜牧《清明》英译文的逻辑功能分析[J].外语与翻译, 2002,（1）: 1–6.

[88] HUANG G.黄国文.语篇分析概要[M].长沙: 湖南教育出版社,1988.

[89] JIANG F.江帆.他乡的石头记:《红楼梦》百年英译史研究[D].上海: 复旦大学,2007.

[90] KEHLER A, KEHLER A. Coherence, Reference, and the Theory of Grammar [M]. Stanford, CA: CSLI Publications, 2002.

[91] KIERAS D E. Initial mention as a signal to thematic content in technical

passages [J]. Memory & Cognition, 1980, 8(4): 345–353.

[92] KIM M, HUANG Z. Theme choices in translation and target readers' reactions to different theme choices [J]. T&I Review, 2012, 2: 79–112.

[93] KIM M. A Discourse Based Study on Theme in Korean and Textual Meaning in Translation [D]. Sydney: Macquarie University, 2007a.

[94] KIM M. Meaning-oriented assessment of translations [G]// JACOBSON H E, ANGELELLI C V. Testing and Assessment in Translation and Interpreting Studies. Amsterdam: John Benjamins, 2009: 123–157.

[95] KIM M. Using systemic functional text analysis for translator education: An illustration with a focus on textual meaning [J]. The Interpreter and Translator Trainer, 2007b, 1(2): 223–246.

[96] KINTSCH W, VAN DIJK T A. Toward a model of text comprehension and production [J]. Psychological Review, 1978, 85(5): 363.

[97] KNOTT A, DALE R. Using linguistic phenomena to motivate a set of coherence relations [J]. Discourse Processes, 1994, 18(1): 35–62.

[98] KNOTT A, SANDERS T. The classification of coherence relations and their linguistic markers: An exploration of two languages [J]. Journal of Pragmatics, 1998, 30(2): 135–175.

[99] KOCH H. A Functional Perspective of Cohesion in English [M]. Munich: GRIN Verlag, 2007.

[100] KREIN-KÜHLE M. Cohesion and coherence in technical translation: The case of demonstrative reference [J]. Linguistica Antverpiensia NS, 2002, 1: 41–51.

[101] LAVIOSA S. Corpus-based translation studies: Where does it come from? Where is it going? [J]. Language Matters, 2004, 35(1): 6–27.

[102] LI C N, THOMPSON S. A. Mandarin Chinese: A Functional Reference Grammar [M]. Berkley, Los Angeles, California: University of California Press, 1981.

[103] LI D, ZHANG C, LIU K. Translation style and ideology: A corpus-assisted analysis of two English translations of Hong Lou Meng [J]. Literary and Linguistic Computing, 2011, 26(2): 153–166.

[104] LI E S H. A Text-based Study of the Grammar of Chinese from a Systemic Functional Approach [D]. Sydney: Macquarie University, 2003.

［105］LI S.李绍年.《红楼梦》翻译学刍议［J］.语言与翻译,1993,33（1）:
　　　30-36.

［106］LI S.李绍年.红楼梦翻译学概说［J］.语言与翻译,1995,42（2）: 62-71.

［107］Lian S.连淑能.英汉对比研究［M］.北京: 高等教育出版社,1993.

［108］Liu M.刘宓庆.英汉对比研究与翻译［M］.南昌: 江西教育出版社,
　　　1991.

［109］Liu Z, Liu C, Zhu H.刘泽权,刘超朋,朱虹.《红楼梦》四个英译本的
　　　译者风格初探: 基于语料库的统计与分析［J］.中国翻译,2011,32
　　　（1）: 60-64.

［110］Liu Z.刘泽权.《红楼梦》中英文语料库的创建及应用研究［M］.北
　　　京: 光明日报出版社,2010.

［111］LORENTZ, G. Learning to Cohere: Causal links in native vs. non-native
　　　argumentation writing [G]. // W. BUBLITZ, U. LENK, E. VENTOLA.
　　　Coherence in Spoken and Written Discourse: How to Create It and How
　　　to Describe It. Amsterdam: John Benjamins Publishing, 1999: 55-75.

［112］Lu J. 陆俭明.探索与创新: 王力先生现代汉语语法研究之基本精神
　　　［J］.北京大学学报（哲学社会科学版）,2010,（5）: 135-139.

［113］LUKIN, A. Examining Poetry: A Corpus Based Enquiry into Literary
　　　Criticism [D]. Sydney: Macquarie University, 2002.

［114］LUKIN, A. What do texts do? The context-construing work of news [J].
　　　Text & Talk, 2013, 33(4-5): 523-551.

［115］LV S.吕叔湘.现代汉语八百词［M］.北京: 商务印书馆,2008.

［116］MANFREDI, M. Translating Text and Context: Translation Studies
　　　and Systemic Functional Linguistics (Vol. 1: Translation Theory) [M].
　　　Bologna: Dupress, 2008.

［117］MANN, W. C., MATTHIESSEN, C. M. I. M. Functions of Language in
　　　Two Frameworks [M]. Los Angeles: University of Southern California,
　　　Information Sciences Institute, 1990.

［118］MANN, W. C., MATTHIESSEN, C., THOMPSON, S. A. Rhetorical
　　　Structure Theory and Text Analysis [M]. Los Angeles: University of
　　　Southern California, Information Sciences Institute, 1989.

［119］MANN, W. C., THOMPSON, S. A. Rhetorical Structure Theory: A
　　　Theory of Text Organization [M]. Los Angeles: University of Southern

California, Information Sciences Institute, 1987.

［120］ MANN, W. C., THOMPSON, S. A. Toward a theory of reading between the lines: An exploration in discourse structure and implicit communication [C]// The 7th IPrA International Pragmatics Conference, 2000.

［121］ MARKELS, R. B. Cohesion Patterns in English Expository Paragraphs [D]. Columbus: Ohio State University, 1981.

［122］ MARTIN, J., R. English Text: System and Structure [M]. Amsterdam: John Benjamins Publishing, 1992.

［123］ MATTHIESSEN, C. Combining clauses into clause complexes [G]// BYBEE J L, NOONAN M. Complex Sentences in Grammar and Discourse: Essays in Honor of Sandra A. Thompson. Amsterdam: John Benjamins Publishing, 2002: 235−319.

［124］ MATTHIESSEN, C. Lexicogrammatical Cartography: English Systems [M]. Tokyo, Taipei, and Dallas: International Language Science Publishers, 1995.

［125］ MATTHIESSEN, C. The environments of translation [G]// E. STEINER & C. YALLOP, Exploring Translation and Multilingual Text Production: Beyond Content (Vol. 3). Berlin and New York: Walter de Gruyter, 2001.

［126］ MATTHIESSEN, C., THOMPSON, S. A. The structure of discourse and "subordination" [G]// HAIMAN J, THOMPSON S A. Clause Combining in Grammar and Discourse. Amsterdam: John Benjamins Publishing, 1988, 18: 275−329.

［127］ MCDONALD, E. Clause and Verbal Group Systems in Chinese: A Text-based Functional Approach [D]. Sydney: Macquarie University, 1998.

［128］ MOORE, J. D., POLLACK, M. E. A problem for RST: The need for multi-level discourse analysis [J]. Computational Linguistics, 1992, 18(4): 537−544.

［129］ MORRIS, J., HIRST, G. The subjectivity of lexical cohesion in text [G]// SHANAHAN J G, QU Y, WIEBE J. Computing Attitude and Affect in Text: Theory and Applications. Dordrecht: Springer, 2006, 20: 41−47.

［130］ MUNDAY, J. Issues in translation studies [G]// J. MUNDAY, The Routledge Companion to Translation Studies. New York: Routledge, 2009.

［131］ MUNDAY, J. Problems of applying thematic analysis to translation between Spanish and English [J]. Cadernos de tradução, 1998, 1(3): 183–213.

[132] MUNDAY, J. Systems in Translation: A Computer-assisted Systemic Approach to the Analysis of the Translation of García Márquez [D]. Bradford: University of Bradford, 1997.

[133] NESBITT, C., PLUM, G. Probabilities in a systemic-functional grammar: The clause complex in English [G]. M. A. K. HALLIDAY, R. P. FAWCETT, D. J. YOUNG. New Developments in Systemic Linguistics: Theory and Application. London: Pinter, 1988, 2: 6–38.

[134] NEUBERT, A., SHREVE, G. M. Translation as Text [M]. Kent: Kent State University Press, 1992.

[135] NEWMARK, P. Communicative and Semantic Translation [J]. Babel: International Journal of Translation, 1977, 23(4): 163–180.

[136] NEWMARK, P. The use of systemic linguistics in translation analysis and criticism [G]// R. STEELE & T. THREADGOLD, Language Topics: Essays in Honour of Michale Halliday. Amsterdam and Philadelphia: John Benjamins Publishing, 1987, 1: 293–304.

[137] NIDA. E. A. Language, Culture, and Translating [M]. Shanghai: Shanghai Foreign Language Education Press, 1993.

[138] NIDA. E. A. Science of translation [J]. Language, 1969: 483–498.

[139] NORD, C. Translating as a Purposeful Activity [M]. Manchester: St. Jerome, 1997.

[140] OLOHAN, M. Introducing Corpora in Translation Studies [M]. New York: Routledge, 2004.

[141] PAGANO, A. Decentering translation in the classroom: An experiment [J]. Perspectives: Studies in Translatology, 1994, 2(2): 213–217.

[142] PARSONS, G. Cohesion coherence: Scientific texts [G]// VENTOLA E. Functional and Systemic Linguistics: Approaches and Uses. Berlin and New York: Walter de Gruyter, 1991.

[143] Pin, W. A systemic functional interpretation of ergativity in Classical Tibetan [C]. // J. KNOX. Papers from the 39th International Systemic Functional Congress, 2012: 105–110.

[144] PRINCE, G., TRAUGOTT, E. C., PRATT, M. L. Linguistics for

Students of Literature [J]. Style, 1981, 15(4): 490–492.

[145] QUIRK, R., CRYSTAL, D. A Comprehensive Grammar of the English Language (Vol. 6) [M]. Cambridge: Cambridge University Press, 1985.

[146] REINHART, T. Conditions for text coherence [J]. Poetics Today, 1980, 1(4): 161–180.

[147] RENKEMA, J. Discourse, of Course: An Overview of Research in Discourse Studies [M]. Amsterdam: John Benjamins Publishing, 2009.

[148] SANDERS, T. J., NOORDMAN, L. G. The role of coherence relations and their linguistic markers in text processing [J]. Discourse Processes, 2000, 29(1): 37–60.

[149] SANDERS, T. J., SPOOREN, W. P., NOORDMAN, L. G. Toward a taxonomy of coherence relations [J]. Discourse Processes, 1992, 15(1): 1–35.

[150] SASAKI, M. An analysis of the clause relations in the three english translations of The Tale of Genji [J]. The Faculty Journal of Aichi Gakuin Junior College, 1995, (3): 36–64.

[151] SEIDLHOFER B, WIDDOWSON H. Coherence in Summary: The Contexts of Appropriate Discourse [G]// W. BUBLITZ, U. LENK, E. VENTOLA. Coherence in spoken and written discourse: how to create it and how to describe it. Amsterdam: John Benjamins Publishing, 1999: 205–219.

[152] Shu D, Liu Z, Xu S.束定芳,刘正光,徐盛桓.引进与借鉴:我国国外语言学研究六十年[J].外语教学与研究:外国语文双月刊,2009,(6):431–437.

[153] SINCLAIR, J. Corpus, Concordance, Collocation [M]. Oxford: Oxford University Press, 1991.

[154] STEDE, M. Rhetorical structure and thematic structure in text generation [C]. // Processings of LORID, 1999: 44–50.

[155] STEINER, E. H., YALLOP, C. Intralingual and interlingual versions of a text — how specific is the notion of translation? [G]// E. STEINER & C. YALLOP. Exploring Translation and Multilingual Text Production: Beyond Content (3). Berlin: Mouton de Gruyter, 2001.

[156] STEWART, D. Conventionality, creativity and translated text: The

implications of electronic corpora in translation [G]// OLOHAN M. Intercultural Faultlines: Research Models in Translation Studies I: Textual and Cognitive Aspects. Manchester: St Jerome, 2000: 73–92.

[157] STUART-SMITH V. The hierarchical organization of text as conceptualized by rhetorical structure theory: A systemic functional perspective [J]. Australian Journal of Linguistics, 2007, 27(1): 41–61.

[158] Sun, L.孙良明.谈《马氏文通》到《新著国语文法》前中国的语法研究（上）: 纪念劭西师《新著国语文法》出版九十年［J］.励耘语言学刊,2014,（1）: 1–36.

[159] SUNDAY, B. L. R. Cohesion and Coherence in the Language Production of a Selected Group of Secondary Bilingual Students [D]. Champaign: University of Illinois at Urbana-Champaign, 1983.

[160] TABOADA, M. Cohesion as a measure in generic analysis [J]. Círculo de lingüística aplicada a la comunicación, 2000, (3): 6.

[161] TABOADA, M. Discourse markers as signals (or not) of rhetorical relations [J]. Journal of Pragmatics, 2006, 38(4): 567–592.

[162] TABOADA, M. Implicit and explicit coherence relations [G]// J. RENKEMA. Discourse, of Course: An Overview of Research in Discourse Studies. Amsterdam: John Benjamins Publishing, 2009: 127–140.

[163] TABOADA, M. T. Building Coherence and Cohesion: Task-oriented Dialogue in English and Spanish [M]. Amsterdam: John Benjamins Publishing, 2004.

[164] TABOADA, M., LAVID, J. Rhetorical and thematic patterns in scheduling dialogues: A generic characterization [J]. Functions of Language, 2003, 10(2): 147–178.

[165] TABOADA, M., Mann, W. C. Rhetorical structure theory: Looking back and moving ahead [J]. Discourse Studies, 2006, 8(3): 423–459.

[166] TANSKANEN, S. K. Collaborating towards Coherence: Lexical Cohesion in English Discourse [M]. Amsterdam: John Benjamins Publishing, 2006.

[167] TAYLOR TORSELLO, C. Grammatica e traduzione [G]// G. CORTESE, Tradurre i linguaggi settoriali. Torino: Edizioni Libreria Cortina, 1996: 87–119.

[168] TAYLOR, C., BALDRY, A. Computer assisted text analysis and translation: A functional approach in the analysis and translation of advertising texts [G]// E. STEINER & C. YALLOP, Exploring Transaltion and Multilingual Text Production: Beyond Content. Berlin: Mouton de Gruyter, 2001.

[169] THOMPSON, S. Aspects of cohesion in monologue [J]. Applied Linguistics, 1994, 15(1): 58-75.

[170] TIERNEY, R. J., MOSENTHAL, J. H. Cohesion and textual coherence [J]. Research in the Teaching of English, 1983: 215-229.

[171] TRAUGOTT, E. C. P., LOUISE, M. Language, Linguistics and Literary Analysis [M]. New York: Routledge, 2008.

[172] TROSBORG, A. Discourse analysis as part of translator training [J]. Current Issues in Language & Society, 2000, 7(3): 185-228.

[173] VAN DIJK, T. A. Semantic discourse analysis [G]// DURANTI A. Handbook of Discourse Analysis. Orlando: Academic Press, 1985, 2: 29-56.

[174] VAN DIJK, T. A. Semantic macro-structures and knowledge frames in discourse comprehension [J]. Cognitive Processes in Comprehension, 1977: 3-32.

[175] VAN DIJK, T. A. Text grammar and text logic [G]// PETOFI J S, RIESER H. Studies in Text Grammar. Berlin: Springer, 1973: 17-78.

[176] VAN DIJK, T. A., Kintsch, W. Strategies of Discourse Comprehension [M]. New York: Academic Press New York, 1983.

[177] VENTOLA, E. Thematic development and translation [G]// GHADESSY M. Thematic Development in English Texts. London: A&C Black, 1995: 85-104.

[178] VINAY, J.P., DARBELNET, J. Comparative Stylistics of French and English: A Methodology for Translation [M]. Amsterdam: John Benjamins Publishing, 1995.

[179] WANG D.王东风.小说翻译的语义连贯重构[J].中国翻译,2005,26(3):37-43.

[180] WANG D.王东风.有标记连贯与小说翻译中的连贯重构:以意识流小说Ulysses的翻译为例[J].外语教学与研究,2006,38(5):303-308.

［181］WANG D. 王东风. 语篇连贯与翻译初探［J］. 外语与外语教学, 1998, 6：39-42.

［182］WANG L. 王力. 中国现代语法［M］. 北京：商务印书馆, 1959［1985］.

［183］WANG L. 王力. 中国语法理论［M］. 北京：商务印书馆, 1945.

［184］WANG L. 王力. 中国语言学史［M］. 上海：复旦大学出版社, 1980.

［185］WANG W. 王伟. 修辞结构理论评介（上）［J］. 国外语言学, 1994,（4）：8-13.

［186］WEBSTER, J. An introduction to continuum companion to systemic functional linguistics [G]// HALLIDAY M A K, WEBSTER J. Continuum Companion to Systemic Functional Linguistics. London: A&C Black, 2009.

［187］WEI Z. 魏在江. 英汉语篇连贯认知对比研究［D］. 上海：华东师范大学, 2004.

［188］Wen J, Ren Y. 文军, 任艳. 国内《红楼梦》英译研究回眸（1979—2010）［J］. 中国外语, 2012, 9（1）：81-93.

［189］WERTH, P. Focus, Coherence and Emphasis [M]. New York: Taylor & Francis, 1984.

［190］WIDDOWSON, H. G. Discourse Analysis [M]. Oxford: Oxford University Press Oxford, 2007.

［191］WIDDOWSON, H. G. Teaching Language as Communication [M]. Oxford: Oxford University Press, 1978.

［192］WIJEYEWARDENE I. Transitivity/ergativity in Thai political science texts [C]// J. KNOX, Papers from the 39th International Systemic Functional Congress, 2012: 129-134.

［193］WOLF F, GIBSON E. Coherence in Natural Language: Data Structures and Applications [M]. Philadelphia: The MIT Press, 2006.

［194］WU C, FANG J. (2007). The semiotics of university introductions in Australia and China [C]// Proceedings of the 33rd International Systemic Functional Congress, 2007.

［195］Xu J. 徐珺. 功能语法用于《儒林外史》汉英语篇的研究：情景语境观［J］. 现代外语, 2003, 26（2）：128-134.

［196］Yan M. 闫敏敏. 二十年来的《红楼梦》英译研究［J］. 外语教学, 2005, 26（4）：64-68.

［197］YANG X, YANG G. A Dream of Red Mansions [M]. Beijing: Foreign

Languages Press, 1994.

［198］ZANETTIN F. Designing an English Italian translational corpus [J]. Language and Computers, 2002, 42(1): 329–343.

［199］Zeng, L. 曾蕾. 英汉 "投射" 小句复合体的功能与语义分析［J］. 现代外语, 2000, 2: 163–173.

［200］ZHANG D. New Developments in the Theory of Discourse Analysis and Its Application [M]. Beijing: Foreign Language Teaching and Research Press, 2012.

［201］ZHANG D. Some characteristics of Chinese mood system [C]// Current Issues in Systemic Functional Linguistics — Papers from the 8th Chinese Systemic Week, 2008: 91–116.

［202］ZHANG D. 张德禄. 从衔接到连贯: 语篇连贯的解码过程探索［J］. 外国语言文学研究, 2004, 4: 002.

［203］ZHANG D. 张德禄. 语篇连贯研究纵横谈［J］. 外国语(上海外国语大学学报), 1999, 6: 24–31.

［204］Zhang G, Liao X. 张拱贵, 廖序东. 重印《新著国语文法》序［J］. 语言教学与研究, 1985, (3): 27–29.

［205］Zhang M, Huang G. 张美芳, 黄国文. 语篇语言学与翻译研究［J］. 中国翻译, 2002, (3): 3–7.

［206］Zhao, Q. 赵晴.《红楼梦》汉英翻译语料库的衔接显化研究［J］. 重庆理工大学学报(社会科学), 2011, 25(11): 110–116.

［207］Zhao, Y. 赵彦春. 翻译中衔接: 连贯的映现［J］. 外语与外语教学, 2002, 7: 23–27.

［208］ZHENG, Y. Text coherence in translation [J]. English Language Teaching, 2009, 2 (3): 53.

［209］Zhou, R. 周汝昌. 红楼梦新证［M］. 北京: 中华书局, 1953[2012].

［210］Zhu, J. 朱军. 衔接恰当, 译文生辉: 评《红楼梦》的两种译本［J］. 外语学刊, 1998, 4: 89–93.

［211］ZHU, Y. Modality and modulation in Chinese [J]. Advances in Discourse Processes, 1996, 57: 183–210.

［212］ZHU, Y., ZHENG, L., MIAO, X. A Contrastive Study of Cohesion in English and Chinese [M]. Shanghai: Shanghai Foreign Language Education Press, 2001.

Index